The Economics of Sport, Health and Happiness

NEW HORIZONS IN THE ECONOMICS OF SPORT

Series Editors: Wladimir Andreff, *Department of Economics, University of Paris 1 Panthéon Sorbonne, France* and Marc Lavoie, *Department of Economics, University of Ottawa, Canada*

For decades, the economics of sport was regarded as a hobby for a handful of professional economists who were primarily involved in other areas of research. In recent years, however, the significance of the sports economy as a percentage of GDP has expanded dramatically. This has coincided with an equivalent rise in the volume of economic literature devoted to the study of sport.

This series provides a vehicle for deeper analyses of the demand for sport, cost–benefit analysis of sport, sporting governance, the economics of professional sports and leagues, individual sports, trade in the sporting goods industry, media coverage, sponsoring and numerous related issues. It contributes to the further development of sports economics by welcoming new approaches and highlighting original research in both established and newly emerging sporting activities. The series publishes the best theoretical and empirical work from well-established researchers and academics, as well as from talented newcomers in the field.

Titles in the series include:

The Economics of Sport, Health and Happiness

The Promotion of Well-being through Sporting Activities

Edited by

Plácido Rodríguez

University of Oviedo, Spain and Fundación Observatorio Económico del Deporte (FOED)

Stefan Késenne

University of Antwerp and Catholic University of Leuven, Belgium

Brad R. Humphreys

University of Alberta, Canada

NEW HORIZONS IN THE ECONOMICS OF SPORT

Edward Elgar

Cheltenham, UK • Northampton, MA, USA

Published by
Edward Elgar Publishing Limited
The Lypiatts
15 Lansdown Road
Cheltenham
Glos GL50 2JA
UK

Edward Elgar Publishing, Inc.
William Pratt House
9 Dewey Court
Northampton
Massachusetts 01060
USA

A catalogue record for this book
is available from the British Library

Library of Congress Control Number: 2011925730

MIX
Paper from
responsible sources
FSC
www.fsc.org   FSC® C018575

ISBN 978 0 85793 013 2

Typeset by Servis Filmsetting Ltd, Stockport, Cheshire
Printed and bound by MPG Books Group, UK

Contents

Contributors

Christoph Breuer is Full Professor of Sport Management, German Sport University Cologne. He has published in several journals such as *European Sport Management Quarterly*, *Sport Management Review* and *European Journal of Sport Science*.

Charlotte Cabane is Assistant Professor in Labour Economics and Employment Policies at Sciences-Po Paris and in Microeconomics and General Introduction to Economics at the University of Paris 1 Panthéon-Sorbonne, France. Charlotte is a PhD candidate in the Centre d'Economie de la Sorbonne, Paris. Her research activities focus on labour economics, sports economics and economics of education. She has participated in important congresses such as the First European Conference in Sports Economics.

Michael C. Davis is Associate Professor of Economics in Missouri University of Science and Technology, USA. His primary fields are macroeconomics, applied econometrics and sports economics. He has published in several journals such as *International Journal of Sport Finance* and *Journal of Sports Economics*.

Paul Downward is Senior Lecturer in Sport Management and Director of the Institute of Sport and Leisure Policy at Loughborough University, UK. He is a member of UK Sport's research advisory group. He is the author of two books on sports economics and has published a number of articles on a range of issues connected to sports, tourism, economics and philosophy in journals such as *Oxford Economic Papers*, *Cambridge Journal of Economics*, *Applied Economics* and *European Sport Management Quarterly*. He belongs to several editorial boards.

Christian M. End is Associate Professor of Psychology at Xavier University, USA. His research interests focuses on social identity theory, self-presentation tactics, and gender differences within the sport fan context. He has published in journals such as *Journal of Sport Behaviour* and the *Journal of Applied Social Psychology.*

David Forrest is Professor of Economics in the University of Salford, UK and Honorary Professor in the Macao Polytechnic Institute. He specializes in the analysis of the sports and gambling industries and advises both the National Lottery Commission and the Gambling Commission in the UK. Recent outlets for his research include articles in *Economic Inquiry, Southern Economic Journal, Journal of the Royal Statistical Society, International Journal of Forecasting* and *European Journal of Operational Research.*

Jaume García Villar is Professor of Econometrics, Departament d'Economia i Empresa, Universitat Pompeu Fabra, Spain. He has published articles in the *Journal of Sports Economics, European Sport Management Quarterly, Health Economics, Oxford Bulletin of Economics and Statistics.* He is the current President of Spanish Statistical Institute (INE).

Haifang Huang is Assistant Professor of Economics at the University of Alberta, Canada. His fields of research include economics of well-being and macroeconomics. He has published articles in the *British Journal of Political Science* and the *Industrial and Labour Relation Review.*

Brad R. Humphreys is Professor in the Department of Economics at the University of Alberta, Canada, where he holds the Chair in the Economics of Gaming. He belongs to several editorial boards and has published articles in the *Southern Economic Journal, Applied Economics, Journal of Sport Management, Journal of Sports Economics* or *Contemporary Economic Policy.*

Georgios Kavetsos is Research Fellow at the Faculty of Finance at Cass Business School, London. His primary research interests are in the area of public, welfare and behavioural economics. He has previously conducted research on the happiness impact of hosting major sporting events and is currently investigating the links between health, physical activity and well-being.

Stefan Késenne is Professor of Economics at the Universiteit Antwerpen and K.U.Leuven, Belgium. He is editor with C. Jeanrenaud of the books *Competition Policy in Professional Sports* and *The Economics of Sport and the Media*. He has published numerous articles in *European Economic Review*, *Journal of Industrial Economics*, *Scottish Journal of Political Economy*, *Journal of Sports Economics* and *European Sport Management Quarterly*, and is author of the book *The Economic Theory of Professional Team Sport*: *An Analytical Treatment*.

Michael Lechner is Professor of Econometrics at the University of St Gallen, Switzerland. His primary research interests are applied labour market, health and sports economics and microeconometrics with a focus on policy evaluation. He has published in many journals such as *Journal of Labor Economics*, *The Economic Journal*, *The European Economic Review* and *Journal of Health Economics*. He is Associate Editor of the *Journal of Labor Economics* and *Econometric Reviews*, among several others.

Jorge Leyva is Research Assistant at the Institute of Sport Economics and Sport Management. He has been Supply Chain Manager at Flextronics International. He is currently doing a Master of Sciences in Sport Management at the German Sport University Cologne.

Ian G. McHale is Senior Lecturer in Statistics in the University of Salford, UK. His current research interests include statistics in sport and the statistical analysis of gambling-related issues. He was co-creator of the EA Sports Player Performance Index, the official player-rating system of the English FA Premier League.

Sonia Oreffice is Assistant Professor of Economics in the Universitat d'Alacant, Spain, Ramón y Cajal Fellow and IZA Research Fellow. Her research interests are family economics, labor economics, and health economics. She has published articles in *Journal of Political Economy*, *Labour Economics*, *Economic Inquiry*, *Review of Economics of the Household*, *Environmental and Resource Economics* and *Economics and Human Biology*.

Tim Pawlowski is Junior/Assistant Professor of Sport Economics at the German Sport University Cologne. His main fields of research are the analysis of the demand for sport (influencing factors/effects on sport participation) as well as the economics of (league) competition. He has published in journals such as *Applied Economics*, *Journal of Sports Economics* and *European Sport Management Quarterly*.

 Joseph Price is an Assistant Professor at the Department of Economics in Brigham Young University, USA. He focuses on empirical economics related to family, labour and health. He has published in journals such as the *Quarterly Journal of Economics*, *Journal of Health Economics*, *Journal of Human Resources*, *Journal of Sports Economics* and *Industrial and Labor Relations Review*.

 Climent Quintana-Domeque is Assistant Professor of Economics in the Universitat d'Alacant, Spain, Juan de la Cierva Research Fellow and IZA Research Fellow. His research interests are health economics, labour economics and development economics. He has published articles in journals such as *Demography*, *Economics and Human Biology*, *Oxford Bulletin of Economics and Statistics*, *Journal of Housing Economics* and *Social Science and Medicine*.

 Simona Rasciute is Lecturer in the Department of Economics at Loughborough University, UK. Her academic interest is foreign direct investment and discrete choice methodology economics. She has published papers in *Economic Modelling* and *European Sport Management Quarterly*.

 Plácido Rodríguez is Professor EU of Economics in the Department of Economics at the University of Oviedo, Spain. He is co-editor of the books *Sports Economics after Fifty Years: Essays in Honour of Simon Rottenberg, Governance and Competition in Professional Sports Leagues, Threats to Sports and Sports Participation* and *Social Responsibility and Sustainability in Sports*. He was President of Real Sporting de Gijón Football Club, current President of the International Association of Sports Economics (IASE) and the Director of the Sports Economics Observatory Foundation (FOED).

Jane E. Ruseski is Assistant Professor in the Department of Economics at the University of Alberta, Canada. Her research interests include health economics, sports economics and industrial organization. She has published articles in *Southern Economic Journal, Applied Health Economics and Health Policy, Journal of Sports Economics* and *Contemporary Economic Policy*.

 Nazmi Sari is Associate Professor in the University of Saskatchewan, Department of Economics, Canada. He also belongs to the Saskatchewan Population Health and Evaluation Research Unit (SPHERU). His specific research interests are economics of physical activity and smoking, quality and efficiency in hospital markets, provider reimbursements and healthcare financing reforms. He has published articles in *Health Economics, International Journal of Industrial Organization, Journal of Socio-economics, Lancet, Health Policy and Planning* and *Advances in Health Economics and Health Services Research*.

 Daniel H. Simon is Assistant Professor of Strategic Management in the Department of Applied Economics and Management at Cornell University, USA. He teaches and conducts research on a variety of issues relating to business and competitive strategy, and managerial economics. His research has appeared or has been accepted for publication in the *Strategic Management Journal, Journal of Law and Economics, Managerial and Decision Economics, Applied Economics, Information Economics and Policy, Journal of Management* and other journals.

Introduction

Plácido Rodríguez, Stefan Késenne and Brad R. Humphreys

The majority of previous research on individual participation in sport and physical activity in the social sciences has come from sociology, policy studies or management. Much of this research is qualitative and descriptive in nature. Other disciplines like sports medicine, sports psychology or sports training have examined individual participation in sport and physical activity from a clinical perspective, focusing on physiological and medical aspects of participation in sport and physical activity. Economic analysis of individual participation in sport and physical activity, and its relationship to health, is not well developed. To address this lack of economic research, the V Gijón Conference on Sports Economics, titled 'Sport and the Promotion of Health and Well Being', focused on economic analysis of the relationship between sports participation, health and well-being. The conference took place on 7–8 May 2010 in the auditorium of the Faculty of Trade, Tourism and Social Sciences Jovellanos of the University of Oviedo, located in Gijón, Spain. The conference was organized by Professors Stefan Késenne (University of Antwerp and Leuven), Brad Humphreys (University of Alberta) and Plácido Rodríguez (University of Oviedo).

The conference was presided over by the Rector of the University of Oviedo, Mr Vicente Gotor Santamaría. The conference opened with presentations by Mr Herminio Sastre Andrés, Vice-counsellor of Science and Tecnology of the Principalty of Asturias; Mr Joaquín Miranda Cortina, Director of the Tourism Society of the local (Gijón) government; Mr Rafael Pérez Lorenzo, Dean of the Jovellanos Faculty, and Mr Plácido Rodríguez, representing the conference organizers. These presentations highlighted the importance of the conference focus.

This book is the outcome of the V Gijón Conference, which was organized by the Sport Economics Observatory Foundation of the University of Oviedo. Twelve researchers from Europe and North America presented papers at the conference. These authors were introduced by the following Spanish professors and researchers: Mikel Urdangarín (President of EASM), Vicente Liern (Valencia University), Leonor Gallardo and Julio del Corral (Castilla-La Mancha University), Benito Pérez (Camilo José Cela University), Francesc Pujol (University of Navarra), Patricio Sánchez (University of Vigo), Levi Pérez, Juan Prieto and Cristina Muñiz (University of Oviedo) and José M. Sánchez (A Coruña University).

The book is of great importance, as it focuses on a relatively unexplored field in economics. It emphasizes and affirms that sport is an important determinant of the health and well-being of communities, economies and society, and that economics plays an important role in the decision to participate in sport and physical activity. The book also emphasizes why governments should continue subsidizing sport and physical activity in an environment of reduced public resources.

The chapters in this book fall into three broad areas. The first focuses on the relationship between sport and health. This issue was addressed by professors Jane Ruseski, Paul Downward, Climent Quintana-Domeque and Nazmi Sari.

In Chapter 1, Jane Ruseski and Brad Humphreys empirically investigate the relationship between participation in physical activity and health using a bivariate probit model. In this analysis, participation in physical activity is statistically identified with an exclusion restriction on a variable reflecting sense of belonging to the community. Estimates based on data from the Canadian Community Health Survey indicate that participation in physical activity reduces the reported incidence of diabetes, high blood pressure, heart disease, asthma and arthritis. Increasing the intensity and frequency of participation in physical activity appears to have a diminishing marginal impact on adverse health outcomes above the moderate level.

In Chapter 2, Paul Downward and Simona Rasciute also use a bivariate probit model to simultaneously analyse the effect of physical activity on self-reported health and well-being, using multiple waves of survey data from the UK. Their results indicate that physical activity has a positive effect on both individual health and well-being in this population. However, some activities, like cycling, have both health benefits and involve some disutility. A willingness-to-pay analysis is also performed. The results indicate a positive and significant willingness to pay for participation in physical activity and sport, but the authors argue that caution should be used when interpreting the willingness-to-pay results in the context of policy evaluation.

In Chapter 3, Jaume García Villar, Sonia Oreffice and Climent Quintana-Domeque analyse the relationship between physical activity and obesity in Spain, using data from the 2006 Spanish National Health Survey. Obesity and the body mass index (BMI) are found to be negatively correlated with leisure physical activity, even when controlling for: physical effort in the primary daily work activity, food consumption, smoking behaviour, educational level, household income, the number of children present in the home, marital status, health and dieting. The reported negative associations are similar for men and women. The intensity and type of physical activity are also negatively related to obesity, as measured by BMI, with the most strenuous exercising exhibiting the strongest correlation.

Recent epidemiological evidence shows that regular physical activity is effective in preventing several chronic diseases, and is associated with a reduced risk of premature death. In an effort to estimate the impact of physical activity on demand for hospital services, previous studies used cross-sectional data-sets. Estimated association in cross-sectional studies could be due to factors that cannot be controlled in a cross-sectional design. These factors could be time-variant or unobserved time-invariant characteristics of the individuals. Hence, the cross-sectional studies overestimate or underestimate the true effects of exercise on demand for hospital services. In Chapter 4, Nazmi Sari, using a panel data-set from Canada and panel data regression models, fills this gap in the literature. The results show that physical exercise decreases the demand for hospital services, and its marginal effect decreases as physical activity increases.

The second area focuses on the relationship between sport and labour market outcomes. The issue was addressed by Michael Lechner, Charlotte Cabane and Michael Davis.

In Chapter 5, Michael Lechner investigates the correlates of individual sports participation in Switzerland as well as the effects of sports participation on health and labour market outcomes using the first eight waves of the Swiss household panel (SHP) survey. Based on results from parametric econometric discrete choice models, better subjective health and health investments, as well as socio-economic status, are positively associated with increased participation in sport and physical activity. Furthermore, the probability of sports participation in the German-speaking part of Switzerland is much higher than in the rest of the country. The econometric analysis of the effects of participation in sport and physical activity on labour market outcomes are limited by the comparatively small sample sizes in the SHP, but nevertheless reveal positive earnings effects of participation in physical activity for men and negative effects for women.

Very little attention has been paid to the impact of sports participation on labour market outcomes in the European academic literature, even though it has received significant attention in North America. In Chapter 6, Charlotte Cabane considers sports participation as a way to improve or signal non-cognitive skills endowments in the labour market. It is known that non-cognitive skills are an important determinant of success in life, therefore Cabane analyses its impact on employment in Germany. She tests the hypothesis that sporty people – *ceteris paribus* – have access to higher-quality jobs because of the non-cognitive skills they have gained during past participation in sport. Using objective measures of job quality, she demonstrates that participating in sport, or 'being sporty' matters for labour market outcomes and that its effect cannot be attributed to any other extra-curricular activities.

In Chapter 7, Michael Davis and Christian End examine the relationship between team sport success and income in the surrounding community. This study focuses on success in the National Football League (NFL) in the USA. They examine two ways that NFL team success can influence income in the local communities: consumption, that is, improved team performance leads to higher levels of buying and giving; and productivity, whereby improved team performance leads to greater workplace productivity. Using a panel data from 1969 to 2007, they analyse two different samples: the 50 largest US metropolitan areas in 2007 and any US metropolitan area with a Major League Baseball (MLB), National Basketball Association (NBA), NFL or National Hockey League (NHL) team during the sample period. While some of their results do not show the expected effect of a positive relationship between winning and economic impact, a model with real per capita income growth rate as the dependent variable reveals that there is an impact of winning on income.

The third area focuses on the relationship between sport and happiness and well-being. The issue is addressed by Brad Humphreys, David Forrest, Joseph Price, Georgios Kavetsos and Tim Pawlowski.

In Chapter 8, Haifang Huang and Brad Humphreys investigate the relationship between participation in physical activity and self-reported happiness in the USA. Four different empirical models, based on data from the Behavioral Risk Factor Surveillance System and US County Business Patterns data, all suggest that individuals living in a county with greater access to sports facilities are more likely to participate in physical activity and also report higher life satisfaction. The contribution of participation in physical activity to increased happiness is three times the size of the increased happiness associated with employment. The results indicate that both men and women gain happiness from participation in physical activity, and men appear to benefit more from participation than women.

David Forrest and Ian G. McHale examine the relationship between subjective well-being and participation in sport (narrowly defined here, to exclude non-competitive exercise activities), in Chapter 9. Analysis of survey data for more than 28 000 adults in England reveals that those who take part in sport are (slightly) happier than those who do not, even after controlling for a rich variety of covariates controlling for factors such as demography, income, employment and state of health. A two-step treatment effect model is estimated to investigate whether this positive association can be attributed to causation running from sport to happiness. Negative correlation between the error terms in step I (participation) and step II (happiness) implies that sports participants possess unobserved characteristics unfavourable to happiness such that the benefit to them from participation is in fact greater than appears from the raw data or from ordinary least squares regression. It is shown that access to sports facilities is a significant predictor of participation in sport, and therefore public provision of sport facilities can be justified in terms of the criterion that public expenditure should have a demonstrable impact on well-being.

Past studies find that high school athletes are much less likely to experience a teenage birth in the USA. Joseph Price and Daniel H. Simon show, in Chapter 10, that evidence of a link between participation in high school athletics and teen pregnancy depends crucially on the control variables included in the empirical model. They exploit the rapid expansion of sports participation among girls in the USA created by Title IX to investigate the relationship between athletic participation and teen pregnancy and find that, overall, a 10 percentage point increase in the fraction of girls playing sports in a US state increased the teen birth rate by 0.3 percentage points (about a 10 per cent increase). They also document racial differences in the effect of sports participation on the teen birth rate. The increase in the teen birth rate is most pronounced for young white women with some suggestive evidence that sport decreases teen birth rates among young black women.

Sedentary lifestyles are likely to have adverse tangible and intangible (that is, psychological) effects on individuals, including lower self-reported happiness. Focusing on the latter, Georgios Kavetsos, who unfortunately was unable to attend the conference, tests whether physical activity is related to increased levels of well-being, in Chapter 11. Tests based on cross-sectional data, including self-reported measures of individual happiness, from 34 countries confirms this hypothesis. The empirical evidence presented here suggests that higher levels of participation in sport are related to higher levels of happiness and lower levels of happiness are reported by physically inactive individuals.

In Chapter 12, Tim Pawlowski, Christoph Breuer and Jorge Leyva analyse the relationship between subjective well-being (SWB) and the availability of public sports facilities in Germany. Their empirical results indicate that the availability of public sports facilities positively influences SWB. Empirical evidence indicates that, in addition to other important factors, people are more likely to be satisfied with their life, health and leisure status, the closer they live to a public sports facility. Since governments are not only composed of benevolent politicians, in reality, the maximization of a national happiness indicator is not the obvious ultimate goal of public policies. However, these insights might serve as inputs into the political process when deciding on the allocation of sports facilities.

Plácido Rodríguez thanks Cajastur, the Council of Education and Science of the Government of Asturias, FICYT Asturias, the Tourism Society of the Gijón municipal government, the University of Oviedo, the Department of Economics of the University of Oviedo, the Faculty of Trade, Tourism and Social Sciences Jovellanos of the University of Oviedo and the Sports Economics Observatory, Spain for financial support given for the organization of the Conference.

1. Participation in physical activity and health outcomes: evidence from the Canadian Community Health Survey

Jane E. Ruseski and Brad R. Humphreys

1. INTRODUCTION

Lifestyle choices, more narrowly defined as health-related behaviors, are widely recognized in the epidemiological and economics literature as important non-medical determinants of health. Belloc and Breslow (1972) analysed survey data from a random sample of 7000 residents in Alameda County in 1965 and identified seven lifestyle choices that are associated with better health. These practices include eating breakfast, maintaining proper weight, not snacking between meals, never smoking cigarettes, regular physical activity, moderate or no use of alcohol, and getting seven to eight hours of sleep regularly, and are known as the 'Alameda Seven'. The benefits of regular physical activity are well documented in the clinical and public health literature. Benefits include reduced risk of many chronic diseases, reduced stress and depression, and increased emotional well-being, energy level, self-confidence and satisfaction with social activity (Sherwood and Jeffery, 2000). Seven chronic diseases have been consistently associated with physical inactivity: coronary heart disease, hypertension, stroke, colon cancer, breast cancer, type 2 diabetes and osteoporosis. Physically inactive people are also more likely to be obese which is itself an important risk factor for many chronic diseases, including coronary, artery disease, stroke, hypertension, diabetes and cancer. (See Brown et al., 2007; Katzmaryzk and Janssen, 2004; Sherwood and Jeffery, 2000; and US Department of Health and Human Resources, 1996 Warburton et al., 2006; for reviews of the literature on the effects of physical activity on health and disease.)

The economic costs of physical inactivity are undoubtedly substantial but difficult to accurately quantify since physical inactivity is one of several modifiable risk factors for some chronic diseases. In addition, the economic costs include the direct health care costs to treat diseases linked with physical inactivity as well as indirect costs such as work loss due to disability. Katzmarzyk and Janssen (2004) estimated the costs of physical inactivity to be $5.3 billion in Canada in 2001, or 2.6 per cent of total health care costs. Sari (2009) estimated that moderately active individuals, compared with active individuals, use between 2.4 per cent to 9.6 per cent more health care services. Recent estimates from the USA of annual medical spending attributable to obesity were $147 billion per year in 2008, or about 10 per cent of all health care spending (Finkelstein et al., 2009). Sander and Bergemann (2003) estimated the economic burden of obesity for Germany in 2001 to be between €2.7 and €5.6 million per year. Although the USA and Germany studies are not specifically about the costs of physical inactivity, estimates of the economic costs of obesity provide some idea of the costs of physical inactivity, since physically inactive people are more likely to be obese.

Given the health benefits of regular physical activity and the costs of physical inactivity, promoting regular physical activity is a public health priority in many countries. In Canada, the prevalence of meeting physical activity guidelines is improving but still remains low. A comparison of the results from the 1996/97 National Population Health Survey (NPHS) with those from the 2005 Canadian Community Health Survey (CCHS) shows that Canadians who reported at least moderately active leisure time rose from 43 per cent to 52 per cent (Gilmour, 2007). Based on estimates from the 2003 and 2008 CCHS, the number of physically active Canadians rose from 13 389 032 in 2003 to 13 924 281 in 2008 – a modest 4 per cent increase (Statistics Canada, 2010). Two-thirds of adult Canadians (over age 20) do not meet the guidelines for sufficient physical activity as defined in Canada's Physical Activity Guide (Public Health Agency of Canada, 2006). This statistic is a motivating factor for the Canadian Sport Policy goal of enhancing Canadians' participation in sport and physical activity at all levels by 2012.

Although regular physical activity is commonly included in epidemiological studies as a health practice that is associated with good health, it has not been as extensively studied as a determinant of health in the health economics literature. In particular, questions about the frequency and intensity needed to provide health benefits remain. The objective of this chapter is to examine the impact of physical activity on health outcomes. Motivated by the Grossman (1972) health production approach, we specify bivariate probit models of health outcomes and measures of physical activity. We estimate the structural parameters of the health outcome equation together with the reduced form parameters for the physical activity equation using data from the 2005 CCHS using maximum likelihood.

2. ECONOMIC FRAMEWORK

The economic framework underlying the empirical analysis is Grossman's health production or human capital model (1972). Grossman builds on the concept of home production introduced by Becker (1965) to develop a model of the demand for health. The model links household production and investment in human capital theories in describing the demand for health, by ascribing both a consumption and investment motive to health. Health is a consumption good because people derive satisfaction from being healthy. It is an investment good because it determines the total amount of time available for all activities. The health production framework motivates the econometric analysis of the relationship between non-medical inputs such as physical activity and health outcomes. In this framework, individuals are described by a utility function U(C, H; X_U, μ_U) where utility depends a stock of health (H) and on the consumption of other commodities (C). X_U is a set of exogenous observable factors that affect utility and μ_U is a set of unobservable factors that affect utility. Commodities are produced by combining purchased market goods and time. Consumers invest in their stock of health by combining medical and non-medical inputs and time to produce health. The stock of health has the classic characteristic of an investment good that depreciates as people age. Individuals make choices about how to allocate their time and resources to health investments and other activities subject to time and monetary budget constraints.

Grossman posits that health is an investment good that depreciates with age. The health production model has been expanded to allow factors other than age to affect the stock of health. For example, the expanded health production model assumes that the stock of health is affected by health behaviors (or lifestyle choices). The health production function can be written as H(L, X, M, N; H_{t-1}, E) where H is the stock of health; L is a vector of lifestyle choices or health-related behaviors; X represents non-medical purchased inputs to health; M is purchased medical inputs; N is environmental inputs; H_{t-1} is existing health stock and E is education.

Health can be thought about as current health or future health, recognizing the influence of health behaviors on health is not immediate. Some activities, like smoking, may provide current utility but can be expected to decrease the stock of health over the long run. Conversely, other activities, like healthy eating habits and regular exercise may increase or decrease current utility but can be expected to increase health stock net of normal depreciation.

The health production framework recognizes that individuals are heterogeneous in terms of health production. The investment in health realized by any individual depends on the initial endowment and decisions about engaging in healthy behaviors. The optimality conditions arising from this type of model describe the trade-offs individuals face between choices that provide direct satisfaction and other behaviors that improve health. In this context, physical activity is a health-promoting activity. The optimality conditions provide the basis for constructing and estimating empirical models of health outcomes.

3.   HEALTH PRODUCTION STUDIES

The Grossman health production framework has been used in numerous empirical studies that examine the demand for health. This literature is quite diverse. The focus of the first studies was on the demand for health inputs, mainly medical care (for example, Goldman and Grossman, 1978; Leibowitz and Friedman, 1979). However, Fuchs (1986) convincingly argued that lifestyle choices are responsible for a substantial portion of variation in health. Recognizing that variation in medical care utilization can only partially explain differences in health, a substantial literature has developed that explores the relationship between lifestyle choices (or health behaviors), education, income and health.

The critical empirical challenges in the estimation of health production functions is accounting for unobservable heterogeneity and endogeneity of health inputs. Rosenzweig and Schultz (1983) and Mullahy and Portney (1990) are among the first to tackle these issues by employing instrumental variable techniques to estimate single equation health production functions. Rosenzweig and Schultz (1983) estimated a health production function in which birth weight is the health outcome of interest. The inputs affecting birth weight are prenatal medical care, characteristics of the mother such as employment status while pregnant, smoking while pregnant, age and number of births, prices and income. Mullahy and Portney (1990) examined the effect of cigarette smoking, air pollution, climatological conditions and other risk factors on the production of respiratory health. Treating smoking as an endogenous variable, they found that increased smoking results in more days of respiratory illness.

Several studies examine the effects of multiple lifestyle choices and health behaviors on various measures of health and health status. Kenkel (1995) used the 1985 Health Interview Survey data to examine the effects of the Alameda Seven on health in a health production framework. He estimated individual health production functions using five output measures: self-reported health status; presence of activity limitations; number of restricted activity days in the past two weeks; systolic blood pressure and a measure of proper weight. He found that excessive weight, cigarette smoking, heaving drinking, excessive or insufficient sleep, and stress to have negative effects on health and harmful, while exercise and moderate alcohol consumption had positive effects on health.

Contoyannis and Jones (2004), Balia and Jones (2008) and Schneider and Schneider (2009) modeled the production of health as recursive structures with reduced form equations for health behaviors or lifestyle choices and a structural equation for the health production function. Contoyannis and Jones (2004) examined the effects of socio-economic status and lifestyle on health. Using data from the 1984 and 1991 British Health and Lifestyle Survey (HALS), they estimated the structural parameters of a health production function together with the reduced form parameters for lifestyle equations. Health was measured by a binary indicator of self-assessed health status. The endogenous health behavior (lifestyle) variables were based on the Alameda Seven and include eating breakfast, smoking, exercise, alcohol consumption, sleep and weight. They found that sleeping well, exercising and not smoking had positive effects on the probability of reporting excellent or good health, but eating breakfast and moderate alcohol consumption were not indicators of health status.

The correlation between socio-economic status and health is well documented in the literature. However, lifestyle choices may mediate the relationship between socio-economic characteristics and health. Contoyannis and Jones (2004) in fact find this to be the case in their study of socio-economic status, health and lifestyle. Balia and Jones (2008) also used the British HALS (1984 and 2003) to further examine this issue. Their studied focused on the effect of lifestyle choices on mortality and evaluated their contribution to the observed socio-economic gradient of mortality. Like Contyannis and Jones, health was measured by a binary indicator of self-assessed health status and the lifestyle variables are based on the Alameda Seven. Mortality was measured as a binary variable taking on the value of 1 if the respondent had died before the May 2003 survey and zero otherwise. They found that all of the lifestyle indicators had a negative sign but only non-smoking, eating breakfast and obesity were statistically significant. Regular exercise was not found to be an important determinant of health. They also found that lifestyle choices do, indeed, contribute in an important way to the socio-economic gradient of mortality.

Schneider and Schneider (2009) examined the impact of smoking, alcohol consumption and obesity on self-assessed health status using data from the 2006 German Socio-economic Panel (SOEP). Like Contayannis and Jones (2004) and Balia and Jones (2008), they estimated the structural parameters of a health production function and reduced form parameters of the three health behavior equations as a recursive system. They found differential effects of smoking, alcohol consumption and obesity on health status by gender. Drinking and obesity had a negative impact on male health but no significant effect of smoking was found. For females, drinking positively influenced health status but smoking and obesity were not significant.

Grossman's model (1972) incorporates an important role for education in the production of health by assuming that education increases the efficiency of household health production. Educational attainment is often found to be positively and strongly correlated with health outcomes or health status. However, empirically establishing the mechanisms through which education affects health is challenging because there are at least three alternative explanations about the structural relationship between education and health. The first view argues that there is a direct causal effect whereby additional education allows individuals to more effectively achieve health with a given set of inputs. The second explanation is that unobserved factors such as preferences, upbringing and rate of time preference affect both health and education in the same direction. The third explanation is reverse causality, that is, better health allows one to attain a higher level of education.

Kenkel (1991, 1995) and Gilleski and Harrison (1998) are examples of empirical studies of the causal relationship between schooling and health outcomes. Kenkel (1991) tests a hypothesis of allocative efficiency, that is, education improves the choice of health inputs or health behavior by improving an individual's health knowledge. Kenkel estimates the separate effects of health knowledge and schooling on (un)healthy behaviors of cigarette smoking, alcohol consumption and exercise. He finds that part of the relationship between schooling and health behavior is explained by differences in health knowledge, but most of schooling's effects on health behavior still remain after controlling for differences in health knowledge. In a related paper, Kenkel (1995) explores the notion of productive efficiency by examining the effect of education on the marginal products of other health inputs, such as smoking, drinking, exercise and sleep habits. He finds that for some health measures, education increases the positive marginal products of healthy inputs and decreases the negative marginal product of some unhealthy inputs. Gilleski and Harrison (1998) study both productive and allocative efficiency of schooling on health and find evidence of both.

This chapter adds to the empirical literature on health production by focusing the effect of physical activity on several health outcomes that have been explicitly linked with physical activity in the clinical literature. Some of the previous studies include regular exercise as an input in the health production function (for example, Kenkel, 1995; Contoyannis and Jones, 2004; Balia and Jones, 2008). Kenkel and Contoyannis and Jones find that regular exercise is associated with better health, but Balia and Jones do not find a significant effect of exercise on health status. We take a closer look at the role of physical activity in producing health by considering both the intensity and frequency of physical activity in our models.

4. EMPIRICAL ANALYSIS

Empirical analyses of the effects of health-related behaviors on health are challenging due to the econometric problems of unobserved individual heterogeneity and the endogeneity of health and health-related behaviors. Some empirical analyses use single equation instrumental variable approaches, such as two-stage least squares, to address these issues. (Gilleskie and Harrison, 1998; Kenkel, 1991, 1995; Lindhal, 2005; Mullahy and Portney, 1990; Rozenweig and Schultz, 1983, are examples.) An alternative approach is to specify a recursive bivariate or multivariate probit model including a system of equations for the health production function and health behaviors to control for unobserved heterogeneity and endogeneity (Balia and Jones, 2008; Contoyannis and Jones, 2004; Rascuite and Downward, 2010; Schneider and Schneider, 2009).

We take the second approach to develop evidence about the relationship between participation in physical activity and health outcomes. We estimate a bivariate probit model:

$$Y_{pi}^* = \beta_p X_{pi} + u_{pi}$$

$$Y_{hi}^* = \alpha y_{pi} + \beta_h X_{hi} + u_{hi} \tag{1.1}$$

where Y_{hi}^* represents the latent stock of health of individual i, and Y_{pi}^* represents the latent benefit that individual i derives from participation in physical activity p. Y_{pi}^* and Y_{hi}^* are unobservable, but we observe y_{pi} and y_{hi} which are indicator variables. $y_{hi} = 1$ if $Y_{hi}^* < 0$ and $y_{pi} = 1$ if $Y_{pi}^* > 0$. Otherwise, both variables are equal to 0. X_{pi} and X_{hi} are vectors of explanatory variables that affect participation in physical activity and health outcomes. These variables include demographic, physiological, and economic characteristics of individuals in the sample. β_p, β_h, and a are unknown parameters to be estimated. u_{pi} and u_{hi} are unobservable, normally distributed, mean 0, constant variance error terms that capture all other factors that affect participation in physical activity and health outcomes.

Note the system is recursive in that health outcomes depend on the exogenous variables X_{hi} and participation in physical activity, y_{pi}. The physical activity equation is a reduced form equation and the health outcome equation is a structural equation with participation in physical activity as an explanatory variable. Maddala (1983) described methods for estimating recursive systems of equations like (1.1). In order for the parameters to be consistently estimated, the system must be identified; in this case, an explanatory variable must appear in X_{pi} that does not appear in X_{hi}. Wilde (2000) shows that an exclusion restriction is not required to identify the parameters in the system of equations, as long as X_{pi} and X_{hi} each contain one varying explanatory variable.

5.   DATA SOURCE AND DESCRIPTION

We use data from the Canadian Community Health Survey (CCHS) cycle 3.1. The CCHS is a cross-sectional, nationally representative survey that collects data on health status, health care utilization and health determinants. The CCHS also contains detailed demographic and economic variables about the survey respondents and their households. The target population is all Canadians over the age of 12, excluding those living on First Nations reserves and in institutions and serving in the armed forces. Data are collected through a random digit dial telephone survey. Cycle 3.1 of the CCHS was conducted in 2005. This wave of the survey contained 132 221 usable observations after those with missing values were dropped.

The lifestyle variable of interest in this study is physical activity. The CCHS asks detailed questions about participation in leisure time physical activity and contains a number of variables describing the type of participation and intensity. We use three derived binary variables to examine the effects of different levels of participation and intensity. The first two, an indicator for individuals who are 'active' and an indicator for individuals who are 'moderately active', are based on the average daily energy expended on leisure time physical activity, based on the CCHS Physical Activity Index. The energy expenditure measure in the CCHS is based on the frequency and duration of reported sessions of physical activity and the metabolic equivalent for task (MET) value of the specific activity. METs reflect metabolic energy cost relative to resting, so a leisure time physical activity like ice hockey with a MET value of 6 requires six times the energy as during rest. 'Active' is the highest level of physical activity based on the Physical Activity Index, and 'moderately active' is the second highest level. The third measure of physical activity is an indicator for individuals who participated daily in leisure time physical activity. This variable was based on responses about leisure time physical activity over the preceeding three months. These three indicator variables identify individuals who frequently and intensely engage in physical activity. The two variables based on daily energy expenditure reflect both intensity and frequency of physical activity, and the indicator variable for daily participation reflects high-frequency participation but not intensity. This delineation in the physical activity variables should allow us to evaluate the extent and intensity of physical activity needed for health benefits.

Health is measured using the detailed information in the CCHS about health outcomes. We focus on five health outcomes in this study: individuals who report having arthritis, high blood pressure, diabetes, heart disease and asthma. These are also the most frequently reported negative health outcomes in the CCHS, and most of them, primarily high blood pressure, diabetes and heart disease, have been linked to lifestyle choices and can be influenced by physical activity. Each health outcome is measured as a binary variable taking on the value of 1 if the individual reported having any of these conditions and zero otherwise.

We also include a number of socio-economic and demographic characteristics that are commonly included in determinants of health studies. Positive relationships between income and education and health have been documented in numerous studies. In our data, household income is measured in categories. The categorical income variables allow us to account for differences in the relative income position of the households in the analysis and for a nonlinear relationship between income and physical activity and health. Education is also measured in discrete categories: high school, some college and college graduate. We include employment status, home ownership and welfare as the primary source of income as additional measures of the economic environment. Home ownership can be thought of as a measure of social class. Individual characteristics included are age, marital status, gender, size of household, presence of young children in the household, and native-born Canadian. All empirical models include a vector of indicator variables for province of residence to account for unobservable heterogeneity in provincial characteristics that affect health and physical activity. Finally, we include height as a continuous exogenous variable because it is known to be a good predictor of mortality and morbidity risks, and captures heterogeneity in initial health endowments (Bali and Jones, 2008). Table 1.1 contains summary statistics for the leisure time physical activity, health

Table 1.1   Summary statistics

Variable	Mean
Has asthma	0.088
Has arthritis	0.213
Has high blood pressure	0.187
Has diabetes	0.062
Has heart disease	0.065
Daily active participant in physical activity	0.372
Physical Activity Index 'active'	0.259
Physical Activity Index 'moderate'	0.244
Age	46.10
Height in meters	1.686
Male	0.458
Single	0.304
Employed	0.613
Household income < $15000	0.082
Household income $15000 to $30000	0.154
Household income $30000 to $50000	0.190
Household income $50000 to $80000	0.212
Household income more than $80000	0.211
Welfare is primary source of income	0.038
Owns home	0.717
High school education	0.146
Some college	0.077
College graduate	0.470
Number of persons in household	2.415
Children under 12 in household	0.209
Native-born Canadian	0.840
Expressed sense of belonging to community	0.651

outcome, demographic and economic variables used in the empirical analysis.

Arthritis and high blood pressure are the most frequently reported negative health outcomes in the sample. More than one person in five in the sample reports suffering from arthritis. Participation in physical activity is relatively common in the sample; more than one-third of the sample participates daily, and more than one-quarter scored in the 'active' range of the Physical Activity Index. There is not complete overlap in these two categories of physical activity, because daily participation does not reflect intensity of participation; 65 per cent of the individuals who participated in physical activity daily fell into the 'active' category.

6.   RESULTS AND DISCUSSION

We estimate models for different health outcomes and levels of participation in physical activity. Recall that y_{pi} is an indicator variable that is
equal to 1 if individual i participated in physical activity at level p and 0
otherwise. The three levels of physical activity participation used, daily
participation, an 'active' level of participation based on the Physical
Activity Index and energy expended, and a 'moderately active' level of
participation, represent different levels of frequency and intensity of
participation. These three levels of participation in physical activity can
be interpreted as choices available to individuals who become physically
active. By devoting more time and effort to participation in physical activity, individuals can select themselves into one of these categories; these
different levels of participation in physical activity may also affect the
individual's stock of health. We estimate different models for each of the
five negative health outcomes (asthma, arthritis, high blood pressure, diabetes and heart disease) that have been related to participation in physical
activity.

Wilde (2000) showed that the recursive, bivariate probit model, equation (1.1), could be identified without any exclusion restrictions. While
this may be possible, we were unable to achieve convergence of any of
the empirical models estimated without imposing an exclusion restriction, suggesting that this case does not match the situation described by
Wilde (2000). In general, an exclusion restriction identifying participation in physical activity should be a variable that is related to participation but unrelated to u_{hi}, the error term capturing unobservable factors
that affect an individual's stock of health. Our exclusion restriction
was based on the variable describing an individual's 'sense of belonging' to the local community. Forrest and McHale (2009) and Huang
and Humphreys (2010) showed that individuals living in communities with more sports facilities are more likely to participate in leisure
time physical activity. We assume that individuals who report a very
strong or strong sense of belonging in the community are living in areas
with either adequate local amenities including physical activity related
facilities, or with a generally supportive culture that includes support for
being physically active. These factors should be unrelated to the stock
of health.

Table 1.2 contains estimated parameters and p-values for the bivariate
probit model for individuals with an 'active' level of physical activity on
the Physical Activity Index and a health outcome indicator variable that
is equal to one if the individual reports having diabetes. The estimated
parameters on the provincial indicator variables are not reported. There

Table 1.2   Bivariate probit results, active physical activity and incidence of diabetes

Variable	Structural Health eq.		Reduced Form PA eq.	
	parameter	p-val.	parameter	p-val.
Age	0.013	<0.001	−0.013	<0.001
Male	0.232	<0.001	0.102	<0.001
Single	−0.051	0.013	0.152	<0.001
Employed	−0.206	<0.001	−0.190	<0.001
Household income $15000 to $30000	0.019	0.244	−0.038	0.004
Household income $30000 to $50000	−0.004	0.795	−0.031	0.012
Household income $50000 to $80000	−0.017	0.376	0.006	0.633
Household income more than $80000	−0.091	<0.001	0.109	<0.001
Welfare is primary source of income	0.211	<0.001	−0.067	0.002
Owns home	−0.044	0.004	0.118	<0.001
High school education	−0.063	0.001	0.006	0.660
Some college	−0.031	0.206	0.017	0.270
College graduate	−0.010	0.506	0.102	<0.001
Height in meters	−0.279	0.001	0.433	<0.001
Children under 12 in household	−0.217	<0.001	−0.117	<0.001
Native-born Canadian	0.045	0.003	0.002	0.880
Sense of belonging to community	—	—	0.276	<0.001
Physical Activity Index 'active'	−1.010	<0.001	—	—

were 131110 observations, and the log likelihood value was −97228. The estimated parameters of the reduced form equation for participation in physical activity are similar to other results in the literature (Humphreys and Ruseski, 2007, 2009). Active participation in physical activity falls with age and rises with income and education. Males are more likely to be active participants than females, and unmarried individuals are more likely to participate than married individuals; the presence of children under the age of 12 reduced active participation in physical activity. Based on the structural health outcome equation, the incidence of diabetes in the sample rises with age and falls with income. Males are more likely to have diabetes, as are individuals on welfare. The incidence of diabetes is unrelated to education, and falls with height of the individual and the presence of small children in the household.

The primary parameter of interest in this model is the estimated parameter on the physical activity participation variable in the structural health outcome equation. This parameter shows the effect of participation in that level of physical activity on the probability that

Table 1.3   Estimated marginal impact of physical activity level on health outcomes

Participation	Diabetes	High BP	Heart disease	Arthritis	Asthma
Daily	−0.021*	−0.039*	−0.033**	−0.074**	−0.021*
Active	−0.048**	−0.133**	−0.013*	−0.113**	−0.001
Moderate	−0.121**	NC	−0.093**	−0.183**	−0.062

a physically active individual has diabetes. In this case, the parameter on active participation in physical activity is negative and significant. Active participants in physical activity are less likely to report having diabetes in this sample. The marginal effect of participation on the probability of having diabetes is −0.021, or a 2.1 per cent reduction in the probability of having diabetes, relative to any other level of participation in physical activity.

The relationship between the level of participation in physical activity and health outcomes is the primary focus of this investigation. Instead of reporting full regression results for each of the different levels of participation in physical activity and health outcome in the body of the chapter, we report the estimated marginal impacts for each on Table 1.3. An asterisk (*) identifies parameter estimates significant at the 1 level and two asterisks (**) identify parameter estimates significant at lower than a 1 per cent level. The regression model would not converge for a moderate level of physical activity and the health outcome high blood pressure. The full set of results are reported in Appendix Tables 1.A1–1.A10.

A striking result is that moderate physical activity has the largest marginal impact on health outcomes. There are diminishing returns to physical activity in reducing the probability of chronic disease. For diabetes, the marginal impact of physical activity declines from 12 per cent for moderate to 4.8 per cent for active to 2.1 per cent for daily. Similar patterns emerge for high blood pressure, heart disease and arthritis. The only chronic condition for which this pattern does not hold is asthma where only daily physical activity reduces the probability of having asthma. People who engage in daily physical activity are 2.1 per cent less likely to report having asthma. This result is not surprising since asthma is not as strongly linked with physical activity as the other health outcomes. Asthma is more likely to be influenced by other lifestyle choices such as not smoking. Taken together, these findings have potentially important implications for recommendations about the frequency and intensity of physical activity required for health benefits.

7. CONCLUSION

We use the Grossman health production framework to examine the influence of health-related behavior on health outcomes. The lifestyle choice or health behavior of interest is physical activity. We focus on physical activity because sedentary lifestyles have been recognized as a modifiable risk factor for several chronic diseases like diabetes, heart disease, stroke, arthritis and some types of cancer. However, questions remain as to the frequency and intensity of physical activity needed to reduce the incidence of disease. To explore the effect of different levels of physical activity on health outcomes, we estimate the structural parameters of a series of health production functions together with the reduced form parameters for various physical activity equations specified as bivariate probit models using data from the 2005 CCHS. The models are estimated using maximum likelihood for a bivariate probit model with discrete indicators of physical activity and health outcomes.

We use three derived binary variables to examine the effects of different levels of participation and intensity on health outcomes. The first two, an indicator for individuals who are 'active' and an indicator for individuals who are 'moderately active', are based on the average daily energy expended on leisure time physical activity, based on the CCHS Physical Activity Index. The third measure is an indicator for individuals who participated in leisure time physical activity daily. We focus on four health outcomes that have been linked with physical activity in the epidemiological literature: arthritis, high blood pressure, diabetes and heart disease. We also examine asthma as a fifth health outcome. Each health outcome is measured as a binary variable taking on the value of 1 if the individual reported having any of these conditions and 0 otherwise. In keeping with Grossman's health production framework, socio-economic and individual characteristics are included as explanatory variables in the analysis.

We find that any level of physical activity reduces the probability of reporting having diabetes, high blood pressure, heart disease and arthritis but that moderate physical activity has the largest marginal impact. These results suggest that there are diminishing marginal returns to physical activity. Moderate participation appears to be sufficient to generate tangible health benefits. Physical activity is not as important in influencing the probability of reporting having asthma. Our results are consistent with previous studies examining the relationship between health-related behaviors and health that found a positive relationship between physical activity and health (Contayannis and Jones, 2004; Kenkel, 1995; Rascuite and Downard, 2010). Our results add to these findings by examining the contribution of different frequencies and intensities of physical activity to health.

REFERENCES

Balia, S. and Jones, A.M. (2008), 'Mortality, lifestyle and socio-economic status', *Journal of Health Economics*, **27**, 1–26.

Becker, G. (1965), 'A theory of the allocation of time', *The Economic Journal*, **75**, 493–513.

Belloc, N.B. and Breslow, L. (1972), 'Relationship of physical health status and health practices', *Preventive Medicine*, **1**, 409–21.

Brown, W., Burton, N. and Rowan, P. (2007), 'Updating the evidence on physical activity and health in woman', *American Journal of Preventive Medicine*, **33**, 404–11.

Contoyannis, P. and Jones, A.M. (2004), 'Socio-economic status, health and lifestyle', *Journal of Health Economics*, **23**, 965–95.

Finkelstein, E.A., Trogdon, J.G., Cohen, J.W. and Dietz, W. (2009), 'Annual medical spending attributable to obesity: payer- and service-specific estimates', *Health Affairs*, **28** (5), w822–w831.

Forrest, D. and McHale, I.G. (2009), 'Public policy, sport, and happiness: an empirical study', paper presented at the Annual Conference Arbeitskreis Sportökonomik, Sport and Urban Economics, Berlin, 2009.

Fuchs, V. (1986), *The Health Economy*, Cambridge, MA: Harvard University Press.

Gilleskie, D.B. and Harrison, A.L. (1998), 'The effects of endogenous health inputs on the relationship between health and education', *Economics of Education Review*, **17** (3), 279–97.

Gilmour, H. (2007), 'Physically active Canadians', *Health Reports*, **18** (3), 45–66, Statistics Canada, Catalogue 82-003.

Goldman, F. and Grossman, M. (1978), 'The demand for pediatric care: an hedonic approach', *The Journal of Political Economy*, **86** (2), 259–80.

Grossman, M. (1972), 'On the concept of health capital and the demand for health', *The Journal of Political Economy*, **80**, 223–55.

Huang, H. and Humphreys, B. (2010), 'Sports participation and happiness: evidence from U.S. micro data', Working Paper WP 2010-08, University of Alberta, Department of Economics.

Humphreys, B. and Ruseski, J. (2007), 'Participation in physical activity and government spending on parks and recreation', *Contemporary Economic Policy*, **25**, 538–52.

Humphreys, B. and Ruseski, J. (2009), 'The economics of participation and time spent in physical activity', Working Paper WP 2009-09, University of Alberta, Department of Economics.

Katzmarzyk, P. and Janssen, I. (2004), 'The economic costs associated with physical inactivity and obesity in Canada: an update', *Canadian Journal of Applied Physiology*, **29**, 90–115.

Kenkel, D.S. (1991), 'Health behavior, health knowledge and schooling', *The Journal of Political Economy*, **99** (2), 287–305.

Kenkel, D.S. (1995), 'Should you eat breakfast? Estimates from health production functions', *Health Economics*, **4**, 15–29.

Leibowitz, A. and Friedman, B.S. (1979), 'Family bequests and the derived demand for health inputs', *Economic Inquiry*, **17**, 419–34.

Lindahl, M. (2005), 'Estimating the effect of income on health and mortality using lottery prizes as an exogenous source of variation in income', *The Journal of Human Resources*, **40** (1), 14–168.

Maddala, G. (1983), *Limited Dependent and Qualitiative Variables in Econometrics*, Cambridge, MA: Cambridge University Press.

Mullahy, J. and Portney, P.R. (1990) 'Air pollution, cigarette smoking and the production of respiratory health', *Journal of Health Economics*, **9**, 193–205.

Public Health Agency of Canada (2006), 'Facts on current physical activity levels of Canadians', available at: http://www.phac-aspc.gc.ca/pau-uap/paguide/back3e.html.

Rascuite, S. and Downward, P. (2010), 'Health or happiness? What is the impact of physical activity on the individual?', *Kyklos*, **63** (2), 256–70.

Rosenzweig, M.R. and Schultz, T.P. (1983), 'Estimating a household production function: heterogeneity, the demand for health inputs and their effects on birth weight', *The Journal of Political Economy*, **91** (5), 723–46.

Sander, B. and Bergemann, R. (2003), 'Economic burden of obesity and its complications in Germany', *European Journal of Health Economics*, **4**, 248–53.

Sari, N. (2009), 'Physical inactivity and its impact on healthcare utilization', *Health Economics*, **18**, 885–901.

Schneider, B. and Schneider, U. (2009), 'Determinants and consequences of health behavior: new evidence from German micro data', SOEP Working Paper 253, DIW Berlin, The German Socio-Economic Panel (SOEP).

Sherwood, N. and Jeffery, R. (2000), 'The behavioral determinants of exercise: implications for physical activity interventions', *Annual Review of Nutrition*, **20**, 21–44.

Statistics Canada. (2010), 'Physical activity during leisure-time, by sex, provinces and territories', *CANSIM*, Catalogue 82-221-X, Table 105-0501.

US Department of Health and Human Resources (1996), *Physical Activity and Health: A Report of the Surgeon General*, Centers for Disease Control and Prevention, National Center for Chronic Disease Prevention and Health Promotion, Atlanta, pp. 81–172.

Warburton, D., Nicol, C. and Bredin, S. (2006), 'Health benefits of physical activity: the evidence', *Canadian Medical Association Journal*, **176**, 801–8.

Wilde, J. (2000), 'Identification of multiple probit models with endogenous dummy regressors', *Economics Letters*, **69**, 309–12.

APPENDIX

Table 1A.1   *Bivariate probit results: structural health equation – incidence of diabetes*

Variable	PA Index – Active		PA Index – Moderate		PA Index – Daily	
	Parameter	*p*-value	Parameter	*p*-value	Parameter	*p*-value
Age	0.013	<0.001	0.013	<0.001	0.018	<0.001
Male	0.232	<0.001	0.109	<0.001	0.205	<0.001
Single	−0.051	0.013	−0.095	<0.001	−0.098	<0.001
Employed	−0.206	<0.001	−0.105	<0.001	−0.177	<0.001
Household income $15 000 to $30 000	0.019	0.244	0.038	0.007	0.031	0.072
Household income $30 000 to $50 000	−0.004	0.795	0.038	0.011	0.003	0.858
Household income $50 000 to $80 000	−0.017	0.376	0.034	0.034	−0.024	0.227
Household income more than $80 000	−0.091	<0.001	−0.030	0.114	−0.133	<0.001
Welfare is primary source of income	0.211	<0.001	0.184	<0.001	0.269	<0.001
Owns home	−0.044	0.004	−0.035	0.003	−0.079	<0.001
High school education	−0.063	0.001	0.011	0.507	−0.054	0.005
Some college	−0.031	0.206	0.045	0.033	−0.022	0.408
College graduate	−0.010	0.506	0.065	<0.001	−0.018	0.283
Height in meters	−0.279	0.001	−0.254	<0.001	−0.382	<0.001
Children under 12 in household	−0.217	<0.001	−0.158	<0.001	−0.214	<0.001
Native-born Canadian	0.045	0.003	0.059	<0.001	0.047	0.004
Expressed sense of belonging to community						
Physical Activity Index 'active'	−1.010	<0.001				
Physical Activity Index 'moderate'			−1.384	<0.001		
Physical Activity Index 'daily'					−0.472	<0.000

Table 1A.2   Bivariate probit results: reduced form activity equation –
incidence of diabetes

Variable	PA Index – Active		PA Index – Moderate		PA Index – Daily	
	Parameter	*p*-value	Parameter	*p*-value	Parameter	*p*-value
Age	−0.013	<0.001	−0.001	<0.001	−0.006	<0.001
Male	0.102	<0.001	−0.084	<0.001	−0.061	<0.001
Single	0.152	<0.001	−0.024	0.030	0.110	<0.001
Employed	−0.190	<0.001	0.007	0.477	−0.154	<0.001
Household income $15 000 to $30 000	−0.038	0.004	0.027	0.036	−0.017	0.146
Household income $30 000 to $50 000	−0.031	0.012	0.061	<0.001	−0.025	0.030
Household income $50 000 to $80 000	0.006	0.633	0.092	<0.001	−0.011	0.350
Household income more than $80 000	0.109	<0.001	0.129	<0.001	0.063	<0.001
Welfare is primary source of income	−0.067	0.002	−0.008	0.723	0.031	0.118
Owns home	0.118	<0.001	0.055	<0.001	0.064	<0.001
High school education	0.006	0.660	0.115	<0.001	0.069	<0.001
Some college	0.017	0.270	0.133	<0.001	0.087	<0.001
College graduate	0.102	<0.001	0.180	<0.001	0.150	<0.001
Height in meters	0.433	<0.001	0.136	0.010	0.390	<0.001
Children under 12 in household	−0.117	<0.001	−0.038	<0.001	−0.103	<0.001
Native-born Canadian	0.002	0.880	0.043	<0.001	0.008	0.434
Expressed sense of belonging to community	0.276	<0.001	0.094	<0.001	0.278	<0.001

Table 1A.3 Bivariate probit results: structural health equation – incidence of heart disease

Variable	PA Index – Active		PA Index – Moderate		PA Index – Daily	
	Parameter	p-value	Parameter	p-value	Parameter	p-value
Age	0.024	<0.001	0.020	<0.001	0.024	<0.001
Male	0.328	<0.001	0.198	<0.001	0.286	<0.001
Single	−0.083	<0.001	−0.089	<0.001	−0.076	<0.001
Employed	−0.330	<0.001	−0.226	<0.001	−0.329	<0.001
Household income $15 000 to $30 000	0.002	0.897	0.019	0.199	0.004	0.833
Household income $30 000 to $50 000	−0.027	0.155	0.012	0.467	−0.027	0.140
Household income $50 000 to $80 000	−0.050	0.018	0.006	0.720	−0.053	0.010
Household income more than $80 000	−0.111	<0.001	−0.034	0.101	−0.109	<0.001
Welfare is primary source of income	0.223	<0.001	0.172	<0.001	0.234	<0.001
Owns home	−0.070	<0.001	−0.040	0.002	−0.066	<0.001
High school education	−0.061	0.002	0.006	0.736	−0.041	0.041
Some college	−0.002	0.953	0.063	0.006	0.020	0.449
College graduate	−0.003	0.829	0.073	<0.001	0.023	0.181
Height in meters	−0.349	<0.001	−0.248	0.001	−0.295	0.001
Children under 12 in household	−0.139	<0.001	−0.104	<0.001	−0.144	<0.001
Native-born Canadian	0.115	<0.001	0.114	<0.001	0.115	<0.001
Physical Activity Index 'active'	−0.548	<0.001				
Physical Activity Index 'moderate'			−1.305	<0.001		
Physical Activity Index 'daily'					−0.710	<0.001

Table 1A.4 Bivariate probit results: reduced form activity equation –
incidence of heart disease

Variable	PA Index – Active		PA Index – Moderate		PA Index – Daily	
	Parameter	p-value	Parameter	p-value	Parameter	p-value
Age	−0.013	<0.000	−0.001	<0.000	−0.006	<0.001
Male	0.102	<0.000	−0.084	<0.000	−0.061	<0.001
Single	0.155	<0.000	−0.023	0.037	0.110	<0.001
Employed	−0.190	<0.000	0.008	0.436	−0.154	<0.001
Household income $15000 to $30000	−0.039	0.003	0.024	0.059	−0.018	0.140
Household income $30000 to $50000	−0.032	0.012	0.061	<0.000	−0.025	0.030
Household income $50000 to $80000	0.006	0.643	0.091	<0.000	−0.011	0.349
Household income more than $80000	0.110	<0.000	0.129	<0.000	0.063	<0.001
Welfare is primary source of income	−0.068	0.001	−0.009	0.686	0.030	0.121
Owns home	0.117	<0.000	0.052	<0.000	0.063	<0.001
High school education	0.006	0.636	0.114	<0.000	0.069	<0.001
Some college	0.018	0.252	0.133	<0.000	0.087	<0.001
College graduate	0.102	<0.000	0.181	<0.000	0.150	<0.001
Height in meters	0.435	<0.000	0.132	0.013	0.390	<0.001
Children under 12 in household	−0.116	<0.000	−0.038	<0.000	−0.103	<0.001
Native-born Canadian	0.002	0.878	0.043	<0.000	0.008	0.422
Expressed sense of belonging to community	0.286	<0.000	0.104	<0.000	0.278	<0.001

Table 1A.5 Bivariate probit results: structural health equation – incidence of arthritis

Variable	PA Index – Active		PA Index – Moderate		PA Index – Daily	
	Parameter	*p*-value	Parameter	*p*-value	Parameter	*p*-value
Age	0.023	<0.001	0.021	<0.001	0.028	<0.001
Male	−0.226	<0.001	−0.255	<0.001	−0.296	<0.001
Single	−0.087	<0.001	−0.124	<0.001	−0.143	<0.001
Employed	−0.158	<0.001	−0.068	<0.001	−0.126	<0.001
Household income $15000 to $30000	0.036	0.005	0.051	<0.001	0.049	<0.001
Household income $30000 to $50000	−0.017	0.181	0.025	0.034	−0.008	0.547
Household income $50000 to $80000	−0.043	0.002	0.012	0.357	−0.052	<0.001
Household income more than $80000	−0.083	<0.001	−0.029	0.037	−0.127	<0.001
Welfare is primary source of income	0.371	<0.001	0.310	<0.001	0.455	<0.001
Owns home	0.006	0.605	−0.001	0.915	−0.022	0.049
High school education	−0.043	0.001	0.022	0.070	−0.025	0.083
Some college	0.000	0.982	0.063	<0.001	0.021	0.269
College graduate	−0.023	0.035	0.046	<0.001	−0.020	0.103
Height in meters	0.173	0.005	0.092	0.091	0.111	0.088
Children under 12 in household	−0.231	<0.001	−0.161	<0.001	−0.237	<0.001
Native-born Canadian	0.128	<0.001	0.125	<0.001	0.135	<0.001
Physical Activity Index 'active'	−1.129	<0.001				
Physical Activity Index 'moderate'			−1.424	<0.001		
Physical Activity Index 'daily'					−0.633	<0.001

*Table 1A.6   Bivariate probit results: reduced form activity equation –
            incidence of arthritis*

Variable	PA Index – Active		PA Index – Moderate		PA Index – Daily	
	Parameter	p-value	Parameter	p-value	Parameter	p-value
Age	−0.013	<0.001	−0.001	<0.001	−0.006	<0.001
Male	0.098	<0.001	−0.093	<0.001	−0.061	<0.001
Single	0.149	<0.001	−0.027	0.013	0.109	<0.001
Employed	−0.189	<0.001	0.006	0.509	−0.153	<0.001
Household income $15 000 to $30 000	−0.039	0.003	0.024	0.053	−0.018	0.123
Household income $30 000 to $50 000	−0.033	0.008	0.058	<0.001	−0.026	0.027
Household income $50 000 to $80 000	0.004	0.771	0.090	<0.001	−0.011	0.330
Household income more than $80 000	0.107	<0.001	0.128	<0.001	0.062	<0.001
Welfare is primary source of income	−0.066	0.002	0.000	0.997	0.030	0.120
Owns home	0.119	<0.001	0.054	<0.001	0.064	<0.001
High school education	0.003	0.811	0.104	<0.001	0.068	<0.001
Some college	0.016	0.307	0.128	<0.001	0.086	<0.001
College graduate	0.101	<0.001	0.172	<0.001	0.149	<0.001
Height in meters	0.424	<0.001	0.127	0.016	0.389	<0.001
Children under 12 in household	−0.119	<0.001	−0.041	<0.001	−0.104	<0.001
Native-born Canadian	−0.002	0.829	0.040	<0.001	0.008	0.437
Expressed sense of belonging to community	0.267	<0.001	0.090	<0.001	0.277	<0.001

Table 1A.7   Bivariate probit results: structural health equation – incidence of asthma

Variable	PA Index – Active		PA Index – Moderate		PA Index – Daily	
	Parameter	p-value	Parameter	p-value	Parameter	p-value
Age	−0.005	<0.001	−0.005	<0.001	−0.006	<0.001
Male	−0.117	<0.001	−0.135	<0.001	−0.124	<0.001
Single	0.016	0.322	0.007	0.614	0.028	0.064
Employed	−0.096	<0.001	−0.084	<0.001	−0.112	<0.001
Household income $15 000 to $30 000	0.026	0.108	0.031	0.039	0.024	0.134
Household income $30 000 to $50 000	−0.054	0.001	−0.030	0.090	−0.056	<0.001
Household income $50 000 to $80 000	−0.046	0.005	−0.012	0.536	−0.046	0.004
Household income more than $80 000	−0.024	0.180	0.020	0.371	−0.017	0.333
Welfare is primary source of income	0.228	<0.001	0.205	<0.001	0.228	<0.001
Owns home	−0.089	<0.001	−0.062	<0.001	−0.080	<0.001
High school education	−0.113	<0.001	−0.069	0.004	−0.106	<0.001
Some college	0.044	0.026	0.080	<0.001	0.052	0.009
College graduate	−0.026	0.053	0.032	0.167	−0.011	0.453
Height in meters	−0.404	<0.001	−0.330	<0.001	−0.362	<0.001
Children under 12 in household	−0.066	<0.001	−0.069	<0.001	−0.075	<0.001
Native-born Canadian	0.247	<0.001	0.239	<0.001	0.246	<0.001
Physical Activity Index 'active'	−0.022	0.870				
Physical Activity Index 'moderate'			−0.868	<0.001		
Physical Activity Index 'daily'					−0.296	0.004

Table 1A.8   Bivariate probit results: reduced form activity equation –
incidence of asthma

Variable	PA Index – Active		PA Index – Moderate		PA Index – Daily	
	Parameter	*p*-value	Parameter	*p*-value	Parameter	*p*-value
Age	−0.013	<0.001	−0.001	<0.001	−0.006	<0.001
Male	0.102	<0.001	−0.084	<0.001	−0.061	<0.001
Single	0.155	<0.001	−0.022	0.051	0.110	<0.001
Employed	−0.190	<0.001	0.007	0.458	−0.154	<0.001
Household income $15000 to $30000	−0.038	0.004	0.024	0.061	−0.018	0.132
Household income $30000 to $50000	−0.031	0.012	0.060	<0.001	−0.025	0.029
Household income $50000 to $80000	0.006	0.616	0.091	<0.001	−0.011	0.338
Household income more than $80000	0.110	<0.001	0.129	<0.001	0.062	<0.001
Welfare is primary source of income	−0.068	0.001	−0.008	0.710	0.031	0.117
Owns home	0.117	<0.001	0.054	<0.001	0.064	<0.001
High school education	0.006	0.651	0.114	<0.001	0.068	<0.001
Some college	0.018	0.262	0.134	<0.001	0.087	<0.001
College graduate	0.102	<0.001	0.180	<0.001	0.149	<0.001
Height in meters	0.435	<0.001	0.137	0.010	0.390	<0.001
Children under 12 in household	−0.115	<0.001	−0.037	<0.001	−0.103	<0.001
Native-born Canadian	0.001	0.905	0.043	<0.001	0.008	0.428
Expressed sense of belonging to community	0.285	<0.001	0.103	<0.001	0.279	<0.001

Table 1A.9 *Bivariate probit results: structural health equation – incidence of high blood pressure*

Variable	PA Index – Active		PA Index – Daily	
	Parameter	*p*-value	Parameter	*p*-value
Age	0.022	<0.001	0.031	<0.001
Male	0.058	<0.001	0.012	0.360
Single	−0.033	0.033	−0.117	<0.001
Employed	−0.150	<0.001	−0.095	<0.001
Household income $15 000 to $30 000	0.016	0.221	0.034	0.014
Household income $30 000 to $50 000	0.038	0.004	0.060	<0.001
Household income $50 000 to $80 000	0.041	0.003	0.043	0.004
Household income more than $80 000	0.049	0.002	0.001	0.968
Welfare is primary source of income	0.191	<0.001	0.291	<0.001
Owns home	0.060	<0.001	0.024	0.038
High school education	−0.034	0.012	−0.022	0.141
Some college	−0.034	0.062	−0.027	0.173
College graduate	−0.014	0.199	−0.034	0.008
Height in meters	−0.203	0.002	−0.389	<0.001
Children under 12 in household	−0.217	<0.001	−0.228	<0.001
Native-born Canadian	0.030	0.008	0.028	0.026
Physical Activity Index 'active'	−1.299	<0.001		
Physical Activity Index 'daily'			−0.419	<0.001

Note: PA Index – moderate did not converge.

Table 1A.10   Bivariate probit results: reduced form activity equation –
incidence of high blood pressure

Variable	PA Index – Active		PA Index – Daily	
	Parameter	*p*-value	Parameter	*p*-value
Age	−0.014	<0.001	−0.006	<0.001
Male	0.093	<0.001	−0.062	0.010
Single	0.147	<0.001	0.110	0.010
Employed	−0.190	<0.001	−0.153	0.009
Household income $15000 to $30000	−0.040	0.002	−0.018	0.012
Household income $30000 to $50000	−0.032	0.010	−0.025	0.012
Household income $50000 to $80000	0.004	0.763	−0.011	0.012
Household income more than $80000	0.106	0.000	0.062	0.012
Welfare is primary source of income	−0.068	0.001	0.030	0.020
Owns home	0.122	<0.001	0.064	0.009
High school education	0.004	0.742	0.069	0.012
Some college	0.014	0.384	0.087	0.015
College graduate	0.101	<0.001	0.150	0.009
Height in meters	0.428	<0.001	0.391	0.050
Children under 12 in household	−0.119	<0.001	−0.103	0.010
Native-born Canadian	0.000	0.999	0.008	0.010
Expressed sense of belonging to community	0.252	<0.001	0.278	0.008

Note: PA Index – moderate did not converge.

2. An economic analysis of the subjective health and well-being of physical activity?

Paul Downward and Simona Rasciute

INTRODUCTION

Internationally a large number of policy initiatives emphasize the need for policy to promote well-being and health. The same is true of the UK in which there has been a focus on the need to increase physical activity such as sport, as well as walking and cycling as active modes of transport (DCMS/Strategy Unit, 2002; Department of Health, 2004; Department for Transport, 2004; Cycling England, 2007).

Drawing upon two waves of a unique, but not panel, data-set for England, this chapter extends Rasciute and Downward (2010), to explore the links between physical activity and active travel on subjectively reported health and well-being. Key contributions of the chapter are to examine the relationships for the separate waves of the data and also to produce willingness-to-pay measures of the impacts of physical activity and active travel results. The former explores the robustness of the findings of Rasciute and Downward (2010), which was based on pooled data, while the latter provides an attempt to add some scale to the benefits associated with physical activity and active travel. This can help to inform policy priorities.

The chapter is organized as follows. In Section 2 the interrelated nature of subjectively stated health and well-being are discussed. In Section 3 the literature on well-being generally is reviewed, as well as contributions focusing upon the impact of physical activity. In Section 4 the data employed in the analysis is introduced and discussed. In Section 5 the econometric methods are discussed. The results are presented in Section 6, and Section 7 offers conclusions.

1. SUBJECTIVELY STATED HEALTH AND WELL-BEING

Public policy documents often bracket together health and well-being. This is not surprising as reductions in well-being can be linked to the lack of psychological health through the incidence of mental disorders, such as anxiety and depression, as well as stress, sleeping disorders and loss of cognitive function. However matters are more complex than this as well-being is also linked to levels of physiological health, as measured by obesity, cardiovascular diseases, high blood pressure, hypertension, diabetes, strokes, heart disease, osteoarthritis and osteoporosis. Further, both well-being and health can also be affected by social as well as individual determinants; such as communities, neighbourhoods and social exclusion. In general it is argued that physical activity can have a positive effect on both well-being and health (Scully et al., 1999; WHO World Health Day, 2002; Department of Health, 2004; Biddle and Ekkakkis, 2005).

There is similar overlap between the investigation of health and well-being in the academic literature. Psychologists and economists have both contributed to this literature. The seminal work by economists began with the Leyden School (Kahneman et al 1999; Van Praag and Frijters, 1999) but this has grown into a large literature. A key distinguishing feature of the economic literature is the analysis of large-scale secondary data-sets (Clarke et al., 2008; Dolan et al., 2008).[1] Theoretically, too, the economic approach treats statements about well-being and dimensions of health as essentially statements about the utility of individuals (Shields and Wheatley Price, 2005; Kahneman and Krueger, 2006; Gardner and Oswald, 2006). However, it is important to recognize that utility in the economics literature is not just concerned about individual private and self-interested welfare. Rather, it can also include altruism, utility stemming from social comparison, and the social interactions implied in much consumption activity (Frey and Stutzer, 2002, 2005).[2]

While Dolan et al. (2008) provide a thorough review of the measurement of well-being in the economics literature, it is worth noting that the most common measures have included single-item statements about the respondent's happiness or satisfaction with life as a whole (for example, Blanchflower and Oswald, 2004a; Golden and Wiens-Tuers, 2006; Shields et al., 2009; or, for example, Winkelman and Winkelman, 1998; Winkelman, 2005; Gardener and Oswald, 2006; Frijters et al., 2008).[3] In contrast Shields and Wheatley Price (2005) examine personal social support as an indicator of well-being. However, and particularly pertinent for this chapter, multi-item measures of well-being have been used, such as the General Health Questionnaire 12 Score (GHQ12), developed by Goldberg (1972). In this respect, health and well-being are treated as synonymous by authors such as Brown et al. (2005) and Gardener and Oswald (2006).[4]

A key motivation of this chapter, therefore, as with Rasciute and Downward (2010) is to examine the impact of physical activity and active transport on both well-being and health. The aim is to recognize the potential joint determination of the latter two variables, but also that they may have distinctive determinants as well. Before attempting that task, however, the well-being literature is reviewed both generally and in terms of the emergent findings connected with physical activity. Regressors other than physical activity and active travel in the current chapter are included in the analysis drawing upon the general literature.

2.   THE WELL-BEING LITERATURE

The main findings of the well-being literature are documented in Dolan et al. (2008) and can be summarized and updated as follows, making use of a distinction between 'internal' and 'external' characteristics affecting well-being developed in Shields et al. (2009). In the former case it is argued that ethnicity or levels of education are not closely linked to levels of well-being (Shields and Wheatley Price, 2005). In contrast it has been argued that there is a quadratic effect of age upon well-being, with there being a minimum in middle age. The effect is identified in cross-section data (Shields and Wheatley Price, 2005), panel data (Winkelmann and Winkelmann, 1998; Winkelmann, 2005) or pooled data, with cohorts accounted for (Blanchflower and Oswald, 2008a). The reasons for the non-linearity could be linked to age measuring unobserved social status that has accrued over time and a feeling of being more in control of one's life and environment (Ryff, 1995); that ageing produces lower aspirations that are met more easily (Campbell et al., 1976), or that older people are happier precisely because they have lived longer (Argyle, 1999). It is also argued that being older is associated with an increased sense of seeking emotional meaning from life and a decreasing motivation to expand one's horizons (Carstensen at al., 1999; Charles et al., 2001). As Blanchflower and Oswald (2008a) also argue, it could be that cheerful people live longer so that the well-being U-shape in age is identifying a selection effect. In this chapter it is postulated that the quality of person's health and physical abilities worsen with age. Consequently, the level of health needs to be controlled for explicitly in assessing the impact of age on well-being.

Other temporal patterns for well-being are identified in the effects of marital status, family organization and relationships upon well-being.

It is found that being married raises well-being compared with being divorced, separated or having suffered bereavement, the latter of which has the largest (and negative) effect (Gardner and Oswald, 2006). Further, it is shown that becoming married generates a positive 'shock' to well-being that eventually returns to previous levels after about five years. In contrast, the reduction in well-being from suffering the bereavement of a partner dissipates more slowly over eight years (Lucas et al., 2003). In the case of divorce, it is found that well-being reduces more for females than for males (Clark et al., 2008) but that those who remarry recover their levels of well-being (Johnson and Wu, 2002). In contrast Gardner and Oswald (2006) identify that while divorce can reduce well-being, once one allows for higher initial stress levels, the apparent reductions in well-being are actually a return to normal levels. Further, Stutzer and Frey (2006) identify that there are selection effects in household composition. In this regard marriage is more likely for happier people. Consequently, Frijters et al. (2008) argue that events such as separation have anticipation, selection and adaptation effects. More generally, the well-being of members in a family are identified to be positively correlated (Shields and Wheatley Price, 2005; Winkelmann, 2005; Bruhin and Winkelmann, forthcoming), and, in an innovative investigation, it is identified that more regular sex involving fewer partners among higher-educated people may be connected with this (Blanchflower and Oswald, 2004b). Significantly, de Mello and Tiongson (2009) identify that while health is a determinant of well-being, the health of a spouse, if not their children, also affects their well-being, while Powdthavee and Vignoles (2008) identify that parental distress can subsequently affect the life satisfaction of children. Finally, Powdthavee (2008), has shown that well-being is also generally higher through social interactions with friends as well as relatives.

Similar dynamics are identified for the impact of income on well-being revealed in discussion of the 'Easterlin paradox' (Easterlin, 1974). This arises when rising real incomes are not correlated with rising levels of self-reported well-being over time and, yet, cross-sectional studies identify a positive effect of income on well-being (Blanchflower and Oswald, 2004b; Shields and Wheatley Price, 2005), as do panel data studies (Winkelmann and Winkelmann, 1998; Ferrer-i-Carbonell and Frijters, 2004; Ferrer-i-Carbonell, 2005; Clark et al., 2005). Of course in a cross-section context for any given comparator income, absolute and relative incomes will be perfectly correlated as income is simply rescaled.[5]

Clark et al. (2008) suggest a solution to the paradox by arguing that a stronger relationship between income and well-being will occur within a country at a point in time, rather than over time across countries, because of the status benefits or losses accrued by having relative differences in income to others. Over time, well-being will also be connected to the level of consumption facilitated by income. Consequently, diminishing marginal consumption benefits, and thus well-being, will occur as income increases over time. This supports the explanation offered by Frey and Stutzer (2002) that it is relative income that ultimately affects well-being as an example of the relativity of individual's judgement of their well-being.[6]

The literature argues that employment and self-employment tends to increase well-being, in contrast to unemployment (Winkelmann and Winkelmann, 1998; Shields and Wheatley Price, 2005; Andersson, 2008). Once again it is argued that this is not only because of access to income but also because of identity, self-esteem, social recognition and the provision of a sense of purpose and opportunities for social interaction (Shields and Wheatley Price, 2005).

Finally, a number of papers now also assess how 'external' factors have affected well-being. For example, in the context of the macroeconomy, Frijters et al. (2004) identified that German reunification enhanced the life satisfaction of East Germans, while Frijters et al. (2006) show how the transition of the Russian economy affected the well-being of Russians. On a more regional level, Shields and Wheatley Price (2005) identify that location factors contribute a relatively small amount to well-being in Australia, while Carroll et al. (2009) argue that drought can reduce well-being for rural residents of Australia.

Leaving aside the general literature on well-being, there is a large literature addressing the impacts of physical activity and sport and health. For example Biddle et al. (2004) note the links between physical activities such as active travel, sport and the availability of active play opportunities and the physical and psychological health of young people. More generally, Pate et al. (1995), Oja et al. (1998) WHO World Health Day, (2002), Cevero and Duncan (2003), Wendel-Vos et al. (2004), Smith and Bird (2004), Basset et al. (2008) and Shephard (2008) argue that active travel and, particularly walking and cycling may be the main answer to questions raised about declining population health. This is because they suggest greater possibilities for achieving 'health-enhancing physical activity' (HEPA) levels, which are defined as 30 minutes or more of regular, moderate-intensity physical exercise on most days of the week for adults, and at least twice a week for children, of at least 60 minutes duration.[7] A number of measurements of health have been addressed in such research. For example, Oja et al. (1998) examined the impact upon VO_2max (maximal oxygen consumption), heart rates and cholesterol, and Bassett et al. (2008) analyse the relationship between transport and body mass index (BMI).

In contrast there has been limited research on the links between well-being and physical health. As well as the contribution by de Mello and Tiongson (2009) noted earlier, in the context of the family, there have been some papers, for example by Blanchflower and Oswald (2008b) and Oswald and Powdthavee (2007), that analyse the links between blood pressure (as a proxy for hypertension) and happiness, using separate regressions and a common set of covariates including countries, and life satisfaction regressions including a BMI indicator respectively. In the first case regressions identify that respondents in countries that have high levels of happiness also report low blood pressure. The implication is that (reduced) blood pressure is an indicator of well-being, which helps to validate measures of subjective well-being. In the latter case BMI variables are included in regressions for Life Satisfaction and Psychological distress. It is shown that greater BMI values are associated with lower happiness and levels of mental health.

Finally in reviewing the well-being literature, there has also been relatively little economic analysis of the impact of physical activity well-being (Dolan et al. 2008). Becchetti et al. (2008) identify significant impacts of an aggregate binary-measured sports variable, as a measure of a relational good, on happiness. Lechner (2009) identifies positive impacts of an ordinally defined aggregate sports variable on measures of subjective health and well-being. Lee and Park (2010) find positive effects of ordinally defined aggregate physical activity measures on the life-statisfaction of the disabled. Finally, Rasciute and Downward (2010) identify similar results exploring the impact of active travel modes, such as walking and cycling, on well-being as well as participation in forms of physical activity generally, while Downward and Rasciute (forthcoming) identify increases in well-being associated with different types of sports and, particularly, those that involve more social interactions.[8] This chapter extends the analysis of Rasciute and Downward (2010) by disaggregating the results over time, and also calculating the implied monetary benefits of this activity.

3. DATA

This research makes use of the first two waves of the Taking Part Survey that are currently available.[9] The survey, commissioned by the Department for Culture Media and Sport, was conducted by the British Market Research Bureau and began in 2005. One individual, aged 16 years or older, from a randomly sampled household in England was interviewed. The first wave of data comprised 28 117 respondents, and the second comprised 24 174 respondents.

The dependent variables in this data are captured by well-being,

Table 2.1   Distribution of happiness and health

Happiness scale value	Data-set 1		Data-set 2	
	Frequency	Percentage	Frequency	Percentage
1	100	0.60	76	0.53
2	103	0.62	76	0.53
3	287	1.72	180	1.26
4	361	2.17	278	1.94
5	1 296	7.79	948	6.61
6	1 231	7.40	1 073	7.48
7	3 079	18.50	2 644	18.44
8	5 006	30.07	4 308	30.04
9	2 881	17.31	2 518	17.56
10	2 302	13.83	2 241	15.63
Total	16 646	100.00	14 342	100.00
Health scale value	Frequency	Percentage	Frequency	Percentage
1	95	0.57	115	0.80
2	609	3.66	523	3.65
3	2 845	17.09	2 483	17.31
4	6 998	42.04	6 201	43.24
5	6 099	36.64	5 020	35.00
Total	16 646	100.00	14 342	100.00

measured as a 'happiness' variable investigated by the question: 'Taking all things together, how happy would you say you are?' Respondents then have to assign a value between 1 and 10 to this question, with '1' indicating extremely unhappy and '10' extremely happy. Self-reported health is also measured on an ordinal scale investigated by the question: 'How is your health in general?' Respondents can then assign a value between '1' and '5' for the cases of 'very good', 'good', 'fair', 'bad', and 'very bad'.[10] Table 2.1 provides the frequencies of the values of the dependent variables for each sample.[11]

The survey collects data on 67 separate sports activities which are investigated as participation or not over the last 12 months prior to the interview, in the last four weeks prior to the interview, the frequency in days of participation in the last four weeks, as well as the typical time in minutes of participation in these activities. Drawing on this data, physical activity variables for four active travel variables were constructed. These included cycling for health and recreation, cycling for utilitarian purposes such as travel to work, walking generally and walking specifically for health or recreational purposes. Variables measuring cycling for sporting competition as well as participation in any other sport were also derived. As the data on walking were only recorded for activity over the last four weeks, the other physical activity variables measuring activity undertaken in the last four weeks were employed in this research. The other independent variables included in the analysis are based directly upon the determinants identified in the well-being literature. Table 2.2 provides variable definitions and their sample characteristics. They include the personal characteristics age, gender, ethnicity, education levels, marital status and occupational status. Regional variables, not cited in Table 2.2 for brevity, are also included as control variables for other general 'external' factors that can affect well-being.

4.   ESTIMATION

The estimation of well-being models has taken place using a variety of estimators. Studies such as Gardener and Oswald (2006), Becchetti et al. (2008), Clark et al. (2008), Carroll et al. (2009) and de Mello and Tiongson (2009) make use of estimators traditionally associated with cardinal data. However, one can argue that the scales used to measure well-being and health are more properly understood as ordinal variables. What is not at stake in this discussion is an ontological belief that individuals are referring to the same concept. This must apply to all empirical work and, as Ferrer-i-Carbonell and Frijters (2004) argue, is an essential aspect of using scales as a positive monotonic transformation of underlying utility. Rather, the issue reflects further assumptions such as whether or not the censoring implied in discrete ordinal rankings is accounted for and, as a result, whether or not the levels in the data coupled with any measured changes in the levels following changes in any independent variables correspond across individuals; in other words, that the distances between values on the scales are meaningful. In this chapter it is argued that the appropriate form of estimator should try to represent this discrete form of measurement which, as Greene and Hensher (2009) argue, suggests that estimates of genuine ordinal variables will lack a conditional mean function that would be artificially imposed by cardinal estimators.[12]

To try to account for the theorized relationship between well-being and health initially, a bivariate ordered probit estimator was employed. However, the model did not converge. Therefore, the ordinal data were converted to binary data to capture larger discrete shifts between

Table 2.2   Independent variables

Nominal variable	Data-set 1		Data-set 2		Variable description
	Frequency	%	Frequency	%	
single	5491	32.99	4898	34.15	Single = 1, 0 = otherwise
married	8013	48.14	6703	46.74	Married = 1, 0 = otherwise
separate	2284	13.72	2024	14.11	Separated = 1, 0 = otherwise
widow*	858	5.15	717	5.00	Widowed = 1, 0 = otherwise
white	14219	85.42	12638	88.12	White = 1, 0 = otherwise
asian	1246	7.49	872	6.08	Asian = 1, 0 = otherwise
black	775	4.66	551	3.84	Black = 1, 0 = otherwise
othereth*	406	2.44	281	1.96	Other ethnic origin = 1, 0 = otherwise
working	11039	66.32	9344	65.15	Working = 1, 0 = otherwise
student	534	3.21	479	3.34	Student = 1, 0 = otherwise
keephouse	1130	6.79	1007	7.02	Keep house = 1, 0 = otherwise
retired	2504	15.04	2141	14.93	Retired = 1, 0 = otherwise
illnotwork	509	3.06	498	3.47	Ill and can't work = 1, 0 = otherwise
unemployed	504	3.03	474	3.3	Unemployed = 1, 0 = otherwise
otherwk*	426	2.56	399	2.78	Other work = 1, 0 = otherwise
he	7007	42.09	6158	42.94	Higher education or equivalent = 1, 0 = otherwise
alevel	3267	19.63	2752	19.19	A levels = 1, 0 = otherwise
apprentice	888	5.33	736	5.13	Apprentice = 1, 0 = otherwise
olevel5	3141	18.87	2721	18.97	5 GCSEs = 1, 0 = otherwise
othered*	2343	14.08	1975	13.77	Other education = 1, 0 = otherwise
sex: male	7784	46.76	6738	46.98	Male = 1, 0 = female
sex: female*	8862	53.24	7604	53.02	
drinkdaily	1746	10.49	1405	9.80	Drink alcohol every day = 1, 0 = otherwise
drink4to6	1763	10.59	1581	11.02	Drink alcohol 4 to 6 days a week = 1, 0 = otherwise
drink1to3	5764	34.63	5074	35.38	Drink alcohol 1 to 3 days a week = 1, 0 = otherwise
drinkless 1	4507	27.07	3862	26.93	Drink alcohol less than 1 day a week = 1, 0 = otherwise
notdrink	2866	17.22	2420	16.87	Don't drink alcohol = 1, 0 = otherwise

Table 2.2 (continued)

Nominal variable	Data-set 1		Data-set 2		Variable description
	Frequency	%	Frequency	%	
voluntar	4 581	27.52	3 969	27.67	Undertaken any voluntary work = 1, 0 = otherwise
cycles pr	158	0.95	136	0.95	Cycled for sport in the last 4 weeks = 1, 0 = otherwise
cyclehea	1 835	11.02	1 521	10.61	Cycled for health, recreation in the last 4 weeks = 1, 0 = otherwise
cycleuti	877	5.27	771	5.38	Cycled for utility reasons in the last 4 weeks = 1, 0 = otherwise
walk	12 113	72.77	10 376	73.25	Walked for at least 30 minutes in the last 4 weeks = 1, 0 = otherwise
walkrec	9 412	56.54	8 033	56.01	Walked for recreation in the last 4 weeks = 1, 0 = otherwise
any sport	9 790	58.81	8 231	57.39	Participated in any sport in the last 4 weeks = 1, 0 = otherwise

Cardinal variables	Mean	St. dev.	Mean	St. dev.	
Age	43.54	16.35	43.61	16.33	Age in years
nadult	1.98	0.86	1.96	0.85	Number of adults in the household
nchild	0.65	0.99	0.64	0.98	Number of children in the household
Indincn	18.02	13.86	18.3	14.12	Total gross annual personal income £000s
n	**16 646**		**14 342**		

unhappiness to happiness and poor health to good health.[13] While the use of binary variables is more uncommon in the literature it has a rationale. For example, Winkelman and Winkelman (1998) point out that the resulting binary logit estimator is consistent, while de Mello and Tiongson (2009) rescale their health variable as binary to assess its effect on happiness. The bivariate probit model is employed to allow for a correlation between the error term of the two equations, and recognizes that there may be unobserved characteristics of individuals that influence both whether they are happy and healthy. However, it should be noted that the equations estimated are essentially 'reduced form' equations, as happiness and health do not appear as independent variables in the respective equation for the other variable. In this way, simultaneity is bypassed rather than addressed as with Gerdtham and Johannesson (2001) and de Mello and Tiongson (2009). Consequently, no strong causal claims can be derived from the research.

In specifying the bivariate probit model, the explanatory variables may or may not be the same for the two equations and the error terms are assumed to be jointly normally distributed. Following Greene (2008), the general specification for this two-equation model is:

$$y_1^* = x_1'\beta_1 + \varepsilon_1, \, y_1 = 1 \text{ if } y_1^* > 0, \, 0 \text{ otherwise,}$$

$$y_2^* = x_2'\beta_2 + \varepsilon_2, \, y_2 = 1 \text{ if } y_2^* > 0, \, 0 \text{ otherwise,}$$

$$E[\varepsilon_1 \mid x_1, x_2] = E[\varepsilon_2 \mid x_1, x_2] = 0 \tag{2.1}$$

$$Var[\varepsilon_1 \mid x_1, x_2] = Var[\varepsilon_2 \mid x_1, x_2] = 1$$

$$Cov[\varepsilon_1, \varepsilon_2 \mid x_1, x_2] = \rho$$

With two binary variables four possible outcomes are observed, which are: a person who reports good health and the level of well-being above average, a person who reports good health and the level of well-being below average, a person who reports poor health and the level of well-being above average and, finally, a person who reports poor health and the level of well-being below average. These correspond to different values of the latent variables, y_1^* and y_2^*.

The bivariate normal cumulative distribution function is:

$$\text{Prob}(X_1 < x_1, X_2 < x_2) = \int_{-\infty}^{x_2} \int_{-\infty}^{x_1} \phi_2(z_1, z_2, \rho) \, dz_1 dz_2 \tag{2.2}$$

The density is:

$$\phi_2(x_1, x_2, \rho) = \frac{\exp(-(1/2)(x_1^2 + x_2^2 - 2\rho x_1 x_2)/(1 - \rho^2))}{2\pi(1 - \rho^2)^{1/2}} \tag{2.3}$$

To construct the log-likelihood, let $q_{i1} = 2y_{i1} - 1$ and $q_{i2} = 2y_{i2} - 1$. Thus $q_{i1} = 1$ if $y_{ij} = 1$ and -1 if $y_{ij} = 0$ for $j = 1$ and 2. Now let:

$$z_{ij} = x_{ij}'\beta_j \text{ and } w_{ij} = q_{ij}z_{ij}, j=1, 2 \tag{2.4}$$

and

$$\rho_{i*} = q_{i1}q_{i2}\rho \tag{2.5}$$

The probabilities that enter the likelihood function are

$$\text{Prob}(Y_1 = y_{i1}, Y_2 = y_{i2} \mid x_1, x_2) = \Phi_2(w_{i1}, w_{i2}, \rho_{i*}) \tag{2.6}$$

Thus

$$\ln L = \sum_{i=1}^{n} \ln \Phi_2(w_{i1}, w_{i2}, \rho_{i*}) \tag{2.7}$$

The bivariate probability, however, is also not a conditional mean function (Greene, 2008). Therefore, the derivatives do not correspond to regression coefficients. As with the binary probit model, the dependent variables and hence the coefficients are not measured in natural units and can only be given a qualitative interpretation. To aid interpretation, marginal effects can be calculated such as to establish the effects of the explanatory variables on conditional probabilities, for example the probability that someone reports good health, given that they are happy (Jones, 2007). Knowledge of such effects helps to give some comparative scale of the effect of changes in independent variables on the dependent variable. Finally, while individual coefficients may have no obvious meaning, nonetheless their ratio does and, as shown by Boes and Winkelmann (2006), can be used to identify a 'willingness to pay' (WTP) or 'shadow price' for the effects of events on well-being. In this chapter such ratios of coefficients are calculated as the value of participation in physical activity and active travel is desired.

5.   RESULTS

The results are presented in Tables 2.3 and 2.4 where coefficients for all of the variables plus willingness to pay for the physical activity variables are presented for the first and second data-sets respectively. A separate set of estimates were required to distinguish between the walking and walking for recreational purposes variables as the former variable includes cases measured specifically by the latter variable.

The first result to note from the analysis was that ρ was estimated (Rho) to be non-zero, varying from 0.351 to 0.307, and being statistically significant. This was the case with Rasciute and Downward (2010). This suggests the presence of unobserved characteristics affecting both happiness and health, and provides some support for the model. The regression results presented in Tables 2.3 and 2.4 are, broadly consistent across the two

Table 2.3   Regression results data-set 1

Regressors	Happy coefficient	z	Health coefficient	z	Happy coefficient	z	Health coefficient	z
Constant	0.2127	1.2020		0.1668	0.2759	1.5630	0.3579	2.1500
NUMADULT	0.061	3.5840	0.0175	1.1050	0.0608	3.5820	0.0180	1.1340
CYCLESPR	−0.2550	−1.9230	0.0820	0.5430	−0.2498	−1.8860	0.0838	0.5600
CYCLEHEA	0.0164	0.3440	0.2531	5.7030	0.0049	0.1020	0.2414	5.4190
CYCLEUTI	0.1001	1.5970	0.1433	2.3830	0.1133	1.8100	0.1694	2.8110
ANYSPNOT	0.1678	6.0120	0.2244	8.9620	0.1631	5.8380	0.2205	8.7970
WALK	0.1294	4.4960	0.2413	9.1420	n/a	n/a	n/a	n/a
WALKREC	n/a	n/a	n/a	n/a	0.1417	5.2640	0.2215	9.2040
SINGLE	0.2529	3.7740	−0.1319	−2.0790	0.2562	3.8240	−0.1263	−1.9960
MARRIED	0.6127	9.5830	0.0225	0.3840	0.6115	9.5660	0.0211	0.3610
SEPARATE	0.1553	2.3780	−0.1328	−2.1090	0.1589	2.4350	−0.1271	−2.0260
INCOME	0.0072	6.1840	0.0052	4.8500	0.0070	6.0030	0.0049	4.5740
NORTHE	0.2562	4.5370	0.0172	0.3440	0.2588	4.5850	0.0199	0.3980
NORTHW	0.2169	3.9440	0.0990	1.9940	0.2177	3.9590	0.0998	2.0100
YORKS	0.2225	4.0360	0.0833	1.6820	0.2244	4.0730	0.0855	1.7240
EMID	0.2230	3.8280	−0.0427	−0.8590	0.2249	3.8610	−0.0428	−0.8610
WMID	0.1882	3.5040	0.0634	1.3150	0.1953	3.6330	0.0727	1.5050
EAST	0.1823	3.3300	0.0873	1.8080	0.1857	3.3940	0.0924	1.9110
LONDON	0.0040	0.0770	0.0651	1.2980	0.0152	0.2900	0.0808	1.6110
SOUTHE	0.1185	2.3620	0.1193	2.6410	0.1252	2.4960	0.1288	2.8500
WHITE	0.2381	3.1210	0.0517	0.6510	0.2413	3.1580	0.0608	0.7700
ASIAN	0.0090	0.1050	−0.0404	−0.4570	0.0165	0.1910	−0.0285	−0.3230
BLACK	0.1455	1.5890	0.1736	1.8010	0.1577	1.7170	0.1943	2.0210
WORKING	0.2377	2.9530	0.4475	6.5070	0.2411	2.9950	0.4503	6.5200
STUDENT	0.2439	2.2750	0.4956	4.9490	0.2491	2.3240	0.5021	5.0280
KEEPHOUS	−0.0108	−0.1180	0.2335	2.8930	−0.0089	−0.0970	0.2393	2.9540
RETIRED	0.2835	2.8890	0.1523	1.8650	0.2820	2.8740	0.1506	1.8390
ILLNOTWO	−0.4320	−4.3810	−1.3270	−13.4680	−0.4341	−4.4010	−1.3388	−13.5690
UNEMPLOY	−0.2263	−2.2540	0.1846	1.9980	−0.2197	−2.1870	0.1954	2.1110
HE	0.1036	2.5510	0.2367	6.4630	0.0966	2.3720	0.2287	6.2310
ALEVEL	0.1317	2.9650	0.1058	2.6620	0.1271	2.8550	0.1009	2.5330
APPRENTI	0.0465	0.7040	−0.0652	−1.1490	0.0423	0.6400	−0.0710	−1.2490
OLEVEL5	−0.0033	−0.0770	0.1428	3.6290	−0.0084	−0.1950	0.1360	3.4550
SEX	−0.0548	−1.8960	−0.0754	−2.9020	−0.0516	−1.7840	−0.0722	−2.7820
AGE	−0.0225	−4.5060	−0.0069	−1.4950	−0.0245	−4.8810	−0.0096	−2.0730
AGESQUAR	0.0002	4.4130	−.182200 D-04	−0.3740	0.0003	4.7020	.173067 D-05	0.0350
VOLUNTAR	0.1087	3.5560	0.0431	1.6140	0.1083	3.5390	0.0447	1.6710
NUMCHILD	−0.0057	−0.3760	−0.0047	−0.3330	−0.0043	−0.2810	−0.0032	−0.2290
RHO(1,2)	0.308	18.005			0.307	18.026		

Table 2.3   (continued)

Regressors	Happy coefficient	z	Health coefficient	z	Happy coefficient	z	Health coefficient	z
WTP £000s								
CYCLESPR								
CYCLEHEA			48.635				49.158	
CYCLEUTI			27.526				34.499	
ANYSPNOT	23.364		43.110		23.366		44.897	
WALK	18.026		46.356					
WALKREC						20.290		45.108

data-sets. Cycling for health and recreation, and for utilitarian purposes such as travel to work, has a positive effect on individual health but has no effect on well-being. This contrasts with a negative effect on well-being identified in Rasciute and Downward (2010). In contrast, too, the effect of cycling activity for sporting competition is shown to be significant in the well-being equations for data-set 2 (Table 2.4). This implies that sporting cycling can add to utility but is not primarily identified with health benefits. The variability in these latter results, however, causes some concern and is perhaps resultant from working with a small sample size for sporting cycling (see Table 2.2). In contrast, participation in any sport contributes positively to both outcomes. Both forms of walking also have a statistically significant and positive effect on both individual health and happiness. Consistent with Rasciute and Downward (2010) therefore, the results suggest a contrast between cycling and walking as modes of active travel which may be connected with the convenience of walking and the fact that, unlike sporting cycling, recreational and utility cycling may experience a degree of disutility from factors such as proximity to motorized transport (Garling et al., 2002; Pucher and Dijkstra, 2003).

While the qualitative results are reasonably robust, Tables 2.3 and 2.4 also present estimates of the willingness to pay for the active travel and physical activity variables. With the exception of the anomalous result for sporting cycling, the results suggest that an episode of walking or participation in any sport generate approximately between £18 000 to £24 000 of well-being to individuals. However, the rank order of these effects changes over the two data-sets concerned. Further, the health benefits of walking are valued at approximately twice this value for data-set 1 and slightly less for data-set 2, with the health values for participation in any sport being approximately £3000 to £6000 less than walking. A further interesting finding is that the health benefits of cycling for health and recreation are

Table 2.4   Regression results data-set 2

Regressors	Happy coeffi- cient	z	Health coeffi- cient	z	Happy coeffi- cient	z	Health coeffi- cient	z
Constant	0.590	2.921	0.715	3.856	0.667	3.313	0.811	4.382
NUMADULT	0.069	3.586	0.007	0.408	0.069	3.613	0.009	0.494
CYCLESPR	0.482	2.144	0.263	1.402	0.495	2.181	0.271	1.452
CYCLEHEA	-0.052	-0.938	0.153	3.072	-0.062	-1.120	0.140	2.805
CYCLEUTI	-0.011	-0.155	0.221	3.177	0.005	0.074	0.242	3.464
ANYSPORT	0.141	4.250	0.198	7.086	0.141	4.237	0.196	6.997
WALK	0.183	5.673	0.237	8.395	n/a	n/a	n/a	n/a
WALKREC	n/a	n/a	n/a	n/a	0.155	5.041	0.209	8.003
SINGLE	0.140	1.761	-0.148	-2.149	0.144	1.817	-0.141	-2.052
MARRIED	0.506	6.612	0.056	0.869	0.501	6.540	0.051	0.793
SEPARATE	-0.017	-0.214	-0.140	-2.074	-0.017	-0.216	-0.139	-2.069
INCOME	0.008	5.588	0.006	5.357	0.008	5.487	0.006	5.170
NORTHE	0.050	0.749	-0.025	-0.450	0.051	0.757	-0.026	-0.458
NORTHW	0.060	0.933	-0.001	-0.018	0.062	0.967	0.001	0.027
YORKS	0.007	0.107	-0.021	-0.391	0.011	0.172	-0.017	-0.318
EMID	0.096	1.417	0.008	0.146	0.104	1.540	0.016	0.287
WMID	0.031	0.488	0.027	0.501	0.034	0.532	0.030	0.563
EAST	0.085	1.293	0.041	0.753	0.093	1.406	0.050	0.924
LONDON	-0.052	-0.859	0.051	0.971	-0.036	-0.608	0.072	1.364
SOUTHE	0.029	0.476	0.027	0.531	0.032	0.527	0.030	0.586
WHITE	0.352	3.675	0.088	0.855	0.349	3.649	0.083	0.810
ASIAN	0.185	1.719	-0.134	-1.202	0.179	1.670	-0.142	-1.268
BLACK	0.254	2.263	0.147	1.220	0.254	2.262	0.145	1.203
WORKING	0.158	1.769	0.276	3.763	0.163	1.830	0.282	3.839
STUDENT	0.158	1.289	0.469	4.289	0.173	1.410	0.487	4.451
KEEPHOUS	-0.151	-1.486	-0.013	-0.157	-0.137	-1.352	0.003	0.040
RETIRED	0.249	2.295	0.045	0.522	0.252	2.328	0.051	0.588
ILLNOTWO	-0.635	-6.076	-1.467	-14.696	-0.640	-6.127	-1.472	-14.735
UNEMPLOY	-0.214	-1.931	-0.080	-0.838	-0.195	-1.766	-0.058	-0.605
HE	0.095	2.078	0.244	6.226	0.093	2.017	0.241	6.128
ALEVEL	0.106	2.089	0.217	5.018	0.107	2.121	0.218	5.042
APPRENTI	0.155	1.963	0.097	1.548	0.147	1.865	0.088	1.402
OLEVEL5	0.003	0.062	0.160	3.769	0.001	0.022	0.157	3.704
SEX	-0.058	-1.735	-0.139	-4.915	-0.053	-1.607	-0.133	-4.684
AGE	-0.026	-4.624	-0.017	-3.394	-0.028	-4.830	-0.018	-3.724
AGESQUAR	0.000	4.228	.453801 D-04	0.879	0.000	4.341	.551407 D-04	1.069
VOLUNTAR	0.114	3.225	0.005	0.181	0.114	3.220	0.006	0.206
NUMCHILD	0.008	0.439	0.012	0.748	0.009	0.509	0.013	0.836
RHO(1,2)	0.350	18.725			0.351	18.866		

Table 2.4   (continued)

Regressors	Happy coeffi-cient	z	Health coeffi-cient	z	Happy coeffi-cient	z	Health coeffi-cient	z
WTP £000s								
CYCLESPR	62.151				65.164			
CYCLEHEA			24.765				23.494	
CYCLEUTI			35.877				40.571	
ANYSPNOT	18.246		32.109		18.543		32.886	
WALK	23.647		38.436					

between approximately £10 000 to £15 000 greater than cycling for utility purposes in data-set 1, but between approximately £6000 to £10 000 less in data-set 2, Further, the health benefits are generally considered to be lower in data-set 2 than data-set 1. What this suggests is that the willingness-to-pay measures are relatively time variant and that longitudinal analysis is really required before trying to establish more refined policy priorities on the basis of such welfare measures. This may be evidence of dynamic effects associated with changes in people's circumstances upon well-being noted in the literature

6. CONCLUSIONS

In this chapter it has been shown that physical activities such as participation in sport, as well as active transport, such as walking for utilitarian and recreational motives, can enhance both well-being and health. In contrast cycling activity for both utilitarian and health and recreational reasons primarily has an impact on health. The results for cycling for sport vary, depending on the periodicity of the data-set. These results suggest some robustness of the results presented in Rasciute and Downward (2010) and, thereby, provide some basis for establishing policy priorities. However, it is also shown that the estimated monetary valuations of these impacts are also sensitive to the periodicity of the data and, as such, do not suggest strong evidence for refining these policy priorities. Rather they suggest a need for more longitudinal research. The results currently suggest and reaffirm that if cycling is to enhance well-being fully, this requires further investigation of this context and possible policy to target the problems that currently preclude it having an effect.

NOTES

1. It is argued that well-being has been more typically explored from direct statements of research subjects by psychologists (Kahneman et al., 1999; Dolan et al., 2008).
2. Social interactions in consumption can be understood as connected to 'relational goods' (Gui, 2000; Becchetti et al., 2008). To the extent that physical activities such as sports, and active travel have such a dimension, then this research is directed at such goods, with the consequent prediction that they will raise well-being. Downward and Riordan (2007) examine the importance of social interactions in determining sports and leisure participation, while Downward and Rasciute (forthcoming) examine how socially interactive sports raise well-being more than individual sports.
3. For example in the US General Social Surveys respondents are asked, if 'Taken all together, how would you say things are these days – would you say that you are very happy, pretty happy, or not too happy'. In Eurobarometers respondents are asked, 'On the whole are you very satisfied, fairly satisfied, not very satisfied, or not at all satisfied with the life you lead'.
4. To derive this score respondents rank their experience of symptoms relative to their usual experience on 12 items using a four-point scale. The location of the usual situation in the scale can vary. The four-point scale can be used in its original form or 'anchored' such that a binary score is allocated across two pairs of adjacent scale points. The scales are then summed. In the latter case this will produce an aggregate score ranging from '0' to '12'. This scale is included, for example in the British Household Panel and the Health Survey for England. The binary recoding and scale items can be adjusted to emphasize positive and negative symptoms.
5. In some respects this could be a problematic relationship to investigate empirically over time, given the potential difference in scaling of income and well-being variables. One might expect the latter to exhibit stationarity as it is measured on a time invariant scale, unlike income which can vary continually in magnitude (see Johns and Ormerod, 2007) A further problem with such trend analysis is that if well-being is a genuine ordinal variable, then its average value is meaningless.
6. This has implications for deriving the implied economic value of life events, following Oswald and Clarke (2002) in that it raises the question of which income value should be used on which to normalize coefficients (see also Clarke et al., 2008). Oswald and Clarke (2002) indicate that normalizations for both absolute and relative income levels are consistent if the comparator group for income is the same. The approach is used by Caroll et al. (2009).
7. See www.euro.who.int/mediacentre/PR/2006/20061117_1 (accessed 16 April 2010).
8. As noted earlier, it is not obvious that sports participation is a relational good in the aggregate as activity can be undertaken by the individual, as opposed to with others in competitive or non-competitive circumstances. Likewise, volunteerism may be more altruistic than relational.
9. The data are available from http://www.data-archive.ac.uk.
10. In the analysis that follows the numerical codings were reversed.
11. The reported sample sizes are smaller than the overall sample sizes to allow for missing values across all of the covariates and dependent variables.
12. It has been argued by Ferrer-i-Carbonell and Frijters (2004) that the results do not differ much between estimators. This is a problematic argument for two reasons. Theoretically it does not address the nature of utility being represented differently in broadly cardinal or ordinal terms. Ordinary least squares (OLS)-type regressions suggest the possibility of direct estimates of marginal utility, whereas ordered models more properly marginal rates of substitution through rations of coefficients. Empirically, too, this suggests that coefficients are not directly comparable across estimators though, under certain circumstances, their signs might be.
13. The value of zero combines ordinal categories from 1 to 5 and the value of one combines the categories from 6 to 10 for the happiness variable. For the health variables,

the value of zero combines ordinal categories from 1 to 3 and the value of one combines the categories from 4 to 5.

REFERENCES

Argyle, M. (1999), 'Causes and correlates of happiness', in D. Kahneman, E. Diener and N. Schwartz (eds), *Well-being: The Foundations of Hedonic Pyschology*, New York: Russell Sage Foundation, ch. 18.

Andersson, P. (2008), 'Happiness and health: well-being among the self-employed', *The Journal of Socio-Economics*, **37**, 213–36.

Bassett, D.R. Jr, Pucher, J., Buehler, R., Thompson, D.L. and Crouter, S.E. (2008), 'Walking cycling and obesity rates in Europe, North America, and Australia', *Journal of Physical Activity and Health*, **5**, 795–814.

Becchetti, A., Pelloni, A. and Rossetti, F. (2008), 'Relational goods, sociability, and happiness', *Kyklos*, **61** (3), 343–63.

Biddle, A.J.H., Goreley, T. and Stensel, D.J. (2004), 'Health-enhancing physical activity and sedentary behaviour in children and adolescents', *Journal of Sports Sciences*, **22**, 679–701.

Biddle, S.J.H. and Ekkekakis, P. (2005), 'Physical active lifestyles and well-being', in F.A. Huppert, N. Baylis and B. Keverne (eds), *The Science of Well-Being*, Oxford: Oxford University Press.

Blanchflower, D.G. and Oswald, A.J. (2004a), 'Well-being over time in Britain and the USA', *Journal of Public Economics*, **88**, 1359–86.

Blanchflower, D.G. and Oswald, A.J. (2004b), 'Money, sex and happiness: an empirical study', *Scandinavian Journal of Economics*, **106** (3), 315–415.

Blanchflower, D.G. and Oswald, A.J. (2008a), 'Is well-being U-shaped over the life cycle?', *Social Science and Medicine*, **66**, 1733–49.

Blanchflower, D.G. and Oswald, A.J. (2008b), 'Hypertension and happiness across nations', *Journal of Health Economics*, **27** (2), 218–33.

Boes, S. and Winkelmann, R. (2006), 'The effect of income on positve and negative subjective well-being', working paper No. 0605, Socioeconomic Institute, University of Zurich.

Brown, S., Taylor, K. and Wheatley Price, S. (2005), 'Debt and distress: evaluating the psychological cost of credit', *Journal of Economic Psychology*, **26**, 642–63.

Bruhin, A. and Winkelmann, R. (forthcoming), 'Happiness functions with preference interdependence and heterogeneity: the case of altruism within the family', *Journal of Population Economics*.

Campbell, A., Converse, P.E. and Rogers, W.L. (1976), *The Quality of American Life*, New York: Sage.

Carroll, N., Frijters, P. and Shields, M.A. (2009), 'Quantifying the costs of drought, new evidence from life satisfaction data', *Journal of Population Economics*, **22**, 445–61.

Carstensen, L.L., Issacowitz, D.M. and Turk-Charles, S. (1999), 'Taking time seriously: a theory of socioeconomic selectivity', *American Psychologist*, **54**, 165–81.

Cevero, R. and Duncan, M. (2003), 'Walking, bicycling and urban landscapes: evidence from the San-Francisco Bay Area', *Americal Journal of Public Health*, **93** (9), 1478–83.

Charles, S.T., Reynolds, C.A. and Gatz, M. (2001), 'Age-related differences and change in positive and negative effects in 23 years', *Journal of Personality and Social Psychology*, **80**, 136–51.

Clark, A.E., Diener, E., Georgellis, Y. and Lucas, R.E. (2008), 'Lags and leads in life satisfaction: a test of the baseline hypothesis', *Economic Journal*, **118**, F222–F243.

Clark, A.E., Etile, F., Postel-Vinnay, F., Senik, C. and Van der Straeten, K. (2005), 'Heterogeneity in reported well-being: evidence from twelve European countries', *Economic Journal*, **115**, C118–C132.

Cycling England (2007), 'Bike for the Future II: a funding strategy for national investment in cycling to 2012', available at: http://www.dft.gov.uk/cyclingengland/site/wp-content/uploads/2008/08/bftfii-executive-summary.pdf (accessed 16 April 2010).

De Mello, L. and Tiongson, E.R. (2009), 'What is the value of (my and my family's) good health', *Kyklos*, **62** (4), 594–610.

Department for Culture, Media and Sport (DCMS)/Strategy Unit (2002), 'Game plan: a strategy for delivering government's sport and physical activity objectives', London: DCMS/Strategy Unit.

Department for Transport (2004), 'Walking and cycling: an action plan', available at: http://www.dft.gov.uk/pgr/sustainable/walking/actionplan/ingandcyclingdocumentinp5802.pdf (accessed 16 April 2010).

Department of Health (2004), 'At least five a week: evidence on the impact of physical activity and its relationship to health. A report from the Chief Medical Officer', available at http://www.dh.gov.uk/en/Publicationsandstatistics/Publications/PublicationsPolicyAndGuidance/DH 4080994 (accessed 16 April 2010).

Dolan, P., Peasgood, T. and White, M. (2008), 'Do we really know what makes us happy? A review of the economic literature on the factors associated with subjective well-being', *Journal of Economic Psychology*, **29**, 94–122.

Downward, P.M. and Rasciute, S. (forthcoming), 'Does sport make you happy? An analysis of the well-being derived from sports participation', *International Review of Applied Economics*.

Downward, P.M. and Riordan, J. (2007), 'Social interactions and the demand for sport: an economic analysis', *Contemporary Economic Policy*, **25** (4), 518–37.

Easterlin, R. (1974), 'Does economic growth improve the human lot? Some empirical evidence', in R. David and R. Reder (eds), *Nations and Households in Economic Growth: Essays in Honor of Moses Abramovitz*, New York: Academic Press.

Ferrer-i-Carbonell, A. (2005), 'Income and well-being: an empirical analysis of the comparison income effect', *Journal of Public Economics*, **89**, 997–1019.

Ferrer-i-Carbonell, A. and Frijters, P. (2004), 'How important is methodology for the estimates of the determinants of happiness' *Economic Journal*, **114**, 641 59.

Frey, B.S. and Stutzer, A. (2002), *Happiness and Economics: How the Economy and Institutions Affect Well-Being*, Princeton, NJ: Princeton University Press.

Frey, B.S. and Stutzer, A. (2005), 'Testing theories of happiness' in L. Bruni and P.L. Porta (eds), *Economics and Happiness: Framing the Analysis*, Oxford: Oxford University Press, pp. 116–46.

Frijters, P., Geishecker, I., Shields, M.A. and Haisken-DeNew, J.P. (2006), 'Can the large swings in Russian life satisfaction be explained by ups and downs in real incomes?', *Scandinavian Journal of Economics*, **108** (3), 433–58.

Frijters, P., Hasken-DeNew, J.P. and Shields, M.A. (2004), 'Money does matter! Evidence from increasing real income and life satisfaction in East Germany following reunification', *American Economic Review*, **94** (3), 730–40.

Frijters, P., Johnston, D.W. and Shields, M.A. (2008), 'Happiness dynamics with quarterly life event data', IZA Discussion Paper No. 3604, July.

Gardner, J. and Oswald, A.J. (2006), 'Do divorcing couples become happier by breaking up', *Journal of the Royal Statistical Society* (A), **169**, Pt 2, 319–36.

Garling, T., Eeka, D., Loukopoulosa, P., Fujiic, S., Johansson-Stenmand, O., Kitamurac, R., Pendyalae, R. and Vilhelmsonet B. (2002), 'A conceptual analysis of the impact of travel demand management on private car use', *Transport Policy*, **9** (1), 59–70.

Gerdtham, U.-G. and Johannesson, M. (2001), 'The relationship between happiness, health, and socioeconomic factors: results based on Swedish microdata', *Journal of Socio-Economics*, **30**, 553–7.

Goldberg, D. (1972), *The Detection of Psychiatric Illness by Questionnaire*, Oxford: Oxford University Press.

Golden, L. and Wiens-Tuers, B. (2006), 'To your happiness? Extra hours of labour supply and worker well-being', *Journal of Socio-Economics*, **35**, 382–97.

Greene, W. (2008), *Econometric Analysis*, Upper Saddle River, NJ: Pearson, Prentice Hall.

Greene, W.H. and Hensher, D.A. (2009), 'Modelling ordered choices', available at: http://pages.stern.nyu.edu/~wgreene/ (accessed 1 June 2009).

Gui, B. (2000), 'Beyond transactions: on the interpersonal dimension of economic reality', *Annals of Public and Cooperative Economics*, **71** (2), 139–69.

Johns, H. and Ormerod, P. (2007), *Happiness, Economics and Public Policy*, London: The Institute of Economic Affairs.

Johnson, D.R. and Wu, J. (2002), 'An empirical test of crisis, social selection, and role explanations of the relationship between marital disruption and psychological distress: a pooled time-series analysis of four-wave panel data', *Journal of Marriage and Family*, **64**, 211–24.

Jones, A. (2007), *Applied Econometrics for Health Economists: A Practical Guide*, Abingdon, UK: Radcliffe Publishing Ltd.

Kahneman, D. and Kreuger, A.B. (2006), 'Developments in the measurement of subjective well-being', *Journal of Economic Perspectives*, **20** (1), 3–24.

Kahneman, D., Diener, E. and Schwartz, N. (eds) (1999), *Well-being: the Foundations of Hedonic Pyschology*, New York: Russell Sage Foundation.

Lechner, M. (2009), 'Long-run labour market and health effects of individual sports activities', *Journal of Health Economics*, **28** (4), 839–54.

Lee, Y.H. and Park, I. (2010), 'Happiness and physical activity in special populations: evidence from Korean survey data', *Journal of Sports Economics*, **11** (2), 136–56.

Lucas, R.E., Clark, A.E., Georgellis, Y.Y. and Diener, E. (2003), 'Re-examining adaptation and the set point model of happiness: reactions to changes in marital status', *Journal of Personality and Social Psychology*, **84**, 527–39.

Oja, P., Vuori, I and Paronen, O. (1998), 'Daily walking and cycling to work: their utility as health-enhancing physical activity', *Patient Education and Counselling*, **33**, S87–S94.

Oswald, A. and Clark, A. (2002), 'A simple statistical method for measuring how life events affect happiness', *International Journal of Epidemiology*, **31** (6), 1139–44.

Oswald, A. and Powdthavee, N. (2007), 'Obesity, unhappiness and the challenge of affluence', *Economic Journal*, **117**, F441–F459.

Pate, R.R., Pratt, M., Blair, S.N., Haskell, W.L., Macera, C.A. and Bouchard, C. (1995), 'Physical activity and public health: a recommendation from the Centers for Disease Control and Prevention and the American College of Sports Medicine', *Journal of the American Medical Association*, **275** (5), 402–7.

Powdthavee, N. (2008), 'Putting a price tag on friends, relatives, and neighbours: using surveys of life satisfaction to value social relationships', *Journal of Socio-Economics*, **37** (4), 1459–80.

Powdthavee, N. and Vignoles, A. (2008), 'Mental health of parents and life satisfaction of children: a within-family analysis of intergenerational transmission of well-being', *Social Indicators Research*, **88** (3), 397–422.

Pucher, J. and Dijkstra, L. (2003), 'Promoting safe walking and cycling to improve public health: lessons from The Netherlands and Germany', *American Journal of Public Health*, **93** (9), 1509–16.

Rasciute, S. and Downward, P.M. (2010), 'Health or happiness? What is the impact of physical activity on the individual', *Kyklos*, **63** (2), 256–70.

Ryff, C.D. (1995), 'Psychological well-being in adult life', *Current Directions in Psychological Science*, **4**, 99–104.

Scully, D., Kremer, J., Meade, M., Graham, R. and Dudgeon, K. (1999). 'Physical exercise and psychological well-being: a critical review', *British Journal of Sports Medicine*, **32**, 11–20.

Shephard, R.J. (2008), 'Is active commuting the answer to population health?', *Sports Medicine*, **38** (9), 751–8.

Shields, M.A. and Wheatley Price, S. (2005), 'Exploring the economic and social determinants of psychological well-being and perceived social support in England', *Journal of the Royal Statistical Society* (A), **168**, Pt 3, 513–37.

Shields, M.A., Wheatley Price, S. and Wooden, M. (2009), 'Life satisfaction and the economic and social characteristics of neighbourhoods', *Journal of Population Economics*, **22**, 421–43.

Smith, A. and Bird, S. (2004), 'From evidence to policy: reflections on emerging themes in health-related physical activity', *Journal of Sports Sciences*, **22**, 791–9.

Stutzer, A. and Frey, B.S. (2006), 'Does marriage make people happy, or do happy people get married?', *The Journal of Socio-Economics*, **35**, 326–47.

Van Praag, B.M.S. and Frijters, P. (1999), 'The measurement of welfare and well-being: the Leyden approach', in D. Kahneman, E. Diener and N. Schwartz (eds), *Well-being: The Foundations of Hedonic Psychology*, New York: Russel Sage Foundation, pp. 413–32.

Wendel-Vos, G.C.W., Schuit, A.J., Feskens, E.J.M., Boshuizen, H.C., Verschuren, W.M.M., Saris, W.H.M. and Kromhout, D. (2004), 'Physical activity and stroke. A meta-analysis of observational data', *International Journal of Epidemiology*, **33**, 787–98.

Winkelmann, L and Winkelmann, R. (1998), 'Why are the unemployed so unhappy? Evidence from Panel Data', *Economica*, **65** (257), 1–15.

Winkelmann, R. (2005), 'Subjective well-being and the family: results from an ordered probit model with multiple random effects', *Empirical Economics*, **30**, 749–61.

World Health Organization (WHO) World Health Day (2002), available at: www.who.int/world-health-day/brochure.en.pdf (accessed 16 April 2010).

3. Physical activity and obesity in Spain: evidence from the Spanish National Health Survey*

Jaume García Villar, Sonia Oreffice and Climent Quintana-Domeque

1. INTRODUCTION

Obesity has become one of the most important public health concerns around the world as a relevant risk factor for several health problems and chronic diseases, such as heart disease, diabetes, certain cancers, arteriosclerosis or apnea (WHO, 2002). According to the Spanish Ministry of Health (MSC, 2005), in Spain 38.5 per cent of adult individuals are overweight and 14.5 per cent are obese. Moreover, with the exception of the UK, Spain is the European Union country with the highest increases in obesity rates over the last decade (WHO, 2002).

In the attempt to reverse this 'epidemic' affecting both adults and children, increasing concern and emphasis has been put on the relationship between weight, physical activity and eating habits, which have been studied in the medical and socioeconomic literatures. For instance, Costa-Font and Gil (2008) account for frequency of physical activity and consumption of certain food items in their analysis of how socioeconomic inequalities affect obesity in Spain. Neira and de Onis (2006) refer to both dietary habits and leisure-time activities in their report on the Spanish Ministry of Health prevention plan for obesity. Interestingly, the importance of walking, cycling and using public transportation is found to be negatively related to obesity rates across countries in Europe, the USA and Australia (for example, Bassett et al., 2008).

In this study, we examine physical activity and obesity in Spain, and investigate the associations between these anthropometric and lifestyle characteristics, focusing on detailed activity information such as the frequency of physical activity both during leisure time and in main daily tasks (job, school or home). We perform our analysis by gender, taking into account nutrition – frequency of consumption of fruit, meat, fish, vegetables, sweets, and so on – education, income, health, smoking status, children, marital status, being on a diet and province of residence.

We use data from the most recent Spanish National Health Survey (Encuesta Nacional de Salud, ENS) of 2006 and focus on adult men and women aged 20 to 50, measuring their body weight by means of an obesity index and of the body mass index (BMI). Body mass index is defined as an individual's body weight (in kilograms) divided by the square of his or her height (in meters), while obesity is a dummy variable that takes value of 1 if the individual BMI is above or equal to 30, and zero otherwise (WHO, 2003).

Assessing the extent to which obesity and BMI are related to the degree of physical activity allows us to consider an effective remedy and prevention mechanism of obesity, especially when a range of individual characteristics are accounted for. Is there a negative association between physical activity and obesity? Is this correlation present only for physical activity during leisure time and/or in main daily tasks? Does it persist once we account for individual heterogeneity? Does it vary by gender?

We find that men's and women's physical activity during leisure time plays a significant role in explaining their obesity status (BMI): both men and women who exercise are 4 per cent less likely to be obese. Interestingly, physical activity during the performance of main daily tasks does not appear to be related to individual weight, which is consistent with Costa-Font and Gil (2008), who use data from the ENS 2003.

Lakdawalla and Philipson (2007) consider US workers and the physical strenuousness of their occupation using the Dictionary of Occupation Titles and do find a negative relationship between BMI and on-the-job physical activity. However, our estimates are not directly comparable with theirs. In the ENS, physical activity in the main task refers to both work and non-work activities, and our sample encompasses both workers and non-workers.

Our evidence concerning leisure physical activity is consistent with a framework in which exercising and going to the gym is a substitution induced by the technological change in the workplace, which made jobs much more sedentary (Lakdawalla and Philipson, 2007; Rosin, 2008). In order to burn calories and stay thin, individuals need to perform off-the-job exercise. Moreover, this association persists when controlling for nutrition, income, education, health, smoking status, children, marital status and physical effort in the main daily (non-leisure) activity. In addition, our empirical analysis reveals that eating healthy food, such as fruits and pasta/bread, measured in terms of frequency of eating episodes, is negatively correlated with obesity (BMI).

This chapter is organized as follows. Section 2 briefly discusses the determinants of obesity. Section 3 describes the data. Section 4 presents the empirical results. Section 5 concludes.

2. THE DETERMINANTS OF OBESITY: A BRIEF REVIEW

Obesity is the result of an imbalance in energy consumption and energy usage; eating more calories (consumption of food) than the total amount of calories burned (physical exercise). As a consequence, the body accumulates the extra calories as fat, and over time this gives rise to obesity. Not everyone, however, gaining weight, becoming obese from the imbalance in the caloric equation; this may be a result of genetics. Indeed, there are genetic factors that determine obesity status and complex biochemical systems that tend to maintain body weight (for example, Rosenbaum et al., 1997; Comuzzie and Allison, 1998; Woods et al., 1998).

Economists have studied the determinants of BMI and have modeled various explanations of obesity, which relate to genetic, behavioral and environmental factors that affect energy intake and energy expenditure. Rosin (2008) presents a survey of the literature on the determinants of BMI and the explanations of obesity offered by economists, such as technological change (Philipson and Posner, 1999; Cutler et al., 2003; Lakdawalla and Philipson, 2007, 2009), relative prices (Chou et al., 2004), and time preference (Komlos et al., 2004).

According to Philipson and Posner (1999) technological change has lowered the cost of food (calories) through agriculture innovation. Lakdawalla and Philipson (2009) show that 40 per cent of the increase in weight was due to expansion in the supply of food, while 60 per cent was due to demand factors through more sedentary lifestyles. However, the empirical analysis by Cutler et al. (2003) points to an increase in food consumption rather than reduced exercise.

Using a sample of older men in the USA, Loh (2009) shows that individuals working more hours may have less time to exercise and be more likely to have a higher BMI. At the same time, they consume more highly caloric food to economize on the scarcity of their time, thus increasing their BMI (Chou et al., 2004).

Using the National Longitudinal Survey of Youth (NLSY), Lakdawalla and Philipson (2007) show that job-related physical activity has causal effects on weight for male workers, but for female workers the effect seems primarily selective. They argue that men working more hours in sedentary jobs have a higher BMI.

Finally, Komlos et al. (2004) argue that a higher rate of time preference could reduce investment in exercise and increase caloric intake, which would increase weight. Their empirical evidence suggests that the link between obesity and the marginal rate of time preference is plausible.

The absence of physical activity seems to be a prominent risk factor for becoming overweight and obese. Despite cross-sectional studies having found only moderate relationships between levels of physical activity and weight status, prospective studies have linked low levels of physical activity with weight gain over time (Dishman et al., 2004).

In this chapter, we provide a cross-sectional analysis of the relationship between leisure physical activity and obesity (and BMI). In addition, we consider the type and intensity of physical activity.

3.   DATA DESCRIPTION

Estimation is carried out on the basis of data from the ENS 2006. The ENS 2006 was administered from June 2006 to June 2007. The Instituto Nacional de Estadística (INE: Spanish National Statistical Institute) was in charge of the fieldwork. The ENS 2006 is a cross-sectional representative national survey of individuals aged 16 or more living in Spanish households, collecting a wide range of individual and household demographic, socioeconomic and health variables. All the information is self-reported by the respondents. The ENS 2006 consists of three questionnaires: household, adults, and minors (aged below 15) whose information was reported by their mother, father or legal representative. For the purpose of this study, we use the first two. Data on life habits, anthropometric characteristics, preventive practices, consumption of food and medicines are specifically collected, along with the region and province of residence.[1]

The total original adult sample (age above 16) is 29478 individuals, who were interviewed in person, and only one adult per household was interviewed. We confine our study to those individuals who were born in Spain and who are between 20 and 50 years old, excluding the elderly due to measurement error concerns. In fact, the error in self-reported anthropometric measures seems to be constant for the 25–55 age group, according to the analyses in Thomas and Frankenberg (2002) and in Ezzati et al. (2006) with US data.[2] Following Conley and Glauber (2007), we discard those couples whose height and weight values include any extremes: a weight of more than 400 pounds or less than 70 pounds, a height above 84 or below 45 inches. In meters and kilos, we have equivalently discarded the very few individuals whose height is below 1.18 meters, the weight range and the upper limit for height being met by the entire adult sample. Our sample thus consists of 4983 observations for men and 7003 for women.

We run regressions of obesity (and BMI) on physical activity during leisure time expressed both in terms of extensive and intensive margin, and on several covariates.

Physical activity during leisure time is defined as a dummy variable that takes a value of 1 if a person reports walking, going to the gym, and so on regularly. Additionally, the frequency (intensity) of practicing the physical activity during the two weeks before the interview is also requested, for activities lasting at least 20 minutes. The type of the activity is also recorded with dichotomous variables, and categorized into light (for example, walking, gardening), moderate (for example, cycling, running) and vigorous (for example, playing soccer, basketball, karate).

We use the following covariates: age, physical exercise in the main activity, food consumption, smoking behavior, educational level, household income, number of adults living in the household, number of children under 15 years of age, cohabiting status (including married couples), good health and being on a diet.

The ENS contains a question about physical activity (exercise) in the main activity (that is, at work, at school, or at home if not working). We construct four dummy variables for the corresponding categories: sitting, standing almost all day, walking and carrying some weight, and performing tasks requiring a vigorous physical effort.

Food consumption is measured by means of 12 variables counting the number of times per week in which the individual eats fruits, meat, eggs, fish, pasta, bread, vegetables, legumes, pork, milk, sweets and sodas. We have assigned the following numbers to the variables: 7 for daily consumption, 4.5 for a frequency of at least three times a week, 1.5 for a frequency of once or twice, 0.5 for less than once, and 0 for never (or almost never).

Smoking behavior is captured by four dummy variables (daily smoker, occasional smoker, stopped smoking, never smoked). Education is also measured by four dummy variables: primary school or less, first stage of secondary (that is, middle school) or medium vocational training, second stage of secondary school (high school) or advanced vocational training, college degree. In the ENS, income is recorded in brackets, and we report it by means of four dummy variables: monthly household income less than €900, between €901 and €1200, between €1201 and €1800, and above €1800. The cohabiting status dummy variable captures whether the individual is living with a partner (spouse or cohabitant) or without a partner. The health status originally recorded by the ENS is a five-category variable (from very good to very bad health); this is the basis of our health dummy variable: 1 if very good or good; 0 if regular, bad or very bad. Finally, we also use a dummy variable for whether the individual is on a diet.

All regressions include a year dummy variable (for whether the interview took place in 2006 or 2007), quarter of interview dummy variables to account for seasonal patterns in weight changes, and province fixed effects to control for constant geographical differences in poverty levels, food prices, eating habits, and cultural attitudes toward obesity and physical activity. Finally, observations are weighed using the individual sample weights available in the ENS (*factor adulto*).

4. EMPIRICAL ANALYSIS

4.1 A First Look at the Data

Table 3.1 summarizes the data used in our analysis. The prevalence of obesity is estimated to be 12 per cent, and the average BMI is 25.1, so the average individual is slightly overweight (BMI $\geq$ 25). Sixty per cent of the respondents report to perform some sort of physical activity during their leisure time. In our sample, 48 per cent of the individuals are women. On average, people are approximately 36 years old. The average number of times in the last two weeks doing physical activity varies between 3.62 for light physical activity to 0.50 for vigorous physical activity.

In terms of physical activity involved in the main activity – either at work for those who are employed, at school for students, or at home – 34 per cent of the individuals report being sitting down most of the time, 46 per cent report being standing up most of the time, 15 per cent report being walking and carrying some weight, and 5 per cent report doing vigorous physical effort.

Regarding food consumption, the most frequently eaten products, on a weekly basis, are Milk (6.53) and Bread (6.43), followed by Fruit (5.16) and Vegetables (4.46). Legumes (2.19), Sodas (2.27), Eggs (2.29) and Fish (2.61) are the least consumed products. Spaniards consume meat (4.18) more regularly than fish.

The smoking prevalence, for daily smokers, is 36 per cent. This increases up to 40 per cent when considering individuals who occasionally smoke. Thirty-nine per cent of Spaniards report having an average monthly income above €1800, while 11 per cent have an average income below €901. Notice that educational categories have been evenly split into the previously defined four categories.

The average individual reports living in a household consisting of 2.82 adults and 0.71 children. We also note that 64 per cent of the individuals live with a partner (including married individuals), 78 per cent report their health status to be good or very good, and 10 per cent are on a diet.

Table 3.2 shows the two main stylized facts in our data. First, the prevalence of obesity is lower for individuals doing physical activity in

Table 3.1   Summary statistics, ENS 2006, individuals aged 20–50

	Observations	Mean (weighted)	Standard deviation	Min.	Max.
Obesity	12119	0.12	0.32	0	1
BMI	12119	25.10	4.16	14.69	58.82
Physical Activity (PA) in Leisure	12522	0.59	0.49	0	1
Female	12674	0.48	0.49	0	1
Age	12674	35.86	8.07	20	50
PA Light in Leisure	12455	3.62	5.51	0	64
PA Moderate in Leisure	12424	1.32	2.95	0	60
PA Vigorous in Leisure	12373	0.50	1.87	0	70
PA 1 Main Activity (sitting)	12554	0.34	0.46	0	1
PA 2 Main Activity (standing almost all day)	12554	0.46	0.50	0	1
PA 3 Main Activity (walking and carrying some weight)	12554	0.15	0.35	0	1
PA 4 Main Activity (vigorous physical effort)	12554	0.05	0.21	0	1
Fruit	12467	5.16	2.47	0	7
Meat	12468	4.18	1.82	0	7
Eggs	12461	2.29	1.60	0	7
Fish	12465	2.61	1.74	0	7
Pasta	12454	3.88	2.02	0	7
Bread	12462	6.43	1.68	0	7
Vegetables	12464	4.46	2.28	0	7
Legumes	12463	2.19	1.60	0	7
Pork	12453	3.30	2.53	0	7
Milk	12464	6.53	1.45	0	7
Sweets	12466	3.41	2.94	0	7
Sodas	12464	2.27	2.62	0	7
Smoking (daily)	12674	0.36	0.48	0	1
Smoking (occasionally)	12674	0.04	0.18	0	1
Smoking (in the past)	12674	0.19	0.41	0	1
Smoking (never)	12674	0.41	0.49	0	1
Income < €901	11452	0.11	0.33	0	1
Income €901–1200	11452	0.20	0.40	0	1
Income €1201–1800	11452	0.30	0.46	0	1
Income > €1800	11452	0.39	0.48	0	1
Education (primary or less)	12603	0.25	0.44	0	1
Education (middle school)	12603	0.23	0.42	0	1
Education 3 (high school)	12603	0.27	0.44	0	1

Table 3.1   (continued)

	Observations	Mean (weighted)	Standard deviation	Min.	Max.
Education 4 (college degree)	12 603	0.25	0.43	0	1
Number of adults in household	12 674	2.82	1.00	1	10
Number of children (below 15)	12 674	0.71	0.92	0	7
Cohabiting (living with a partner)	12 672	0.64	0.47	0	1
Good (or very good) Health	12 674	0.78	0.42	0	1
Diet	12 548	0.10	0.31	0	1

Note: Authors' calculations from the ENS 2006.

their leisure time, for both men and women. Men who report doing some physical activity in their leisure time have an obesity rate of 11.5 per cent, while this rate amounts to 16.3 per cent for those reporting not doing any. The difference, which is around 5 per cent, is statistically significant at the 1 per cent level. For women, the obesity rates are 8.3 per cent and 12.8 per cent, respectively, and the difference is 4.5 per cent, which is also statistically significant at the 1 per cent level. Second, average BMI is lower for individuals doing some physical activity. Men who report doing some physical activity have an average BMI of 25.77, while the average for their counterparts is 26.44. The difference is 0.667, statistically significant at the 1 per cent level. Women who report not doing any physical activity have an average BMI of 24.47, which compares to 23.85 for their counterparts. The difference is 0.621 and it is statistically significant at the 1 per cent level.

The differences in obesity rates and average BMI between those who report doing some physical activity and those who do not are similar for both men and women. Interestingly, the average BMI, independent of physical activity, is always larger for men, who are on average overweight, than for women. The average BMIs for women are below 25, independent of physical activity, so women are not, on average, overweight.

This first look at the data suggests that physical activity and obesity (and more generally BMI) are negatively related for both men and women. Furthermore, these associations do not seem to differ by gender.[3] Needless to say, individuals who report doing some physical activity could differ in several dimensions from those who do not. Tables 3.3 and 3.4 confirm this.

Men who report doing some physical activity are younger than those who do not, but this is not the case for women. The degree of physical

Table 3.2   *Prevalence of obesity and mean BMI by physical activity for*
men and women, aged 20–50, ENS 2006

	Prevalence of obesity	
	Men	Women
Physical Activity = 0	0.163	0.128
	(0.011)	(0.008)
	1894	*2958*
Physical Activity = 1	0.115	0.083
	(0.008)	(0.006)
	3089	*4045*
Difference (PA = 1 – PA = 0)	**−0.048*****	**−0.045*****
	(0.013)	**(0.010)**
	4983	*7003*

	Mean BMI	
	Men	Women
Physical Activity = 0	26.44	24.47
	(0.120)	(0.112)
	194	*2958*
Physical Activity = 1	25.77	23.85
	(0.088)	(0.085)
	3089	*4045*
Difference (PA = 1 – PA = 0)	**−0.667*****	**−0.621*****
	(0.148)	**(0.140)**
	4983	*7003*

Notes:
Each prevalence (mean) is obtained from a regression of obesity (BMI) on a constant using
only the information for the corresponding group (PA = 0 or PA = 1).
The difference in prevalence (mean) across groups is obtained from a regression on a
constant and PA.
Observations have been weighed using individual sampling weights.
Robust standard errors in parentheses. Number of observations in italics.
*** p-value < 0.01, ** p-value < 0.05, * p-value < 0.1.

exercise in the main activity (job, school, home, and so on) differs between
those who report doing some physical activity and those who do not for
men, but not for women. Both men and women who report doing some
physical activity consume more frequently fruit, fish and vegetables, and
less frequently pork, than their counterparts. They are also less likely to
smoke daily, more likely to be highly educated, to report being in good or
very good health, and to be on a diet.

Hence, the negative relationship between physical activity and obesity (or

Table 3.3   Mean characteristics by physical activity status for men aged 20–50, ENS 2006

N = 4442	Physical activity = 0	Physical activity = 1	Adjusted Wald test for the difference F-statistic
Obesity	0.168 (0.012)	0.115 (0.008)	13.86***
BMI	26.54 (0.127)	25.75 (0.093)	25.15***
Age	36.76 (0.279)	35.06 (0.222)	22.84***
PA 1 Main activity	0.32 (0.015)	0.38 (0.013)	12.08***
PA 2 Main activity	0.36 (0.015)	0.38 (0.013)	1.18
PA 3 Main activity	0.20 (0.013)	0.17 (0.010)	3.91**
PA 4 Main activity	0.12 (0.010)	0.065 (0.006)	22.41***
Fruit	4.55 (0.090)	5.16 (0.070)	28.82***
Mcat	4.28 (0.057)	4.27 (0.045)	0.00
Eggs	2.39 (0.053)	2.32 (0.040)	1.09
Fish	2.32 (0.054)	2.55 (0.043)	11.45***
Pasta	3.94 (0.065)	3.90 (0.052)	0.25
Bread	6.54 (0.046)	6.55 (0.038)	0.03
Vegetables	3.85 (0.076)	4.17 (0.062)	10.65***
Legumes	2.35 (0.055)	2.19 (0.045)	4.98**
Pork	3.94 (0.083)	3.65 (0.068)	7.45***
Milk	6.35 (0.061)	6.52 (0.041)	5.16**
Sweets	3.27 (0.092)	3.39 (0.076)	1.06
Sodas	2.77 (0.094)	2.62 (0.076)	1.50
Smoking (daily)	0.50 (0.016)	0.33 (0.012)	75.84***
Smoking (occasionally)	0.022 (0.005)	0.055 (0.006)	17.61***
Smoking (in the past)	0.19 (0.012)	0.20 (0.010)	0.64
Smoking (never)	0.29 (0.015)	0.42 (0.013)	45.67***
Income < €901	0.11 (0.009)	0.10 (0.008)	0.77
Income €901–1200	0.20 (0.013)	0.18 (0.010)	2.07
Income €1201–1800	0.35 (0.015)	0.28 (0.011)	14.69***
Income > €1800	0.33 (0.015)	0.44 (0.013)	30.52***
Education (primary or less)	0.33 (0.015)	0.20 (0.010)	56.36***
Education (middle school)	0.26 (0.014)	0.23 (0.011)	4.19**
Education 3 (high school)	0.25 (0.013)	0.30 (0.012)	10.31***
Education 4 (college degree)	0.16 (0.012)	0.28 (0.012)	50.52***
Number of adults in household	2.75 (0.051)	2.81 (0.043)	0.86
Number of children (below 15)	0.77 (0.029)	0.64 (0.024)	12.21***
Cohabiting (living with a partner)	0.68 (0.016)	0.55 (0.013)	35.23***
Good (or very good) health	0.79 (0.013)	0.84 (0.010)	9.07***
Diet	0.065 (0.008)	0.094 (0.008)	6.57**

Note: *** p-value < 0.01, ** p-value < 0.05, * p-value < 0.1.

Table 3.4   Mean characteristics by physical activity status for women aged 20–50, ENS 2006

N = 6197	Physical activity = 0	Physical activity = 1	Adjusted Wald test for the difference F-statistic
Obesity	0.125 (0.009)	0.085 (0.006)	14.30***
BMI	24.46 (0.117)	23.91 (0.090)	14.00***
Age	35.81 (0.226)	36.31 (0.200)	2.67
PA 1 Main activity	0.30 (0.012)	0.32 (0.010)	1.47
PA 2 Main activity	0.56 (0.013)	0.56 (0.011)	0.00
PA 3 Main activity	0.12 (0.008)	0.10 (0.006)	1.41
PA 4 Main activity	0.027 (0.005)	0.020 (0.003)	1.85
Fruit	5.18 (0.065)	5.67 (0.053)	34.61***
Meat	4.08 (0.047)	3.96 (0.042)	3.76*
Eggs	2.23 (0.039)	2.27 (0.034)	0.63
Fish	2.57 (0.044)	2.88 (0.039)	28.36***
Pasta	3.94 (0.053)	3.78 (0.044)	5.62**
Bread	6.32 (0.045)	6.28 (0.043)	0.42
Vegetables	4.52 (0.059)	5.17 (0.047)	73.71***
Legumes	2.22 (0.043)	2.08 (0.034)	5.94**
Pork	2.94 (0.065)	2.71 (0.055)	7.29***
Milk	6.60 (0.037)	6.66 (0.031)	1.57
Sweets	3.41 (0.074)	3.44 (0.064)	0.06
Sodas	1.99 (0.069)	1.74 (0.058)	7.50***
Smoking (daily)	0.40 (0.013)	0.30 (0.010)	32.72***
Smoking (occasionally)	0.028 (0.004)	0.033 (0.004)	0.73
Smoking (in the past)	0.17 (0.009)	0.21 (0.009)	11.29***
Smoking (never)	0.41 (0.013)	0.45 (0.011)	7.43***
Income < €901	0.13 (0.009)	0.11 (0.007)	2.32
Income €901–1200	0.22 (0.011)	0.21 (0.009)	0.83
Income €1201–1800	0.32 (0.012)	0.29 (0.010)	3.40*
Income > €1800	0.34 (0.012)	0.39 (0.011)	12.84***
Education (primary or less)	0.32 (0.012)	0.22 (0.009)	42.34***
Education (middle school)	0.22 (0.011)	0.23 (0.009)	0.43
Education (high school)	0.26 (0.011)	0.25 (0.010)	0.21
Education (college degree)	0.20 (0.010)	0.30 (0.010)	42.65***
Number of adults in household	2.77 (0.031)	2.80 (0.029)	0.40
Number of children (below 15)	0.86 (0.022)	0.71 (0.019)	25.72***
Cohabiting (living with a partner)	0.72 (0.012)	0.69 (0.011)	3.39*
Good (or very good) health	0.71 (0.012)	0.76 (0.009)	8.62***
Diet	0.095 (0.007)	0.135 (0.007)	14.60***

Note: *** p-value < 0.01, ** p-value < 0.05, * p-value < 0.1.

BMI) could be capturing differences between those who do physical exercise and their counterparts. We investigate this possibility in the next subsection.

4.2 Main Findings

Table 3.5 presents a series of probit regressions for men in which obesity is the dependent variable. Column (1) shows that, controlling for age, men who report doing physical activity are 3.6 per cent less likely to be obese.

Column (2) includes 'physical activity in the main activity' dummy variables. The coefficient on physical activity in leisure time is now −0.039, that is, almost invariant with respect to column (1). The dummy variables capturing 'physical activity in the main activity' are not individually different than zero, though the F-test for their joint significance does reject that their coefficients are simultaneously zero at the 10 per cent level.

In column (3) we add 12 variables regarding food consumption: fruit, meat, eggs, fish, pasta, bread, vegetables, legumes, pork, milk, sweets and sodas. Essentially, the coefficient of interest still remains the same, −0.038. Interestingly, neither the dummy variables capturing 'physical activity in the main activity', nor those controlling for food consumption, are jointly significant determinants of obesity.

Column (4) adds smoking behavior dummy variables. The coefficient on physical activity in leisure time is −0.039, identical to that reported in column (2). We also see that those who smoke occasionally are less likely to be obese than those who have never smoked, while the individuals who used to smoked but do not currently smoke are more likely to be obese than the never-smokers. Notice that food consumption cannot be discarded as an obesity determinant, since the F-test for the joint significance of the 12 food variables does reject that their coefficients are simultaneously zero at the 10 per cent level.

Finally, column (5) accounts for differences in educational level and household income, to further control for individual heterogeneity. We also include number of children and adults in the household and a dummy variable regarding cohabitation status (including married). Surprisingly, the coefficient of interest remains almost intact, −0.037, which is very close to that estimated in column (1). Now, neither 'physical activity in the main activity' nor food consumption can be discarded as obesity determinants, since their respective F-tests for their joint significance do reject that their coefficients are simultaneously zero at the 10 per cent and 1 per cent levels, respectively.

While highly educated men are less likely to be obese, the role of income cannot be clearly disentangled (García Villar and Quintana-Domeque, 2009). Indeed, the F-test for the joint significance of the income dummy variables does not reject that their coefficients are simultaneously zero.

Table 3.5 Probit regressions of obesity on physical activity and other variables, men aged 20–50, ENS 2006, 'marginal effects' (evaluated at the means) are reported

	(1)	(2)	(3)	(4)	(5)
Physical activity in leisure	−0.036***	−0.039***	−0.038***	−0.039***	−0.037***
	(0.013)	(0.012)	(0.013)	(0.013)	(0.013)
Age	0.005***	0.005***	0.005***	0.005***	0.004***
	(0.0006)	(0.0005)	(0.0007)	(0.0007)	(0.0008)
PA 1 Main activity (sitting)		0.032	0.026	0.026	0.041
		(0.026)	(0.026)	(0.026)	(0.027)
PA 2 Main activity (standing almost all day)		0.002	0.003	0.004	0.005
		(0.025)	(0.026)	(0.026)	(0.026)
PA 3 Main activity (walking and carrying some weight)		0.041	0.039	0.039	0.030
		(0.030)	(0.030)	(0.030)	(0.029)
p-value F		*0.0842**	*0.1846*	*0.1866*	*0.0895**
Food consumption	No	No	Yes	Yes	Yes
p-value F			*0.1279*	*0.0962**	*0.0082****
Smoking (daily)				−0.009	−0.015
				(0.015)	(0.016)
Smoking (occasionally)				−0.063**	−0.059**
				(0.020)	(0.020)
Smoking (in the past)				0.028*	0.014
				(0.018)	(0.018)
p-value F				*0.0097****	*0.0628**
Income €901–1200					−0.015
					(0.022)
Income €1201–1800					−0.043**
					(0.020)
Income > €1800					−0.037
					(0.023)
p-value F					*0.1784*
Education (middle school)					−0.008
					(0.017)
Education (high school)					−0.032*
					(0.016)
Education (college degree)					−0.051***
					(0.016)
p-value F					*0.0460***
Number of adults					0.005
					(0.007)

Table 3.5   (continued)

	(1)	(2)	(3)	(4)	(5)
Number of children					0.0003 (0.007)
Cohabiting					0.026 (0.016)
Observed prevalence	0.1344	0.1341	0.1355	0.1355	0.1362
Pseudo-R²	0.0448	0.0488	0.0556	0.0598	0.0792
N	4948	4930	4871	4871	4455

Notes:
All regressions include year and quarter of interview dummy variables and province fixed effects.
The excluded categories are smoking (never), education (primary or less), income < €901, and performing tasks requiring a vigorous physical effort in the main activity (PA 4 main activity).
p-value F: p-value corresponding to the F-test for the joint significance of the dummy variables.
Observations have been weighed using sampling weights.
Robust standard errors are reported in parentheses.
*** p-value < 0.01, ** p-value < 0.05, * p-value < 0.1.

These regressions demonstrate that the associations of physical activity and obesity remain significant and similar when we (over)control for 'physical activity in the main activity', food consumption, smoking behavior, educational level and household income.

Table 3.6 replicates Table 3.5 for women. As before, the coefficient on physical activity in leisure time is almost the same across columns (1)–(4), between −0.039 and −0.042: women who report doing physical activity in their leisure time are around 4 per cent points less likely to be obese. However, the coefficient of interest in column (5) is −0.029, around 75 per cent of the coefficient estimated in columns (1)–(4). Controlling for educational achievement and household income reduces the size of the coefficient on physical activity in leisure time by 25 per cent. Hence, for women, a significant part of the association between physical activity and obesity is due to the differences in educational achievement and household income.

Tables 3.7 and 3.8 present a series of ordinary least squares (OLS) regressions for men and women, respectively, in which BMI is the dependent variable. Although the estimates are qualitatively very similar to those reported in Tables 3.5 and 3.6, some differences emerge. For men, the size of the coefficient on physical activity in leisure time increases (in absolute

Table 3.6   *Probit regressions of obesity on physical activity and other variables, women aged 20–50, ENS 2006, 'marginal effects' (evaluated at the means) are reported*

	(1)	(2)	(3)	(4)	(5)
Physical activity	−0.039***	−0.041***	−0.041***	−0.042***	−0.029***
in leisure	(0.010)	(0.009)	(0.010)	(0.009)	(0.010)
Age	0.003***	0.003***	0.003***	0.003***	0.001*
	(0.0006)	(0.0005)	(0.0007)	(0.0006)	(0.0007)
PA 1 Main activity		−0.056*	−0.056*	−0.058*	−0.024
(sitting)		(0.027)	(0.028)	(0.027)	(0.032)
PA 2 Main activity		−0.039	−0.042	−0.045	−0.036
(standing almost		(0.033)	(0.034)	(0.034)	(0.036)
all day)					
PA 3 Main activity		−0.028	−0.034	−0.034	−0.029
(walking and		(0.027)	(0.026)	(0.026)	(0.028)
carrying some weight)					
p-value F		*0.0710**	*0.1143*	*0.0953**	*0.6134*
Food consumption	No	No	Yes	Yes	Yes
p-value F			*0.0182***	*0.0184***	*0.0062****
Smoking (daily)				−0.021*	−0.023**
				(0.010)	(0.010)
Smoking				0.006	0.020
(occasionally)				(0.025)	(0.028)
Smoking (in the past)				−0.016	−0.010
				(0.011)	(0.011)
p-value F				*0.1806*	*0.1234*
Income €901–1200					0.015
					(0.016)
Income €1201–1800					−0.010
					(0.015)
Income > €1800					−0.022
					(0.017)
p-value F					*0.0897**
Education					−0.044***
(middle school)					(0.009)
Education					−0.059***
(high school)					(0.010)
Education					−0.085***
(college degree)					(0.010)
p-value F					*0.0000****
Number of adults					0.006
					(0.006)
Number of children					0.002
					(0.006)

Table 3.6 (continued)

	(1)	(2)	(3)	(4)	(5)
Cohabiting					0.014
					(0.013)
Observed prevalence	0.1024	0.1016	0.1005	0.1005	0.1018
Pseudo-R^2	0.0398	0.0445	0.0531	0.0550	0.0916
N	7003	6985	6917	6917	6270

Notes:
All regressions include year and quarter of interview dummy variables and province fixed effects.
The excluded categories are smoking (never), education (primary or less), income < €901, and performing tasks requiring a vigorous physical effort in the main activity (PA 4 main activity).
p-value F: p-value corresponding to the F-test for the joint significance of the dummy variables.
Observations have been weighed using sampling weights.
Robust standard errors are reported in parentheses.
*** p-value < 0.01, ** p-value < 0.05, * p-value < 0.1.

value) from -0.403 (the naive specification, column 1) to -0.507 (the most complete specification, column 5). Moreover, for both men and women, cohabiting is positively associated with having a higher BMI.

4.3 Intensity and Type of Physical Activity

So far we have focused on the relationship between physical activity in spare time and obesity (BMI), without distinguishing between types of physical activity and their intensities, which is the topic of this subsection.

According to Caspersen et al. (1995), physical activity is 'any bodily movement produced by skeletal muscles that results in energy expenditure'. More specifically, the Centers for Disease Control and Prevention (CDC) and the American College of Sports of Medicine define physically inactive or sedentary subjects as those who did not engage in at least 150 minutes of physical activities per week (Pate et al., 1995).

As we mentioned in section 3, in the ENS individuals who report doing some physical activity in their spare time are asked about how many times during the last two weeks they did light, moderate or vigorous physical activity for more than 20 minutes. For men, the weighted average numbers of times doing light, moderate and vigorous physical activity are 8.7, 6.3 and 5.1, respectively, with standard deviations of 5.1, 4.1 and 4.2. In other words, 87, 63 and 51 minutes (on average) per week in the last two weeks. For women, the weighted average numbers of times doing light, moderate

*Table 3.7   OLS regressions of BMI on physical activity and other
variables, men aged 20–50, ENS 2006*

	(1)	(2)	(3)	(4)	(5)
Physical activity	−0.403***	−0.457***	−0.483***	−0.527***	−0.507***
in leisure	(0.143)	(0.143)	(0.145)	(0.145)	(0.152)
Age	0.113***	0.113***	0.110***	0.102***	0.084***
	(0.008)	(0.008)	(0.009)	(0.009)	(0.011)
PA 1 Main activity		0.379	0.242	0.213	0.487*
(sitting)		(0.248)	(0.251)	(0.251)	(0.275)
PA 2 Main activity		0.020	−0.040	−0.044	0.087
(standing almost all day)		(0.250)	(0.253)	(0.251)	(0.266)
PA 3 Main activity		0.243	0.192	0.185	0.178
(walking and carrying some weight)		(0.278)	(0.277)	(0.275)	(0.286)
p-value F		*0.1083*	*0.3024*	*0.3773*	*0.0862**
Food consumption	No	No	Yes	Yes	Yes
p-value F			*0.0050***	*0.0044**	*0.0009****
Smoking (daily)				−0.248	−0.250
				(0.161)	(0.171)
Smoking (occasionally)				−0.421	−0.342
				(0.309)	(0.319)
Smoking (in the past)				0.735***	0.577***
				(0.191)	(0.199)
p-value F				*0.0000****	*0.0005****
Income €901–1200					−0.287
					(0.286)
Income €1201–1800					−0.469*
					(0.270)
Income > €1800					−0.424
					(0.278)
p-value F					*0.3557*
Education (middle school)					−0.026
					(0.213)
Education (high school)					−0.224
					(0.213)
Education (college degree)					−0.590**
					(0.233)
p-value F					*0.0268***
Number of adults					0.025
					(0.077)
Number of children					0.067
					(0.086)

Table 3.7   (continued)

	(1)	(2)	(3)	(4)	(5)
Cohabiting					0.679***
					(0.192)
R²		0.0979	0.1004	0.1106	0.1195	0.1407
N		4983	4965	4906	4906	4501

Notes:
All regressions include year and quarter of interview dummy variables and province fixed effects.
The excluded categories are: smoking (never), education (primary or less), income < €901, and performing tasks requiring a vigorous physical effort in the main activity (PA 4 main activity).
p-value F: p-value corresponding to the F-test for the joint significance of the dummy variables.
Observations have been weighed using sampling weights.
Robust standard errors are reported in parentheses.
*** p-value < 0.01, ** p-value < 0.05, * p-value < 0.1.

and vigorous physical activity are 9.4, 5.8 and 5.1, respectively, with standard deviations of 5.2, 3.9 and 6.7. In other words, 94, 58 and 51 minutes (on average) per week in the last two weeks.

In Tables 3.9 and 3.10 we inquire about the role played by type of physical activity and its intensity, including those who do not perform any physical activity, dividing physical activity into three main variables: light physical activity, moderate physical activity and vigorous physical activity. Since we focus on the entire sample of individuals, each of these variables can take a value of zero.

Tables 3.9 and 3.10 present a series of regressions of obesity (probit) and BMI (OLS) on the intensity of physical activity in spare time by type (light, moderate and vigorous) and other variables, for men and women, respectively. The estimates for men suggest that light physical activity is not related to either obesity or BMI, whether (columns 1 and 3) or not (columns 2 and 4) we control for other covariates. However, moderate and vigorous physical activities are negatively related to both obesity and BMI.

According to the estimates in columns (1) and (2), an increase of 10 in the number of times during the last two weeks doing moderate physical activity (that is, an increase of 100 minutes of physical activity per week during the last two weeks) is associated with a reduction in the probability of being obese of around 7 to 8 per cent. If the increase is in vigorous physical activity, the reduction is estimated to be around 22 to 23 per cent. Similar qualitative results emerge in columns (3) and (4) for BMI.

Table 3.10 shows a similar pattern for women, with the important

Table 3.8   OLS regressions of BMI on physical activity and other variables, women aged 20–50, ENS 2006

	(1)	(2)	(3)	(4)	(5)
Physical activity	−0.601***	−0.626***	−0.642***	−0.664***	−0.428***
in leisure	(0.136)	(0.133)	(0.134)	(0.134)	(0.140)
Age	0.124***	0.120***	0.116***	0.117***	0.079***
	(0.008)	(0.008)	(0.009)	(0.009)	(0.010)
PA 1 Main activity		−1.04**	−0.924*	−0.989*	−0.129
(sitting)		(0.507)	(0.530)	(0.533)	(0.585)
PA 2 Main activity		−0.509	−0.416	−0.466	−0.224
(standing almost all day)		(0.497)	(0.520)	(0.523)	(0.573)
PA 3 Main activity		−0.391	−0.410	−0.439	−0.303
(walking and carrying some weight)		(0.521)	(0.540)	(0.544)	(0.594)
p-value F		*0.0010***	*0.0044***	*0.0027***	*0.8640*
Food consumption	No	No	Yes	Yes	Yes
p-value F			*0.0000***	*0.0000***	*0.0000***
Smoking (daily)				−0.413***	−0.572***
				(0.157)	(0.162)
Smoking (occasionally)				0.125	0.106
				(0.400)	(0.404)
Smoking (in the past)				−0.140	−0.157
				(0.167)	(0.172)
p-value F				*0.0571**	*0.0039***
Income €901–1200					−0.022
					(0.256)
Income €1201–1800					−0.249
					(0.247)
Income > €1800					−0.491*
					(0.265)
p-value F					*0.1242*
Education (middle school)					−0.817***
					(0.203)
Education (high school)					−1.67***
					(0.218)
Education (college degree)					−2.39***
					(0.224)
p-value F					*0.0000***
Number of adults					0.163**
					(0.072)
Number of children					−0.022
					(0.088)

Table 3.8 (continued)

	(1)	(2)	(3)	(4)	(5)
Cohabiting					0.605***
					(0.179)
R^2		0.0850	0.0896	0.1059	0.1076	0.1531
N		7003	6985	6917	6917	6270

Notes:
All regressions include year and quarter of interview dummy variables and province fixed effects.
The excluded categories are: smoking (never), education (primary or less), income < €901, and performing tasks requiring a vigorous physical effort in the main activity (PA 4 main activity).
p-value F: p-value corresponding to the F-test for the joint significance of the dummy variables.
Observations have been weighed using sampling weights.
Robust standard errors are reported in parentheses.
*** p-value < 0.01, ** p-value < 0.05, * p-value < 0.1.

gender difference that for them light physical activity also matters, in terms of both obesity and BMI.

Notice that, in Tables 3.9 and 3.10, the most complete specifications control for self-reported good health and being on a diet too. The association between self-reported good health (and very good health) and obesity is negative for both men and women, while the association with BMI is negative only for women. In addition, individuals who report to be on a diet are more likely to be obese and have a higher BMI than those who do not. This 'counterintuitive' association can be explained by the fact that heavier and obese individuals are more likely to be on a diet in order to lose weight. Alternatively, this can be the product of some sort of misreporting behavior related to BMI and obesity. Unfortunately, the cross-sectional nature of the ENS does not allow us to investigate further these hypotheses.

To summarize, our findings document a negative association between physical activity during leisure time and obesity (and BMI), for both men and women.

5. DISCUSSION

The study of the relationship between physical activity and obesity faces several methodological problems (for example, Roman et al., 2009). First, physical activity is a variable that is difficult to measure (Sephard, 2003). Second, obese individuals tend to underestimate their food intake and

Table 3.9   *Probit and OLS regressions of obesity or BMI on type of physical activity and other variables, men aged 20–50, ENS 2006*

	Obesity		BMI	
	(1)	(2)	(3)	(4)
Light physical activity	−0.0002	0.0001	−0.009	−0.011
	(0.001)	(0.001)	(0.013)	(0.014)
Moderate physical activity	−0.0078***	−0.0070***	−0.058***	−0.068***
	(0.002)	(0.003)	(0.020)	(0.020)
Vigorous physical activity	−0.022***	−0.023***	−0.127***	−0.127***
	(0.005)	(0.005)	(0.020)	(0.021)
p-value F	*0.0000***	*0.0000***	*0.0000***	*0.0000***
Age	0.004***	0.003***	0.105***	0.074***
	(0.0008)	(0.0009)	(0.009)	(0.011)
PA 1 Main activity (sitting)		0.038		0.477*
		(0.027)		(0.277)
PA 2 Main activity (standing almost all day)		0.006		0.129
		(0.025)		(0.269)
PA 3 Main activity (walking and carrying some weight)		0.029		0.194
		(0.029)		(0.287)
p-value F		*0.1314*		*0.1436*
Food consumption	No	Yes	No	Yes
p-value F		*0.0474**		*0.0065***
Smoking (daily)		−0.015		−0.248
		(0.015)		(0.168)
Smoking (occasionally)		−0.056**		−0.404
		(0.021)		(0.333)
Smoking (in the past)		0.012		0.538***
		(0.017)		(0.197)
p-value F		*0.0770*		*0.0009***
Income €901–1200		−0.011		−0.283
		(0.021)		(0.286)
Income €1201–1800		−0.035*		−0.438
		(0.020)		(0.270)
Income > €1800		−0.030		−0.409
		(0.022)		(0.280)
p-value F		*0.2888*		*0.4172*
Education (middle school)		−0.006		0.051
		(0.016)		(0.212)
Education (high school)		−0.023		−0.153
		(0.016)		(0.212)

Table 3.9 (continued)

	Obesity		BMI	
	(1)	(2)	(3)	(4)
Education (college degree)		−0.040**		−0.559**
		(0.017)		(0.232)
p-value F		*0.1644*		*0.0296***
Number of adults		0.005		0.034
		(0.006)		(0.077)
Number of children		−0.000		0.080
		(0.007)		(0.086)
Cohabiting		0.031**		0.716***
		(0.016)		(0.192)
Good health		−0.030*		−0.051
		(0.016)		(0.199)
Diet		0.099***		1.39***
		(0.030)		(0.314)
(Pseudo) R^2	(0.0597)	(0.1062)	0.1048	0.1578
N	4855	4377	4919	4442

Note: See Table 3.8.

to overestimate their physical activity patterns (Livingstone and Black, 2003). Third, measurement error in BMI may lead to misclassification of individuals into different weight categories (for example, Danubio et al., 2008). This misclassification not only translates into a loss of precision but also can be translated into a biased estimate of the association between weight classification and physical activity.

It is also clear that our regression analysis using a cross-section of observational data cannot establish a 'causal' relationship between physical activity and obesity (or BMI). Reverse causality cannot be disentangled: obese (heavier) individuals could be less likely to be involved in doing physical exercise. The existence of omitted variables related to both physical activity and BMI, such as the rate of time preference (Komlos et al., 2004), can bias our estimates too. If we were willing to assume that these confounder factors are constant over time, longitudinal data would help us to overcome the omitted variable bias through within-individual fixed effects estimation. However, this approach would remove variation both in BMI and in physical activity, and it could exacerbate measurement error biases. Moreover, this strategy cannot address reverse causality issues.

Although a 'causal' interpretation of our regression estimates must be

Table 3.10 Probit and OLS regressions of obesity or BMI on type of physical activity and other variables, women aged 20–50, ENS 2006

	Obesity		BMI	
	(1)	(2)	(3)	(4)
Light physical activity	−0.002**	−0.002**	−0.023**	−0.035***
	(0.001)	(0.001)	(0.011)	(0.011)
Moderate physical activity	−0.006**	−0.003	−0.094***	−0.050**
	(0.003)	(0.002)	(0.027)	(0.024)
Vigorous physical activity	−0.027***	−0.018**	−0.144***	−0.107**
	(0.008)	(0.008)	(0.043)	(0.043)
p-value F	*0.0003****	*0.0019****	*0.0000****	*0.0001****
Age	0.003***	0.001***	0.122***	0.074***
	(0.0005)	(0.0006)	(0.008)	(0.009)
PA 1 Main activity (sitting)		−0.026		−0.209
		(0.031)		(0.581)
PA 2 Main activity (standing almost all day)		−0.037		−0.303
		(0.035)		(0.568)
PA 3 Main activity (walking and carrying some weight)		−0.032		−0.438
		(0.026)		(0.587)
p-value F		*0.6246*		*0.7397*
Food consumption	No	Yes	No	Yes
p-value F		*0.3432*		*0.0003****
Smoking (daily)		−0.022**		−0.570***
		(0.010)		(0.160)
Smoking (occasionally)		0.022		0.150
		(0.028)		(0.408)
Smoking (in the past)		−0.011		−0.195
		(0.011)		(0.171)
p-value F		*0.0998**		*0.0033****
Income €901–1200		0.018		−0.021
		(0.015)		(0.251)
Income €1201–1800		−0.007		−0.255
		(0.014)		(0.242)
Income > €1800		−0.019		−0.476*
		(0.016)		(0.256)
p-value F		*0.0664**		*0.1232*
Education (middle school)		−0.042***		−0.762***
		(0.009)		(0.197)
Education (high school)		−0.053***		−1.56***
		(0.010)		(0.216)

Table 3.10 (continued)

	Obesity			BMI
	(1)	(2)	(3)	(4)
Education (college degree)		−0.077***		−2.19***
		(0.009)		(0.223)
p-value F		*0.0000****		*0.0000****
Number of adults		0.006		0.161**
		(0.005)		(0.072)
Number of children		0.003		0.009
		(0.006)		(0.088)
Cohabiting		0.012		0.612***
		(0.012)		(0.174)
Good Health		−0.034***		−0.503***
		(0.011)		(0.160)
Diet		0.109***		2.56***
		(0.020)		(0.242)
(Pseudo) R^2	(0.0411)	(0.1165)	0.0873	0.1914
N	6916	6197	6916	6197

Note: See Table 3.8.

done with caution, the fact that for men the size of the association between physical activity and obesity is quite constant across specifications supports the hypothesis that, at least for men, physical activity during leisure time decreases the probability of being obese.

We hope that our findings will help to guide the implementation of preventive policies against the spread of obesity in the Spanish population, and will stimulate future research focused on the causal path between obesity and physical activity.

NOTES

* We thank Francesco Serti and the participants at the V Gijón Conference on Sports Economics for their helpful comments and suggestions. Special thanks go to Plácido Rodríguez. Oreffice and Quintana-Domeque acknowledge financial support from the Spanish Ministry of Science and Innovation (ECO 2008-05721/ECON). Errors are ours.
1. Spain is organized with 18 regions: 17 'autonomous communities' (Comunidades Autónomas) and 'Ceuta y Melilla' (two 'autonomous cities'). Each autonomous community is composed of provinces (Provincias), which serve as the territorial building blocks for the former. There are 50 provinces and two autonomous cities. We use 52 province dummy variables.
2. Cawley (2000, 2004) used the National Health and Nutrition Examination Survey III

(NHANES III) to estimate the relationship between measured height and weight and their self-reported counterparts. First, he estimated regressions of the corresponding measured variable to its self-reported counterpart by age and race. Then, assuming transportability, he used the NHANES III estimated coefficients to adjust the self-reported variables from the NLSY. The results for the effect of BMI on wages were very similar, whether corrected for measurement error or not. Hence, we rely on his findings, and we are confident that our results (based on unadjusted data) are unlikely to be significantly biased.

3. At the same time, the rate of physical activity during leisure is different between men and women: 62.2 per cent for men and 57.4 per cent for women. The prevalence of physical activity for women is approximately 5 per cent lower than for males (a difference that is statistically significant at the 5 per cent level). Bearing in mind that these are just raw means, this is somewhat surprising, given the stronger social pressure that women face with respect to their body size than men, which has been widely documented in the literature (for example, Averett and Korenman, 1996; Oreffice and Quintana-Domeque, 2010).

REFERENCES

Averett, S., Korenman, S. (1996), 'The economic reality of the beauty myth', *Journal of Human Resources*, **31**, 304–30.

Bassett, D., Pucher, J., Buehler, R., Thompson, D. and Crouter, S. (2008), 'Walking, cycling and obesity rates in Europe, North America, and Australia', *Journal of Physical Activity and Health*, **5**, 795–814.

Caspersen, C.J., Powell, K.E. and Christenson, G.M. (1985), 'Physical activity, exercise, and physical fitness: definitions and distinctions for health related research', *Public Health*, **100**, 126–31.

Cawley, J. (2000), 'Body weight and women's labor market outcomes', working paper No. 7841, National Bureau of Economic Research.

Cawley, J. (2004), 'The impact of obesity on wages', *Journal of Human Resources*, **39**, 451–74.

Chou, S., Grossman, M. and Saffer, H. (2004), 'An economic analysis of adult obesity: results from the behavioral risk factor surveillance system', *Journal of Health Economics*, **23**, 565–87.

Comuzzie A. and Allison, D. (1998), 'The search for human obesity genes', *Science*, **280**, 1374–7.

Conley, D. and Glauber, R. (2007), 'Gender, body mass and economic status', in K. Bolin and J. Cawley (eds), *Advances in Health Economics and Health Services Research, The Economics of Obesity*, Vol. 17, Amsterdam: Elsevier, pp. 255–78.

Costa-Font, J. and Gil, J. (2008), 'What lies behind socio-economic inequalities in obesity in Spain? A decomposition approach', *Food Policy*, **33**, 61–73.

Cutler, D., Glaeser, E. and Shapiro, J. (2003), 'Why have Americans become more obese?', *Journal of Economic Perspectives*, **17**, 93–118.

Danubio, M., Miranda, G., Vinciguerra, M., Vecchi, E. and Rufo, F. (2008), 'Comparison of self-reported and measured height and weight: implications for obesity research among young adults', *Economics and Human Biology*, **6**, 181–90.

Dishman, R.K., Washburn, R.A. and Heath, G.W. (2004), *Physical Activity Epidemiology*, Champaign, IL: Human Kinetics.

Ezzati, M., Martin, H., Skjold, S., Vander Hoorn, S. and Murray, C. (2006), 'Trends in national and state-level obesity in the USA after correction for self-report bias: analysis of health surveys', *Journal of the Royal Society of Medicine*, **99**, 250–57.

García Villar, J., Quintana-Domeque, C. (2009), 'Income and body mass index in Europe', *Economics and Human Biology*, **7**, 73–83.

Komlos, J., Smith, P. and Bogin, B. (2004), 'Obesity and the rate of time preference: is there a connection?', *Journal of Biosocial Science*, **36**, 209–19.

Lakdawalla, D. and Philipson, T. (2007) 'Labor supply and weight', *Journal of Human Resources*, **42**, 85–116.

Lakdawalla, D. and Philipson, T. (2009), 'The growth of obesity and technological change', *Economics and Human Biology*, **7**, 283–93.

Livingstone, M.B. and Black, A.E. (2003), 'Markers of the validity of reported energy intake', *Journal of Nutrition*, **133**, 895–920.

Loh, C. (2009), 'Physical inactivity and working hour inflexibility: evidence from a US sample of older men', *Review of Economics of the Household*, **7**, 257–81.

Ministerio de Sanidad y Consumo (MSC) (2005), *Estrategia para la nutrición, actividad física y prevención de la obesidad*, Madrid: Agencia española de seguridad alimentaria, Ministerio de Sanidad y Consumo.

Niera, M. and de Onis, M. (2006), 'The Spanish strategy for nutrition, physical activity and the prevention of obesity', *British Journal of Nutrition*, **96**, 8–11.

Oreffice, S. and Quintana-Domeque, C. (2010) 'Anthropometry and socioeconomics among couples: evidence in the United States', *Economics and Human Biology*, in press.

Pate, R.R., Pratt, M., Blair, S.N., Haskell, W.L., Macera, C.A., Bouchard, C., Buchner, D., Ettinger, W., Heath, G.W., King, A.C., Kriska, A., Leon, A.S., Marcus, B.H., Morris, J., Paffenbarger, R.S., Patrick, K., Pollock, M.L., Rippe, J.M., Sallis, J. and Wilmore, J.H. (1995), 'Physical activity and public health. A recommendation from the Centers for Disease Control and Prevention and the American College of Sports Medicine', *Journal of the American Medical Association*, **273**, 402–7.

Philipson, T. and Posner, R. (1999), 'The long-run growth in obesity as a function of technological change', working paper No. 7423, National Bureau of Economic Research.

Roman, B., Serra-Majem, Ll., Pérez-Rodrigo, C., Drobnic, F. and Segura, R. (2009), 'Physical activity in children and youth in Spain: future actions for obesity prevention', *Nutritional Reviews*, **67**, 94–8.

Rosenbaum, M., Leibel, R. and Hirsch, J. (1997), 'Obesity', *New England Journal of Medicine*, **337**, 396–407.

Rosin, O. (2008), 'The economic causes of obesity: a survey', *Journal of Economic Surveys*, **22**, 617–47.

Sephard, R.J. (2003) 'Limits to measurement of habitual physical activity by questionnaires', *British Journal of Sports Medicine*, **37**, 197–206.

Thomas, D. and Frankenberg, E. (2002), 'The measurement and interpretation of health in social surveys', in C. Murray, J. Salomon, C. Mathers, and A. Lopez (eds), *Measurement of the Global Burden of Disease*, Geneva: WHO, pp. 387–420.

Woods, S., Seeley, R., Porte, D. Jr and Schwarts, M. (1998), 'Signals that regulate food intake and energy homeostasis', *Science*, **280**, 1378–83.

World Health Organization (WHO) (2002), *The World Health Report 2002: Reducing Risks Promoting Healthy Life*, Geneva: WHO.
World Health Organization (WHO) (2003), *Diet, Nutrition, and the Prevention of Chronic Diseases*, WHO Technical Report Series 916, Geneva: WHO.

4. Does physical exercise affect demand for hospital services? Evidence from Canadian panel data*

Nazmi Sari

1. INTRODUCTION

Recent epidemiological literature shows that regular physical activity prevents chronic diseases, improves overall health and reduces risk of premature death (for comprehensive reviews of this literature see US Department of Health and Human Services, 1996; Warburton et al., 2006). In addition to its impacts on health and healthcare utilization, physical activity is also shown to offer an increase in productivity and wages (Barron et al., 2000; Lechner, 2009) and a decrease in absenteeism (Kerr et al., 1993; Heuvel et al., 2005).

In a recent review on the health benefits of physical activity, Warburton et al. (2006) conclude that regular physical activity is effective in preventing several chronic diseases, and is associated with a reduced risk of premature death. The US Surgeon General Report, a comprehensive review of the literature on effects of physical activity on health and disease, also emphasizes the positive role of physical activity on overall mortality (US Department of Health and Human Services, 1996). According to the report, those who are inactive, compared to the most active people, experience between a 1.2-fold to a 2-fold increased risk of dying during the follow-up interval. The report concludes that persons with moderate to high levels of physical activity have a lower mortality rate than those with sedentary habits.

Owing to its health benefits, it is expected that physical exercise decreases utilization of healthcare services. Different streams of researchers examine this issue. One stream focuses on clinical trials of physical fitness and wellness programs for a specific population group (Shephard et al., 1982, 1983; Bowne et al., 1984; Baun et al., 1986; Leigh and Fries,

1992; Shephard, 1996; Dunnagan et al., 1999), while the second stream studies the general population using representative samples (Keeler et al., 1989; Manning et al., 1991; Sari, 2009, 2010). The overall conclusion of these papers suggests that physical exercise decreases hospital stays.

The studies that use clinical trials of physical fitness and wellness programs examine the issue in the context of small population groups specific to an occupation, a company or certain age groups. As an alternative approach, other studies use representative samples for the entire population with a more comprehensive set of control variables (Keeler et al., 1989; Manning et al., 1991; Haapanen-Niemi et al., 1999; Sari, 2009, 2010). However, the latter studies use cross-sectional data-sets.

One of the main shortcomings of a cross-sectional study is that the estimated relationship between inactivity and excess use of healthcare services may not reflect the causal association: the association could be due to other factors, which cannot be controlled in a cross-sectional design. One of the problems may arise from individual specific time invariant characteristics that influence the decision to use services as well as health behavior. This implies that the impact of physical activity on healthcare utilization will be overestimated or underestimated. This can be overcome with a panel study. The current chapter is an attempt to fill this gap in the literature by examining the association between physical activity and healthcare utilization using a panel survey from Canada.

In the following section, a detailed discussion and description of the data sources is introduced. This section also presents descriptive analysis of the exercise and hospital stays. In sections 3 and 4, empirical framework and results from the estimations are discussed. The final section of the chapter provides a summary of the findings, and potential directions for further research on this issue.

2.   DATA SOURCE AND VARIABLES

2.1   Canadian National Population Health Survey

The primary data source for this chapter is the National Population Health Survey (NPHS), a household survey designed to measure the health status of Canadians and to expand knowledge of health determinants. The survey, which was started in 1994, is longitudinal with data being collected for the same members every second year. Currently, the survey is available for seven cycles covering the period 1994–2007 for about 10000 individuals in each cycle. The survey targets household residents in all provinces, and representative for the Canadian population in 1994. For more information on survey design and methodology, see Tambay and Catlin (1995).

2.2 Variables and Measurement Issues

In order to examine impacts of physical activity on demand for hospital services, hospital stays for each individual are used as a dependent variable in this study. These are the stays at a hospital or nursing home, which are measured using annual number of nights spent as a patient in healthcare facilities.

Physical activity is measured using total daily energy expenditure from all leisure time physical activities (LTPAs). The survey has detailed information on LTPAs for each individual. There are a set of questions related to types and duration of LTPAs. Using the detailed information related to LTPAs, the survey has a derived variable which shows total daily energy expenditure (E_j) from all types of LTPAs for each individual.

The derived variable (E_j), which is expressed as total kilocalories (kcal) per kilogram (kg) of body weight, was calculated as follows:

$$E_j = \sum_{k=1}^{K} D_k G_k \qquad (4.1)$$

where D_k stands for hours of daily LTPA k, and G_k denotes hourly energy expenditure from activity k.

Energy expenditure from each LTPA is calculated using the corresponding metabolic rate (MET) for each activity. The METs are multiples of the resting rate of oxygen consumption during physical activity. One MET represents the approximate rate of oxygen consumption of a body at rest, and the equivalent energy cost of 1 MET is 1 kcal/hour per kg of individual's body weight (kcal.hr^{-1}.kg^{-1}) Hence, the energy expenditure from an activity with 2 METs is equal to 2 kcal.hr^{-1}.kg^{-1} (that is, twice the amount of energy expended by a seated adult at rest).

Metabolic rate values can be expressed in three intensity levels: low, medium and high. Survey participants, however, were not asked to specify the intensity level of their activities.

Since individuals tend to overestimate the intensity, frequency and duration of their activities, the MET values used in the data-set correspond to the low intensity value for each activity (Canadian Fitness and Lifestyle Research Institute, www.cflri.ca/). The NPHS also includes information on general health status, chronic conditions, self-perceived stress, socio-economic and demographic factors, other health behaviors (for example, smoking and drinking habits), body mass index, occupation

Table 4.1   Summary statistics for other independent variables

Variable name	Variable description	Mean	S.D.
Walk (non-LTPA)	Usual daily activities or at work (non-LTPA): stand or walk quite a lot, but do not have to carry or lift things very often	0.459	0.498
Light loads (non-LTPA)	Usual daily activities or at work (non-LTPA): usually lift/carry light loads, or climb stairs or hills often	0.216	0.412
Heavy loads (non-LTPA)	Usual daily activities or at work (non-LTPA): heavy work/carry very heavy loads	0.062	0.241
Bike/walk	Estimated daily energy expenditure from biking or walking to work or while doing errands	1.160	2.150
BMI	Body weight in kilograms divided by height in meter squared	25.620	4.823
Alcohol	Average daily number of alcohol consumption	0.453	0.967
Daily smoker	Daily smokers	0.210	0.408
Occas. smoker	Occasional smokers	0.035	0.183
Occas. smoke always	Always occasional smokers	0.012	0.110
F_smoke daily	Former daily smokers	0.278	0.448
F_occas. smok.	Former occasional smokers	0.100	0.299
Poor health	Self-rated poor or fair health	0.091	0.287
# chronic cond.	Number of chronic conditions	1.377	1.567
# injuries	Number of injuries other than repetitive injuries – 12 months	0.192	0.723
Age	Age of respondent	43.300	17.810
HH size	Household size	2.987	1.437
No. of kids<12	Number of children aged less than 12 in the household	0.429	0.822
Live together	Married, has a common-law partner, or lived with a partner	0.596	0.491
Secondary	Respondent's education – secondary school graduation	0.143	0.350
Some post second.	Respondent's education – some post-secondary	0.258	0.437
Post secondary	Respondent's education – post-secondary graduation	0.368	0.482
No. of bedrooms	Number of bedrooms at home	3.006	1.089
Has MD	Has regular medical doctor	0.876	0.330
Employed	Those employed	0.654	0.476

Table 4.1   (continued)

Variable name	Variable description	Mean	S.D.
Occupation1	Management, business, finance, natural, social and health sciences, education	0.267	0.442
Occupation2	Sales and services	0.176	0.381
Occupation3	Trades, transportation, processing, manufacturing, utilities	0.279	0.448
Low income	Household income (<29 999; excl. those with no income)	0.234	0.423
Med income	Household income (30 000–49 999)	0.240	0.427
M_high income	Household income (50 000–79 999)	0.274	0.446
High income	Household income (80 000+)	0.250	0.433
Rural	Respondents living in rural areas	0.191	0.393
Minority	Visible non-aboriginal minority	0.080	0.270
Aboriginal	Aboriginal	0.007	0.080
Male	Male	0.500	0.500

Note: The numbers show the weighted summary statistics in a pooled sample; SD stands for standard deviations.

and work-related information as well as minority status, and place of residence. The list of independent variables with their definitions and descriptive statistics is presented in Table 4.1. The numbers in the table are the weighted mean and standard deviations estimated from the pooled sample. A detailed descriptive analysis for physical activity and inpatient stays is discussed in the following section.

2.3   Descriptive Analysis for Physical Activity and Hospital Stays

Table 4.2 presents the mean and standard deviations for physical activity variables and utilization of hospital services over time. The upper panel of the table represents the hospital stays for all participants, the proportion of users and the utilization among those who are users of hospital services.

During the survey years, there is a decreasing trend for hospital stays, proportion of users and utilization among those who are users. The utilization of hospital services for this cohort is in the range of 0.96 to 0.5 days over time. However, the utilization among those who are users of services ranges from 6.5 days to 10 days in a given year. The decreasing trend in utilization over time for this cohort could be due to a higher death rate of heavy users than that of others. It is also likely that this trend can be associated with the overall decrease in length of stays in Canadian hospitals in the period 1994–2007.

Table 4.2   Mean and standard deviation for LTPAs and hospital stays

	NPHS survey years						
	1994	1996	1998	2000	2002	2004	2006
Annual numbers of hospital stays							
Hospital stays (h)	0.96	0.68	0.69	0.58	0.62	0.79	0.50
	(7.46)	(5.56)	(6.71)	(4.36)	(7.47)	(7.96)	(3.48)
Proportion with $h > 0$	0.10	0.08	0.08	0.08	0.07	0.08	0.08
	(0.31)	(0.28)	(0.27)	(0.27)	(0.25)	(0.27)	(0.26)
Hospital stays for $h > 0$	9.98	8.19	8.94	7.56	8.74	9.95	6.67
group	(23.5)	(19.2)	(24.3)	(15.4)	(29.8)	(28.7)	(11.7)
Leisure time physical activity							
Total energy expenditure	1.75	1.83	2.06	1.80	2.15	2.13	2.36
(E)	(2.14)	(2.14)	(2.41)	(1.92)	(2.14)	(2.17)	(2.27)
$\Delta E = E_t - E_{t-2}$	–	0.01	0.16	−0.32	0.26	−0.10	0.19
		(2.16)	(2.14)	(2.25)	(2.01)	(2.11)	(2.16)
Proportion with $\Delta E > 0$	–	0.47	0.50	0.42	0.53	0.44	0.51
		(0.51)	(0.51)	(0.49)	(0.50)	(0.49)	(0.49)
ΔE for $\Delta E > 0$ group	–	1.39	1.49	1.27	1.51	1.46	1.59
		(1.59)	(1.71)	(1.42)	(1.53)	(1.64)	(1.72)

Note: These are weighted using sample weights; the numbers in parentheses are the standard deviations.

The second part of Table 4.2 presents the means and standard deviations of energy expenditure from all LTPAs. As indicated above, energy expenditure is defined as daily energy expenditure in kilocalories per kg of body weight. Total daily energy expenditure is in the range of 1.7 to 2.4 kcal/kg of body weight.

Few examples related to energy expenditure and corresponding type of LTPAs and their durations would be useful before proceeding with discussions related to the overall trend in energy expenditure. Individuals may burn the same amount of energy, for instance 2 kcal/kg of their body weight, from various LTPAs. Some examples for 2 kcal/kg would be a 40-minute walk for pleasure, or a 40-minute walk with a speed of 2.5 miles per hour on a firm surface, a 15-minute run with a speed of 5 miles per hour or a 20-minute uphill walk with a speed of 3.5 miles per hour (for other examples see Ainsworth et al., 2000).

Table 4.2 presents the proportion of people who improved their physical activity level compared to their previous physical activity level. During these years, about half of the individuals increased their physical activity. Among those who have increased their physical activity, the

Table 4.3   *Mean and standard deviation for LTPAs and hospital stays by sex*

	NPHS survey years						
	1994	1996	1998	2000	2002	2004	2006
Annual numbers of hospital stays							
Female	1.08	0.77	0.82	0.71	0.80	0.83	0.66
	(7.59)	(6.47)	(8.72)	(5.14)	(9.64)	(9.46)	(4.37)
Male	0.83	0.58	0.55	0.45	0.43	0.75	0.34
	(7.26)	(4.59)	(4.27)	(3.50)	(4.89)	(6.34)	(2.42)
Total energy expenditure (E)							
Female	1.55	1.60	1.81	1.63	1.91	1.92	2.14
	(2.04)	(1.91)	(2.12)	(1.83)	(1.95)	(1.98)	(2.11)
Male	1.97	2.08	2.33	1.98	2.40	2.36	2.59
	(2.18)	(2.27)	(2.57)	(1.96)	(2.23)	(2.27)	(2.35)

Note: These are weighted using sample weights; the numbers in parentheses are the standard deviations.

change in daily energy expenditure has been around 1.4 kcal per kg of body weight.

Table 4.3 shows the weighted average for physical activity and hospital stays for the females and males. For each year, females are higher users of hospital services than males, and their physical activity level is lower than that of males. This observation is consistent with the studies from medical sociology and social epidemiology (for example, Andersen, 1995; Pate et al., 1995; Macintyre et al., 1996).

Figure 4.1 presents a scatter plot between inpatient stays and daily energy expenditure from LTPAs. The figure shows the weighted average of inpatient stays by total energy expenditure derived from the Canadian Community Health Survey (CCHS) Cycle 3.1. This cycle of the CCHS has been conducted in 2005, hence representing the most recent population level physical activity and inpatient stays in Canada.

The data suggest that inpatient stays are negatively correlated with energy expenditure. The negative correlation is very distinct as long as daily energy expenditure is below 7 kcal/kg body weight. The negative correlation becomes weaker at the higher level of total energy expenditure. As argued in epidemiology literature, sedentary individuals are expected to gain higher health benefit from increasing their physical activity especially to the level recommended by the Centers for Disease Control and Prevention (CDC), and the American College of Sports Medicine (ACSM).

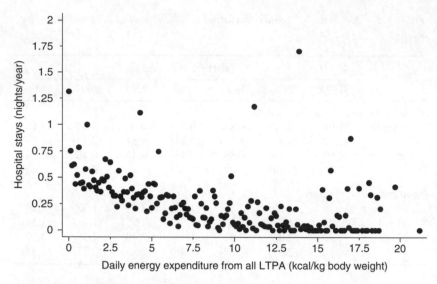

Source: CCHS cycle 3.1.

Figure 4.1   Weighted average of hospital stays by physical activity

The recommendation from the panel of experts brought together by the CDC and the ACSM is to 'accumulate 30 minutes or more of moderate intensity physical activity on most, preferably all, days of the week' (Pate et al., 1995, p. 404). This corresponds to daily energy expenditure of 1.5 kcal.kg^{-1} to 3 kcal.kg^{-1} from all LTPAs (for an update and clarification on 1995 recommendations, see Haskell et al., 2007). Individuals who meet the recommendation are considered moderately active, while those with daily energy expenditure of 3 kcal.kg^{-1} and above are considered physically active. As a body of literature demonstrated since the 1995 recommendation, the benefit from physical activity depends on the initial activity level. As the level of activity increases, the health benefits gained increases but with a decreasing rate (known as the dose-response curve in epidemiology literature). However, as indicated in Haskell et al. (2007), the exact shape of the dose-response curve is unclear and may vary depending on health outcome of interest.

3.   EMPIRICAL FRAMEWORK

The demand for hospital services is estimated using the numbers of annual hospital stay as a dependent variable in the following reduced form model:

$$h_{jt} = \alpha + \beta E_{jt} + \gamma X_{jt} + u_j + \varepsilon_{jt} \qquad (4.2)$$

where h_{jt} is individual j's hospital stay at time t, E_{jt} is individual j's total energy expenditure from all LTPAs at time t, matrix X_{jt} include all other individual characteristics. There are also time-invariant individual characteristics, which impact demand for hospital services. These characteristics are denoted by u_j in equation (4.2)

This model can be estimated by ordinary least squares (OLS). However it may lead to inconsistent estimates due to unobserved individual characteristics which affect both hospital utilization and individuals' health behaviors. This potential bias due to unobserved characteristics is tackled using fixed effect models under the assumption that unobservables are constant overtime.

It is likely that even after controlling for other factors, and time invariant unobserved characteristics through fixed effect models, the results can still be biased. The source of the bias can be due to physical activities during other daily activities. For instance individuals who are active during their non-leisure times may not be as active during their leisure time. Their physical activity in their usual daily activities would also affect the demand for healthcare services. In order to control for these factors, I include a set of dummy variables to capture physical activities during work or other daily activities. These coefficient estimates are presented in the summary regression table (see Table 4.4).

There are other variables measuring non-leisure time physical activities. The participants in the survey were asked to report the number of hours spent walking or biking to work, school or while doing errands in a typical week. These variables are included in the estimations as dummy variables. As an additional approach, I estimated daily energy expenditure from non-leisure time walking and biking using duration of each activity and corresponding MET values for walking and biking. I also used lower MET values than the ones used for leisure time walking and biking. In all cases, these additional variables did not have any effect on LTPA coefficient reported in Table 4.4. The full results, which also include models with variables measuring non-leisure time walking and biking, are presented in the appendix tables.

It is also likely that the coefficient estimate for physical activity variable can be biased due to omitted variables related to earlier health behaviors. Studies suggest that health behavior in earlier years may influence both current health behavior and healthcare utilization. For instance, earlier physical activity may affect current healthcare utilization through its impact on health endowment. As shown in subsequent studies it is also likely that past exercise behavior is a predictor of current physical activity[1]

Table 4.4   Regression results from OLS and fixed effect models

	Pooled OLS (1)	Fixed effect models		Female (4)	Male (5)
		(2)	(3)		
Log E$_t$	−0.118*	−0.065*	−0.073*	−0.154*	0.013
	(−4.24)	(−2.02)	(−2.16)	(−2.81)	(0.33)
Log E$_{t-2}$			−0.025	−0.050	0.003
			(−0.84)	(−1.25)	(0.07)
Walk_nonLTP	−0.537*	−0.361*	−0.226*	−0.429*	−0.030
	(−5.14)	(−3.16)	(−2.19)	(−2.83)	(−0.22)
lightloads_non	−0.455*	−0.352*	−0.270	−0.495*	−0.063
	(−4.32)	(−2.33)	(−1.84)	(−2.54)	(−0.28)
heavyloads_no	−0.558*	−0.536*	−0.399*	−0.613*	−0.223
	(−5.17)	(−3.94)	(−3.22)	(−3.48)	(−1.26)
N	53 465	53 770	44 447	24 833	19 614

Notes:
All fixed effect models include individual fixed effects.
The numbers in parentheses are the robust *t*-statistics.
Full models are presented in the Appendix.
* indicates coefficient estimates significant at 5 per cent or lower.

(Dishman et al., 1985; Kohl and Hobbs, 1998; Trost et al., 2002). As a result, a study which does not take past exercise behavior into account creates biased estimates for the impact of exercise on healthcare utilization. In order to control for bias due to potential omitted variables related to past exercise, the regression equation in (4.1) is also estimated using lagged physical exercise as additional variables.

The differences in health behavior as well as healthcare utilization among female and male groups have been widely studied in medical sociology and social epidemiology (for example, Andersen, 1995; Macintyre et al., 1996). These studies point out that females use more healthcare services and their health behavior is also different from males. As indicated in Table 4.3, the data used in this study also support the overall conclusion from earlier studies related to differences in health behavior and healthcare utilization between females and males. In order to capture this differential impact, regression equation above is also estimated separately for both male and female groups. These results are discussed in the following section, and a summary of the results are presented in Table 4.4.

As indicated earlier, the panel structure of the data is useful in controlling for unobserved time invariant factors that may explain the estimated association between exercise and hospital stays in cross-sectional studies.

However, it is likely that physical activity can still be endogenous, owing to other unobserved time variant factors or to reverse causality especially for those individuals who stay in the hospital for a long time. In order to deal with reverse causality, an additional variable for those individuals who died during the survey years is included. As another robustness check, the regressions have been estimated after excluding heavy users (that is, those who stayed in the hospital for six-months or longer). These additional regressions provide similar estimates with those presented in Table 4.4.

4. RESULTS

Table 4.4 presents the results from the pooled OLS and fixed effect regressions. The first column shows the pooled OLS results while the next columns present the fixed effect results.

The models estimated using the entire sample suggest that physical activity is negatively associated with inpatient stays. The size of the coefficient estimate for the physical activity variable becomes smaller when using fixed effect models rather than a pooled OLS model. This implies that when individual fixed effects are included in the estimations, the size of the coefficient decreases by about 50 per cent.

As a next step, the fixed effect model is extended by using lagged physical activity level for each individual. These results are presented in model (3) in Table 4.4. The coefficient estimate for the natural logarithm of lagged LTPA is statistically insignificant; suggesting that two-year lagged LTPA has no influence on current inpatient stays. However, current physical activity has significant and substantial impact on inpatient stays.

In Table 4.4, coefficient estimates for usual daily activities or work habits in terms of physical activity are also presented. The comparison category is the physically inactive group during their daily life or at work (that is, individuals who usually sit during the day and do not walk around very much). As indicated by the results in the table, physically active people during their non-leisure time use significantly fewer hospital services compared to those who are mostly inactive during their non-leisure time.

The last two columns in Table 4.4 present the coefficient estimates from the regressions based on female or male groups. When the analysis is conducted by each group, the impact of physical activity on hospital stays increases substantially for the females but disappears for the males.

As a next step, using results from the models (3) and (4); marginal effects of exercise for hospital stays are presented in Figures 4.2 and 4.3 for the most relevant values of physical exercise in the sample.

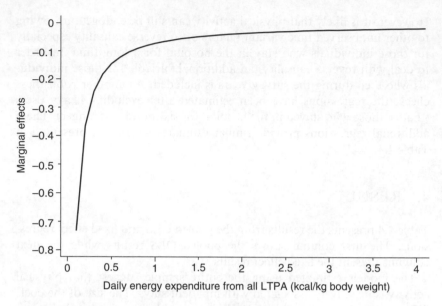

Figure 4.2   Impact of LTPA on hospital stays

Figure 4.2 shows that the marginal effects of physical activity approach to zero as physical activity level reaches 3 kcal per kg of body weight. As pointed out earlier, daily energy expenditure of 3 kcal and above from LTPAs is enough for an individual to derive cardio benefits from exercise. Once this exercise level is achieved, additional exercise does not create substantial benefits for the individuals. As clearly shown in Figure 4.2, physical exercise decreases hospital stays substantially when an individual is physically inactive. For instance, an individual with daily energy expenditure of 1 kcal/kg body weight would have 0.073 hospital stays less if she would increase daily energy expenditure by 1 kcal/kg of body weight. The marginal effects for an individual with daily energy expenditure of 2 kcal and 3 kcal are −0.037 and −0.024 days per year.

Figure 4.3 shows the marginal effects of LTPA for the females. As presented in Table 4.4, physical exercise has substantial impact on hospital stays for the females but has no impact for the males. In order to present marginal effects at different activity level, marginal effects of LTPA has been illustrated in Figure 4.3. The figure, for instance, suggests that a female with daily energy expenditure of 1 kcal/kg body weight would have 0.154 hospital stays less if she would increase her daily energy expenditure by 1 kcal/kg of body weight. The marginal effects for a female with daily energy expenditure of 2 kcal and 3 kcal are −0.077 and −0.051 days per year.

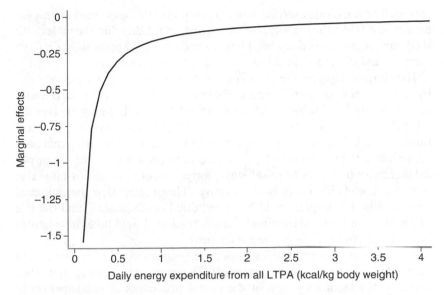

Figure 4.3   Impact of LTPA on hospital stays for females

5.   DISCUSSIONS AND CONCLUDING REMARKS

This study shows that physical exercise and hospital services are substitutable in the production of health. The rate of substitution, however, is decreasing as the level of activity increases. For instance, marginal effect for an inactive individual (those with total daily energy expenditure of less than 1.5 kcal/per kg of body weight) is substantially larger than that of a moderately active individual. The larger gain from exercise has been achieved to the point where the total daily energy expenditure from LTPAs is less than 1.5 kcal per kg of body weight. After this level of activity, the effect gets closer to zero and becomes almost flat. This finding is consistent with the diminishing marginal productivity of physical activity.

As earlier studies in medical sociology and social epidemiology stated, the males and females differ in terms of their utilization of healthcare services and their health behavior. This is also confirmed in this chapter: on average, the males are more active than females, and they use fewer services. To estimate the differential impact of exercise on hospital stays, the demand for hospital stays is estimated separately for both groups. The results confirm the overall findings of negative association between exercise and hospital stays for the females, but the effect disappears for the males. This differential finding is also consistent with the theoretical expectation of diminishing marginal returns from exercise, since the males are the ones who have higher activity level than the females. In other words, it is likely that the males with their current higher activity level have already received potential gain from exercise, and therefore there is no room left for improvement.

The chapter explores the association between exercise and hospital stays by using panel data from Canada. The panel structure of the data is useful in controlling for unobserved time invariant factors that may explain the estimated association between exercise and hospital stays in cross sectional studies. It is, however, important to note that even with panel data approaches, the results could be biased due to reverse causality: as physical inactivity increases hospital stays, longer stays in hospitals may also influence the likelihood of being inactive. This implies that the estimates presented in the chapter could be biased due to endogeneity, and the size of the bias cannot be determined. Hence, readers should take these limitations into account while making inferences.

As widely used in economics, endogeneity issues in this framework can be tackled using instrumental variable (IV) approach. Studies show that access to the facilities is one of the strong predictors of participation in physical activity. Hence, the availability of physical activity facilities can be used as IVs to solve the endogeneity problem. Further research that deals with this empirical problem has the potential to enhance our understanding on this issue.

NOTES

*   The author thanks the participants of the 5th Gijon Conference on Sport and the Promotion of Health and Well-being, and the 9th International Conference on Health Economics, Management and Policy in Athens, Greece for insightful comments and suggestions. While the research and analysis are based on Statistics Canada data provided at the Saskatchewan Research Data Centre (SKY-RDC), the opinions expressed do not represent the views of Statistics Canada. The funding is provided by the University of Saskatchewan through Tri-Council Bridge Fund
1. In the NPHS, the correlation coefficient between the current and two-year lagged physical activity is 0.50.

REFERENCES

Ainsworth, B.E., Haskell, W.L., Whitt, M.C., Irwin, M.L., Swartz, A.M., Strath, S.J., O'Brien, W.L., Bassett Jr, D.R., Schmitz, K.H., Emplaincourt, P.O., Jacobs Jr, D.R. and Leon, A.S. (2000), 'Compendium of physical activities: an update of activity codes and MET intensities', *Medicine and Science in Sports and Exercise*, **32** (9), S498–S516.

Andersen, R.M. (1995), 'Revisiting the behavioral model and access to medical care: Does it matter?', *Journal of Health and Social Behavior*, **36** (1), 1–10.

Barron, J.M., Ewing, B.T. and Waddell, G.R. (2000), 'The effects of high school athletic participation on education and labor market outcomes', *Review of Economics and Statistics*, **82** (3), 409–21.

Baun, W.B., Bernacki, E.J. and Tsai, S.P. (1986), 'A preliminary investigation: effect of a corporate fitness program on absenteeism and healthcare costs', *Journal of Occupational Medicine*, **28**, 19–22.

Bowne, D.W., Russell, M.L., Morgan, J.I., Optenberg, S.A. and Clarke, A.E. (1984), 'Reduced disability and healthcare costs in an industrial fitness program', *Journal of Occupational Medicine*, **26**, 809–16.

Dishman, R.K., Sallis, J.F. and Orenstein, D.R. (1985), 'The determinants of physical activity and exercise', *Public Health Reports*, **100** (2), 158–71.

Dunnagan, T., Haynes, G. and Noland, M. (1999), 'Healthcare costs and participation in fitness programming', *American Journal of Health Behaviors*, **23** (1), 43–51.

Haapanen-Niemi, N., Miilunpalo, S., Vuoir, I., Pasanen, M. and Oja, P. (1999), 'The impact of smoking, alcohol consumption and physical activity on use of hospital services', *American Journal of Public Health*, **89**, 691–8.

Haskell, W.L., Lee, I.M., Pate, R.P., Powell, K.E., Blair, S.N., Franklin, B.A., Macera, C.A., Heath, G.W., Thompson, P.D. and Bauman, A. (2007), 'Physical activity and public health: updated recommendation for adults from the American College of Sports Medicine and the American Heart Association', *Circulation*, **116**, 1081–93.

Heuvel van den, S.G., Boshuizen, H.C., Hildebrandt, V.H., Blatter, B.M., Ariens, G.A. and Bongers, P.M. (2005), 'Effect of sporting activity on absenteeism in a working population', *British Journal of Sports Medicine*, **39** (3), e15.

Keeler, E.B., Manning, W.G., Newhouse, J.P., Sloss, E.S. and Wasserman, J. (1989), 'The external costs of a sedentary life-style', *American Journal of Public Health*, **79**, 975–81.

Kerr, J.H., Marjolein, C. and Vos, H. (1993), 'Employee fitness programmes, absenteeism and general well-being', *Work and Stress*, 7 (2), 179–90.

Kohl III, H.W. and Hobbs, K.E. (1998), 'Development of physical activity behaviors among children and adolescents' *Pediatrics*, **101** (3), 549–54.

Lechner, M. (2009), 'Long-run labour market and health effects of individual sports activities', *Journal of Health Economics*, 28 (4), 839–54.

Leigh, J.P. and Fries, J.F. (1992), 'Health habits, healthcare use and costs in a sample of retirees', *Inquiry*, **29**, 44–54.

Macintyre, S., Hunt, K. and Sweeting, H. (1996), 'Gender differences in health: are things really as simple as they seem?', *Social Science and Medicine*, **42** (4), 617–24.,

Manning, W.G., Keeler, E., Newhouse, J.P., Sloss, E. and Wasserman, J. (1991), *The Costs of Poor Health Habits*, Cambridge, MA: Harvard University Press.

Pate, R.R., Pratt, M., Blair, S.N., Haskell, W.L., Macera, C.A., Bouchard, C., Buchner, D., Ettinger, W., Heath, G.W., King, A.C., Kriska, A., Leon, A.S., Marcus, B.H., Morris, J., Paffenbarger, R.S., Patrick, K., Pollock, M.L., Rippe, J.M., Sallis, J. and Wilmore, J.H. (1995), 'Physical activity and public health: a recommendation from the Centers for Disease Control and Prevention and the American College of Sports Medicine', *Journal of the American Medical Association*, **273**, 402–7.

Sari, N. (2009), 'Physical inactivity and its impact on healthcare utilization', *Health Economics*, **18** (8), 885–901.

Sari, N. (2010), 'A short walk a day shortens the hospital stay: physical activity and the demand for hospital services for older adults', *Canadian Journal of Public Health*, **101** (5), 385–9.

Shephard, R.J. (1996), 'Worksite fitness and exercise programs: a review of methodology and health impact', *American Journal of Health Promotion*, **10** (6), 436–52.

Shephard, R.J., Corey, P., Renzland, P. and Cox, M. (1982), 'The influence of an employee fitness and lifestyle modification program upon medical care costs', *Canadian Journal of Public Health*, **73**, 259–63.

Shephard, R.J., Corey, P., Renzland, P. and Cox, M. (1983), 'The impact of changes in fitness and lifestyle upon healthcare utilization', *Canadian Journal of Public Health*, **74**, 51–4.

Tambay, J. and Catlin, G. (1995), 'Sample design of National Population Health Survey', *Health Reports*, **7** (1), 29–38.

Trost, S.G., Owen, N., Bauman, A.E., Sallis, J.F. and Brown, W. (2002), 'Correlates of adults' participation in physical activity: review and update', *Medicine and Science in Sports and Exercise*, **34** (12), 1996–2001.

US Department of Health and Human Services (1996), *Physical Activity and Health: A Report of the Surgeon General*, Atlanta, GA: US Department of Health and Human Resources, Centers for Disease Control and Prevention, National Center for Chronic Disease Prevention and Health Promotion, pp. 81–172.

Warburton, D.E., Nicol, C.W. and Bredin, S.S. (2006), 'Health benefits of physical activity: the evidence', *Canadian Medical Association Journal*, **174** (6), 801–8.

APPENDIX

Table 4A.1   Regression results from OLS and fixed effect models

	Pooled OLS model	Fixed effect models			
		(1)	(2)	(3)	(4)
Log E_t	−0.118*	−0.065*	−0.069*	−0.076*	−0.073*
	(−4.24)	(−2.02)	(−2.14)	(−2.20)	(−2.16)
Log E_{t-2}				−0.0247	−0.025
				(−0.84)	(−0.84)
Bike/Walk			0.0054	−0.0008	
			(0.38)	(−0.05)	
Walk (non-LTPA)	−0.537*	−0.361*			−0.226*
	(−5.14)	(−3.16)			(−2.19)
Light loads (non-LTPA)	−0.455*	−0.352*			−0.270
	(−4.32)	(−2.33)			(−1.84)
Heavy loads (non-LTPA)	−0.558*	−0.536*			−0.399*
	(−5.17)	(−3.94)			(−3.22)
BMI	−0.017	−0.048	−0.046	−0.058*	−0.060*
	(−1.33)	(−1.86)	(−1.80)	(−2.36)	(−2.40)
Alcohol	−0.073*	−0.051	−0.056	−0.027	−0.024
	(−2.69)	(−1.35)	(−1.50)	(−0.67)	(−0.58)
Daily smoker	0.115	0.276	0.259	0.158	0.161
	(0.96)	(0.73)	(0.69)	(0.36)	(0.36)
Occas. smoker	−0.036	0.140	0.126	0.101	0.100
	(−0.38)	(0.42)	(0.38)	(0.24)	(0.24)
Occas. smoker always	−0.003	0.196	0.155	0.027	0.038
	(−0.02)	(0.98)	(0.79)	(0.11)	(0.15)
F_smoke daily	0.227*	0.528	0.526	0.487	0.479
	(2.59)	(1.36)	(1.36)	(1.01)	(1.00)
F_occas. smok.	0.052	−0.145	−0.149	−0.171	−0.175
	(0.54)	(−0.73)	(−0.74)	(−0.71)	(−0.73)
Minority	0.111	–	–	–	–
	(0.40)				
Aboriginal	−0.213	–	–	–	–
	(−0.98)				
Poor health	1.949*	1.125*	1.152*	1.012*	0.991*
	(6.20)	(4.41)	(4.46)	(3.78)	(3.72)
No. of chronic cond.	0.236*	0.197*	0.197*	0.266*	0.266*
	(4.55)	(2.22)	(2.21)	(2.79)	(2.79)
No. of injuries	0.167*	0.140*	0.137*	0.173*	0.174*
	(3.15)	(2.63)	(2.58)	(2.52)	(2.55)
Age	0.010*	0.009	0.010	0.027*	0.026*
	(3.65)	(0.85)	(1.02)	(2.37)	(2.29)
HH size	0.029	0.032	0.030	0.037	0.038
	(0.77)	(0.58)	(0.54)	(0.73)	(0.75)
No. of kids<12	0.093*	0.063	0.063	0.087*	0.088*
	(2.17)	(1.25)	(1.26)	(2.04)	(2.05)

Table 4A.1   (continued)

	Pooled OLS model	Fixed effect models			
		(1)	(2)	(3)	(4)
Live together	−0.161	0.024	0.010	−0.135	−0.127
	(−1.77)	(0.15)	(0.06)	(−1.19)	(−1.12)
Immigrant	−0.143	–	–	–	–
	(−0.91)				
Secondary	−0.051	−0.305	−0.379	−0.350	−0.302
	(−0.46)	(−1.10)	(−1.35)	(−0.97)	(−0.83)
Some post second.	0.082	0.134	0.090	0.100	0.128
	(0.70)	(0.77)	(0.50)	(0.51)	(0.67)
Post secondary	0.053	0.021	−0.009	0.004	0.025
	(0.46)	(0.11)	(−0.05)	(0.02)	(0.11)
Male	0.129	–	–	–	–
	(1.73)				
No. of bedrooms	−0.070	0.041	0.041	0.036	0.036
	(−1.00)	(0.47)	(0.48)	(0.36)	(0.35)
Has MD	0.235*	0.017	0.023	0.007	0.003
	(2.46)	(0.15)	(0.20)	(0.06)	(0.03)
Employed	−0.480*	−0.332	−0.340	−0.215	−0.208
	(−2.67)	(−1.77)	(−1.80)	(−1.23)	(−1.20)
Occupation1	0.222	0.393	0.388	0.269	0.266
	(1.13)	(1.62)	(1.60)	(1.16)	(1.15)
Occupation2	−0.0004	0.243	0.249	0.094	0.085
	(−0.00)	(1.18)	(1.20)	(0.42)	(0.39)
Occupation3	0.139	0.346	0.325	0.162	0.173
	(0.69)	(1.51)	(1.43)	(0.88)	(0.93)
Low income	0.556*	−0.082	−0.090	−0.158	−0.137
	(2.99)	(−0.37)	(−0.41)	(−0.55)	(−0.48)
Med income	0.292	−0.064	−0.061	−0.132	−0.119
	(1.70)	(−0.30)	(−0.29)	(−0.45)	(−0.41)
M_high income	0.440*	0.0404	0.043	−0.186	−0.172
	(2.33)	(0.17)	(0.18)	(−0.61)	(−0.56)
High income	0.329	−0.064	−0.056	−0.298	−0.288
	(1.86)	(−0.26)	(−0.23)	(−0.95)	(−0.92)
Rural	−0.106	−0.082	−0.086	−0.035	−0.034
	(−1.50)	(−1.45)	(−1.51)	(−0.49)	(−0.48)
Constant	−1.492*	0.360	0.091	0.156	0.292
	(−3.35)	(0.47)	(0.12)	(0.20)	(0.35)
Sample size	53 465	53 770	53 770	44 447	44 447

Notes:
The numbers in parentheses are robust *t*-statistics.
Fixed effect models include provincial dummies and individual effects.
* indicates coefficient estimates significant at 5 per cent or lower.

Table 4A.2   Fixed effect regression results for female and male groups

	Female	Male
Log E$_t$	−0.154*	0.013
	(−2.81)	(0.33)
Log E$_{t-2}$	−0.050	0.003
	(−1.25)	(0.07)
Walk (non-LTPA)	−0.429*	−0.030
	(−2.83)	(−0.22)
Light loads (non-LTPA)	−0.495*	−0.063
	(−2.54)	(−0.28)
Heavy loads (non-LTPA)	−0.613*	−0.223
	(−3.48)	(−1.26)
BMI	−0.051	−0.080*
	(−1.48)	(−2.33)
Alcohol	−0.070	−0.002
	(−1.74)	(−0.04)
Daily smoker	0.641	−0.170
	(0.62)	(−0.76)
Occas. smoker	0.431	−0.089
	(0.44)	(−0.36)
Occas. smoker always	0.249	−0.150
	(0.48)	(−0.83)
F_smoke daily	0.987	0.107
	(0.90)	(0.56)
F_occas. smok.	−0.598	0.215
	(−1.40)	(1.11)
Poor health	0.755*	1.264*
	(2.09)	(3.20)
No. of chronic cond.	0.291*	0.213*
	(1.97)	(2.77)
No. of injuries	0.369*	0.089*
	(2.00)	(2.22)
Age	0.031*	0.026
	(2.29)	(1.46)
HH size	0.031	0.052
	(0.34)	(0.92)
No. of kids<12	0.142*	0.037
	(2.56)	(0.53)
Live together	−0.0634	−0.207
	(−0.39)	(−1.29)
Secondary	−0.0928	−0.543
	(−0.36)	(−0.85)
Some post second.	0.397	−0.129
	(1.44)	(−0.52)

Table 4A.2   (continued)

	Female	Male
Post secondary	0.419	−0.294
	(1.47)	(−0.99)
No. of bedrooms	0.195	−0.108
	(0.99)	(−1.74)
Has MD	0.062	−0.005
	(0.63)	(−0.02)
Employed	−0.411*	0.068
	(−3.68)	(0.20)
Occupation1	0.172	0.372
	(1.04)	(0.79)
Occupation2	0.067	0.127
	(0.44)	(0.28)
Occupation3	0.170	0.209
	(1.01)	(0.57)
Low income	−0.627	0.305
	(−1.34)	(0.76)
Med income	−0.631	0.340
	(−1.35)	(0.82)
M_high income	−0.763	0.344
	(−1.53)	(0.77)
High income	−0.798	0.160
	(−1.55)	(0.36)
Rural	0.025	−0.122
	(0.25)	(−1.14)
Constant	−0.541	−0.0446
	(−0.42)	(−0.04)
Sample size	24 833	19 614

Notes:
The numbers in parentheses are robust *t*-statistics.
Fixed effect models include provincial dummies and individual effects.
* indicates coefficient estimates significant at 5 per cent or lower.

5. Leisure sports participation in Switzerland*

Michael Lechner

1. INTRODUCTION

Recently, there is a renewed interest in the correlates and determinants of sports activities[1] as well as the effects of sports activities on labour market outcomes.[2] However, the evidence on both dimensions is rather limited for Switzerland. Although there is some descriptive evidence (see Lamprecht et al., 2008), econometric analyses are missing. With this chapter I fill this gap in the literature by investigating the correlates of individual sports participation in Switzerland, as well as the impact of doing sports on health and labour market outcomes.

The analysis is based on a very informative individual panel data-set, namely, the Swiss Household Panel (SHP), which currently covers the years 1999 to 2008. The panel structure allows the analysis of dynamic patterns of phenomena under investigation. This advantage comes at a cost, in that the size of samples is fairly moderate.

The econometric analysis of the correlates and determinants of sports participation is based on parametric binary choice models. The complex estimation task of obtaining results for the effects of sports activities on labour market, as well as health and general well-being outcomes, is performed by using robust semi-parametric matching methods that closely follow the approach suggested by Lechner (2009).

With respect to participation in sports, it turns out that better subjective health and health investments as well as socio-economic status are positively associated with positive activity status. Furthermore, the probability of sports participation in the German-speaking part of Switzerland is considerably higher than in the rest of the country. The econometric analysis of the effects of sports activity on labour market outcomes is limited by the comparatively small sample sizes of the SHP, but nevertheless reveals statistically significant earnings effects which are positive for men and negative for women, respectively. However, both results lack some desirable robustness properties.

The next section describes some aspects of sports participation in Switzerland, while section 3 contains the econometric analysis of the correlates with sports activities. Section 4 shows the results of the econometric analysis of the effects of sports and section 5 concludes. Appendix 5A gives some background information on the database and Appendix 5B contains additional results.

2. KEY FEATURE OF LEISURE SPORTS ACTIVITIES IN SWITZERLAND

2.1 Data Sources

In this section we use two data sources to describe key features of leisure sport activities in Switzerland. The main data source is the SHP, a representative annual panel study of Swiss households starting in 1999. The sample we use is a balanced panel of 1325 non-retired individuals of age 18 to 55 in 1999 who are followed until 2008. Clearly, the advantage of the SHP is its panel structure that allows for a cohort perspective. However, the SHP has drawbacks for our study as well: first, the sample size is small which limits the choices of subgroup and semi-parametric analyses that can be performed (this becomes an important problem for the attempted impact analysis in section 5). The second problem is that the information about sports activities is rather limited.

Mainly for the second reason we complement the information obtained from the SHP with information from a large recent representative survey about sports activities of the Swiss population (Sport Schweiz 2008, SS08) in this section. As we have no access to the raw micro data of that survey we rely on the figures published by Lamprecht et al. (2008). When comparing the results from the SHP with the SS08, it should be kept in mind that the latter covers a wider age range (15 to 75) than the SHP. Furthermore, the SHP cohort ages over time. The Appendix contains more details on both data sources.

2.2 Levels and Trends in Sports Participation

Figure 5.1 shows the general trend in sports participation in Switzerland from 1978 to 2008. Although the data quality and comparability of the underlying data over the years is not ideal, the general trend appears to be clear: while the level activity is rising over time, a constant share of about 30 per cent of the population remains inactive.

The SHP cohort (Figure 5.2) shows similar trends (note the use of

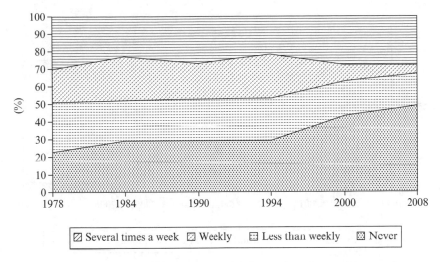

Note: The data comes from different surveys with the number of respondents varying between less than 1000 for the earlier years up to about 10 000 for 2008.

Source: Based on Figure A2.2 in Lamprecht et al. (2008).

Figure 5.1   Activity levels of SHP cohort, 1978 to 2008

different categories), although the share of inactive individuals is some-what lower (20 per cent). The latter is probably due to the 'younger' sample on which these figures are based. Nevertheless, in line with other studies, the share of the inactive individuals is fairly stable over time and similar for men and women. Moreover, the frequency of sport activities also increases over time[3] and is higher for women than for men. Using a more general definition of activities[4] leads to the same conclusions.

The sport intensity numbers in Table 5.1 show that the majority of those active are active for at least 3 to 4 hours per week, with a slightly increasing trend.

Next, Table 5.2 shows the most popular sports performed in Switzerland. Cycling, hiking, swimming and skiing are particularly favoured and are each performed by more than 20 per cent of the population, followed by jogging and other fitness activities. Interestingly, for all activities with a participation rate of at least 10 per cent, the average age of the participants is above 40. The intensity (measured in days per year) varies quite substantially, with skiing at the lower end (10 days) of the top group and fitness activities at the upper end (90 days per year).

Finally, regional diversity appears to be an important issue in Switzerland. As a country with three large regions with different languages and cultures,

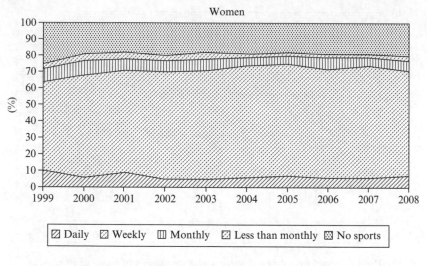

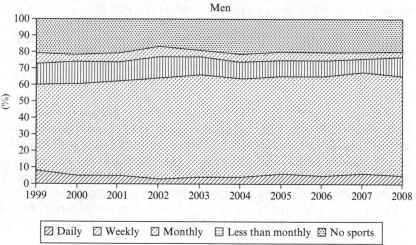

Note: Own computations.

Source: Swiss Household Panel.

Figure 5.2   Activity levels of SHP cohort, 1999 to 2008

Figure 5.3 shows regional differences with respect to sport intensity. From Figure 5.3 it is apparent that activity levels are much higher in the German-speaking part of Switzerland (covering about 60 per cent of the population) than in the French- and Italian-speaking regions respectively.

Table 5.1   Intensity of individual sports

Number of hours per week	2000	2008
Less than one hour	4.0	1.2
1 hour	12.9	14.6
2 hours	20.9	20.0
3 to 4 hours	27.6	29.5
5 to 6 hours	15.7	17.3
7 hours or more	19.0	17.4

Source: Based on Table T2.1 of Lamprecht et al. (2008).

3.   ACTIVITY LEVELS AND SOCIO-DEMOGRAPHIC AND HEALTH CHARACTERISTICS

In this section we relate the activity levels to characteristics of the individuals. To mitigate the obvious endogeneity problems, we take lagged measurements of the characteristics, that is, measured one year earlier than the respective activity status. In Table 5.3 we consider somebody to be active if she performs some sport activity at least once a week.[5] As previous work suggests considerable male–female differences, we perform gender specific estimations. Furthermore, estimating the probit model for the years 2000, 2004 and 2008 allows the detection of changes over time.[6] Table 5.3 shows the marginal effects for particular groups of variables.[7] Usually, many indicators measuring related or the same phenomena are available but are ignored for the sake of a somewhat parsimonious specification. Nevertheless, many of those other variables are included when testing for omitted variables. In addition to the marginal effects, Table 5.3 also shows the p-values for a test of joint significance of the coefficients for groups of related variables.[8]

The first group of variables captures variables closely related to sports activity, namely, own efforts to remain healthy (measured on an 11-point scale) as well as an indicator for voluntary work in non-profit organizations, including sport clubs. The former variable is probably one of the main motives for doing sports and is, as expected, significant throughout all estimations. Furthermore, it is more important for men than for women. The latter variable has become more important recently for both men and women.

Clearly, age plays a role for sports activities, although the relation may be highly non-linear as revealed by the estimations at least for 2000 and 2004. In 2008 the age profile appears to be flat. In addition, the joint tests

Table 5.2　Intensity of individual sports

	Mentions (percentage of whole Swiss population)	Absolute frequency of exercise (average number of days per year)	Average age (in years)	Share of women (percentage)
Cycling, mountain bike	35.0	45	45	46
Hiking, walking, mountain hiking	33.7	40	50	57
Swimming	35.4	30	44	60
Skiing (piste), carving	21.7	10	44	48
Jogging, running, cross-country run	16.8	52	40	44
Fitness, aerobics	14.0	90	43	61
Gymnastics	11.7	50	53	67
Soccer, street soccer	6.9	50	30	9
Snowboarding	4.7	10	26	45
Tennis	4.4	32	42	40
Cross-country skiing	3.9	10	50	49
Tai Chi, Qi Gong, yoga	3.8	48	49	84
Dancing, jazz dance	3.7	45	38	80
Strength training, bodybuilding	3.4	90	39	45
Inline-skating, rollerskate	3.4	20	34	52
Volleyball, beach volleyball	3.3	40	33	49
Badminton	2.7	30	34	41
Ski/snowboard tour, snowshoe	2.5	10	49	52
Combat sports	1.9	90	32	29
Floorball, field hockey, roller hockey	1.7	45	27	23
Riding, equestrian sports	1.7	90	36	84
Climbing, alpine climbing	1.6	20	37	32
Basketball, streetball	1.6	40	25	17
Golf	1.2	30	51	33
Squash	1.2	25	34	28
Shooting	1.1	45	47	17
(Ice) hockey	0.9	45	30	1
Sailing	0.8	20	45	31

Note:　Multiple entries allowed.

Source:　Based on Figure T2.1 of Lamprecht et al. (2008).

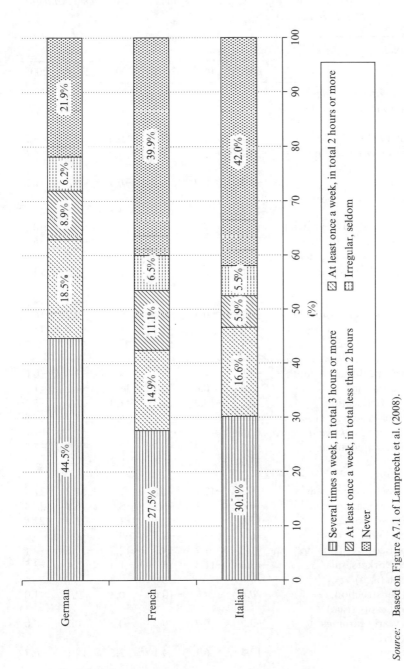

Source: Based on Figure A7.1 of Lamprecht et al. (2008).

Figure 5.3   Intensity of individual sports across language regions

Table 5.3　Correlates with sports activity (sports at least weekly, marginal effects in percentages)

Variable	Women			Men		
	2000	2004	2008	2000	2004	2008
Sports-related activities						
Efforts to remain healthy (0–10)	*3.6*	*2.3*	*3.3*	*6.9*	*5.2*	*5.2*
Voluntary work	3.0	**7.9**	**9.3**	0.6	−2.9	**8.2**
p-value of Wald test in %	*0.0*	*0.0*	*0.0*	*0.0*	*0.0*	*0.0*
Age						
Age in years	**−0.8**	0.2	0.2	**−0.9**	*−0.8*	0.2
Age indicator: 25 or younger	0.6	–	–	*−34.9*	–	–
Age indicator: 25 to 30	**−15.5**	–	–	−4.1	–	–
Age indicator: 30 or younger	–	5.1	8.7	–	10.5	−0.9
Age indicator: 50 to 55	–	−7.3	2.5	–	−4.3	6.0
Age indicator: 56 or older	–	*−15.0*	4.9	–	0.8	12.6
p-value of Wald test in %	*0.6*	42.0	55.0	**1.0**	*5.5*	11.0
Family						
Single	2.1	4.3	6.0	9.5	6.3	**14.9**
Kids < 3 years in household	**−14.3**	0.3	−4.6	0.3	−3.7	**−10.9**
Kids 3–6 years in household	−2.7	−2.2	−1.0	1.4	2.0	−11.9
p-value of Wald test in %	**4.1**	79.0	57.0	42.0	67.0	**3.7**
Social background and education						
Financial problems in youth	**−7.9**	−4.1	−0.7	−4.1	−3.7	−0.0
Basic education	−5.3	0.6	0.1	11.1	−0.1	1.3
University education	0.1	**−13.0**	*−14.3*	11.9	−7.9	−5.1
p-value of Wald test in %	*9.0*	*5.8*	*7.1*	*9.4*	31.0	67.0
Employment (and wealth indicator)						
Full time employment	6.9	*8.3*	*8.7*	*−12.1*	−8.0	−5.3
Not working	−3.2	4.3	1.4	18.2	–	–
Job position:						
Upper management	8.2	**−17.1**	1.8	7.4	*19.1*	*21.0*
Lower management	−4.6	−7.1	−6.1	**15.9**	*16.4*	*23.6*
Skilled worker	**−13.0**	−7.9	−7.5	11.0	*21.4*	*21.8*
Renting home	**−6.7**	−3.4	**−8.1**	−0.2	−1.7	5.1
Clerks (isco)	1.2	−1.7	−1.2	−12.8	−15.4	−9.1
Service workers, sales person (isco)	*−13.6*	**−11.4**	−6.6	1.3	−5.4	−3.5
Craft, construction, machine op. (isco)	*−20.0*	*−24.7*	−10.6	0.3	2.7	1.0
Gross yearly earnings in kCHF	−0.2	*0.2*	*0.2*	0.2	**0.2**	−0.0
Zero earnings	−12.4	6.1	4.1	2.5	14.1	*−6.3*

Table 5.3 (continued)

Variable	Women			Men		
	2000	2004	2008	2000	2004	2008
Nonzero annual earnings < 30kCHF	−9.7	5.3	*9.5*	**19.0**	18.5	−33.8
Annual earnings > 90kCHF	2.1	−10.0	−0.9	−0.5	−1.6	*12.1*
p-value of Wald test in %	*0.1*	*0.8*	**1.5**	**2.8**	*0.2*	*0.1*
Health (objective indicators)						
No bad back or lower back problems (last month)	−0.8	−5.5	3.3	3.0	−4.7	−0.4
No general weakness, weariness, lack of energy	−3.9	−5.2	**7.6**	**−12.3**	1.5	−1.1
No difficulty in sleeping, or insomnia (last month)	3.5	**9.0**	−1.2	−3.7	−5.8	6.7
No headaches or facial pains (last month)	4.8	−1.9	−4.7	1.8	−6.4	*12.0*
Health no impediment for daily work	0.5	4.8	−2.4	4.2	1.6	−2.6
Not in hospital (last 12 months)	3.2	−3.8	−0.0	−7.4	7.1	*0.2*
Accident leading at least 10 days out of work	**−18.5**	−8.6	−1.9	2.9	11.1	1.3
Chronic disease	2.7	–	−1.4	1.3	–	−3.8
Number of doctor visits (last 12 months)	0.3	0.5	0.0	**−1.1**	0.4	−0.0
p-value of Wald test in %	28.0	**3.5**	40.0	*5.6*	40.0	18.0
Subjective health						
Subjective health: very good	*19.2*	7.8	*16.8*	3.9	8.8	*15.1*
good	*9.9*	3.8	*13.6*	2.1	6.2	4.6
p-value of Wald test in %	*0.2*	35.0	**1.6**	84.0	61.0	*9.6*
Regional indicators						
Canton of Geneva	**−9.8**	−8.2	−7.3	−2.1	**−18.0**	−4.3
Espace Mittelland	**−14.6**	−1.6	0.2	−5.0	**−13.1**	**−10.1**
Ticino	**−23.8**	**−19.3**	**−16.4**	**−22.7**	−17.3	−7.3
Type of agglomeration: Centres	−0.7	−0.8	−1.2	−1.7	1.0	−0.6
Industrial and tertiary sector communes	9.0	2.5	−2.0	8.3	−5.5	−6.1
Rural commuter communes	−4.3	−2.5	−4.8	**12.9**	−11.8	−6.0
Agricultural communes	−0.6	4.2	1.9	−7.4	−8.8	**−15.4**
p-value of Wald test in %	*0.1*	17.0	30.0	*5.8*	*0.5*	*6.7*
Sample size (active/non-active)	538/258	581/215	568/228	319/210	333/196	345/184

Table 5.3   (continued)

Notes:
Own calculations from probit model.
Dependent variable is binary indicating sports activities at least once per week.
Independent variables are measured in the year prior to the measurement of the dependent variable.
Marginal effects are averaged over the sample.
Discrete effects are given for the binary regressors.
Constant term included as additional regressor in all estimations.
Bold and italic/**bold**/*italic*: coefficient significant at 1 per cent, 5 per cent, 10 per cent level, respectively.

Source: Swiss Household Panel.

indicate that probably part of the age effects are already absorbed by other variables (for example, marital status).

As regards the variables measuring the number of children in the household, it is not surprising that they are associated with lower sports activity. The ambiguous feature is that it fades away over time for the women, while becoming more important for men. This is in line with the positive marginal effect of single status.

As a measure of the social background of the individual we use information about whether the individual had financial problems in her youth. Indeed this variable is associated with a negative marginal effect, although it is only significant for women in 2000 and fades away over time (as the sample ages). It is surprising that, for women, university education is associated with lower activity levels, in particular for 2004 and 2008 while, for men, this relation is U-shaped for 2000 and not well determined in 2008. It may well be that these 'strange' results for education are coming from the correlation of the educational variables with the characteristics of the labour force status, which are considered next.

While the correlation of the job position and activity status is somewhat erratic for women, for men it is clear that lesser skills are associated with lower activity levels. For women, there are also occupation-specific variations in the activity level. The association with earnings is hard to pin down, which again may stem from the fact that many variables that are usually good predictors of earnings are included in the estimation as well. Finally, as a proxy for wealth (but probably also as proxy for the amount of housework[9]), home ownership is associated with a higher activity level for women, but irrelevant for men. Overall, the joint tests indicate that these variables are important correlates of sports participation for men as well as for women.

The unsystematic results for the detailed health indicators (and the related joint tests) also indicate that the sample size might be smaller than is desirable to exactly pin down these relations. However, the positive associations between subjective health and activity levels appear to be clear.

Finally, the regional indicators reflect the already observed pattern, namely, considerably lower activity levels in the French- and, particularly, Italian-speaking parts of Switzerland.[10]

4. THE EFFECTS OF SPORT ON HEALTH AND LABOUR MARKET OUTCOMES

In this section I shed some light on the effects of leisure sports participation on health, general well-being and labour market outcomes. The empirical research closely follows the approach suggested in a recent paper by Lechner (2009) who analyses the effects of sports participation in Germany. The basic idea is to stratify the sample in an initial year (here 1999) according to gender and sports status. In those strata the probability of being active in the next period is estimated conditional on observables characteristics of that same period. The basic idea of stratifying according to lagged sports status is that the (lagged) potential confounders in those strata are exogenous by construction. Then the propensity score is used as an input into a matching procedure to estimate the effect of activity levels observed in the following year (2000). Those effects are measured some years later to better understand the (expected) long-term effects of being active. Unfortunately, due to the smaller sample in this study compared to the German study, stratification according to sports status is not possible. Instead, we condition on lagged status and perform tests against omitted variables for interaction terms of the confounders and the lagged sports status. Those tests show that such interactions play only a minor role. Owing to the substantial male–female heterogeneity documented in section 3, we decided to stick to the gender stratification despite awareness of potential problems related to the resulting small subsamples. Before presenting the results, a note of caution is appropriate. Owing to the sample size and the corresponding lack of power of the significance tests, most of the estimates are not significant. Even worse, and of course related, the estimation results are lacking robustness with respect to different definitions of the outcome variables and specifications of the propensity scores.

Table 5.4 presents the results for selected outcome variables that cover health, life satisfaction and labour market indicators for selected years (2004, 2006 and 2008). The results show the estimated effect as well as the average level of the respective outcome variable.

Table 5.4   Effect of weekly sports activity in 2000

Outcome variable	2004		2006		2008	
	Level	Effect	Level	Effect	Level	Effect
Women						
Days without health problems (annual)	359	5	360	8	359	4
Subjective health very good (in %)	23	4	20	7	17	−2
No medication required (in %)	76	1	75	**10**	70	9
General life satisfaction (11-p. scale, × 100)	804	18	804	17	795	3
Part time employment (in %)	61	−4	67	−1	68	−3
Full time employment (in %)	18	3	16	**5**	16	1
Cumulated average annual earnings (/100)	343	−5	358	−6	375	−10
Log (cumulated av. annual earnings+1)	9.27	**−0.25**	9.49	**−0.22**	9.73	**−0.12**
Men						
Days without health problems (annual)	360	3	356	−2	358	−0
Subjective health very good (in %)	25	1	23	−4	16	1
No medication required (in %)	73	−1	69	2	68	4
General life satisfaction (11-p. scale, × 100)	804	12	803	10	809	4
Part time employment (in %)	16	−4	15	−5	14	−5
Full time employment (in %)	83	8	85	7	85	5
Cumulated average annual earnings (/100)	871	29	897	31	924	39
Log (cumulated av. annual earnings + 1)	11.04	*0.09*	11.08	*0.04*	11.12	*0.03*

Notes:
Results obtained from smoothed propensity score matching as in Lechner (2009).
Propensity score based on same specification as shown in Table 5.3 plus additional regressor indicating activity level in 1999.
Average treatment effect on the treated shown.
Level: Estimate of mean value of outcome variable if active.
***Bold and italic*/bold**: coefficient significant at 1 per cent, 5 per cent level, respectively.
Symmetric p-values obtained from bootstrapping asymptotic t-values 999 times.

Source: Swiss Household Panel.

As regards the health indicators, almost all of the estimated effects for women (796 observations) are positive and sometimes significant. However, for the smaller male sample (529 observations) none of the estimates are significant and their signs vary.

With respect to the outcome variable related to general life satisfaction, all estimated effects are positive (similar to Lechner, 2009, and Rasciute and Downward, 2010) but, once more, they lack precision. Again similar to Lechner (2009) there seems to be a positive effect on the share of women working full-time (significant in 2006). The same effect appears for men, but as before, it is not significant for any of the years.

The results for the earnings effects are surprising. First, these are the only effects which in their log-specification are significant for all years as well for both sexes.[11] While the effect of being active on future log-earnings is positive for men (as in Lechner, 2009), it turns out to be negative when estimated for women. The positive effects for men can be easily reconciled with theories of investment in health capital (Grossman, 1972) as well as of signalling health, good motivation, social skills and self-discipline and thus higher productivity (for example, Rooth, 2010). However, the large negative effects for women are puzzling. This is particularly so, as the volume of working time seems not to be affected, or if anything, is increasing due to sport activities.

5. CONCLUSIONS

In this chapter I investigated the correlates of individual sports participation in Switzerland as well as their effects on health and labour market outcomes. The empirical analysis is especially concerned about the long-run effects. Therefore, it is based on the first eight waves of the Swiss Household Panel. Investigating the factors associated with sports participation, it turns out that better subjective health and health investments as well as socio-economic status are positively associated with sports activity. It is also shown that there exist considerable regional (cultural?) differences in Switzerland with respect to individual sport activities: the probability of sports participation in the German-speaking part of Switzerland is much higher than in the rest of the country. Finally, the econometric analysis of the effects of sports activity on labour market outcomes is hampered by the comparatively small sample sizes of the SHP, but nevertheless reveals positive earnings effects for men and negative effects for women. Unfortunately, both results lack some desirable robustness properties. The results for health, general well-being and other labour market indicators generally lack precision.

The results of this chapter forcefully document the need for larger and more detailed individual panel databases for Switzerland that allow researchers to resolve the important ambiguities that were demonstrated by the empirical analysis of this chapter.

NOTES

*   The project received financial support from the St. Gallen Research Center in Aging, Welfare, and Labour Market Analysis (SCALA). It has been realized using the data collected by the Swiss Household Panel (SHP), which is based at the Swiss Centre of Expertise in the Social Sciences FORS. The project is financed by the Swiss National Science Foundation. I thank Stefan Legge for his very skilful help in preparing the data used in this chapter and Darjusch Tafreschi for careful proofreading. The usual disclaimer applies.

1. See, for example, Scheerder et al. (2005, 2006) for Belgium, Xiong (2007) for China, Downward (2007) and Farrell and Shields (2002) for England, Becker et al. (2006) and Schneider and Becker (2005) as well as Lechner (2009) for Germany, Drygas et al. (2009) for Poland, Han et al. (2009) for South Korea, as well as Eisenberg and Okeke (2009) and Charness and Gneezy (2009) for the USA.

2. See, for example, Cornelißen and Pfeifer (2008), Lechner (2009) and Rooth (2010). Of course the literature on the effects of general well being (for example, Rasciute and Downward, 2010) as well as on health (for example, Bauman et al., 2002; Gomez-Pinilla, 2008; Hollmann et al., 1981; Lüschen et al., 1993; Rashad, 2007) is also relevant as health and well-being are also relevant for certain labour market outcomes.

3. Note when considering the developments over time that the population considered next year is one year older than in the current year.

4. Physical activities that make one slightly breathless (see Table 5B.1 in the Appendix for details).

5. In Tables 5B.2 and 5B.3 in the Appendix we use different definitions of being active (some sport at all and activities that makes you slightly breathless), but the results are fairly robust.

6. The probit models have been subjected to specification tests against non-normality, heteroscedasticity and omitted variables. No severe specification problems have been detected.

7. Marginal effects averaged over the sample are shown for non-binary variables. For binary variables, we show the average change in the probability of being active when the variable is changed from 0 to 1 for all observations.

8. Note that the t-test for a coefficient being zero is a valid t-test for the average marginal effect being zero, as the latter is zero whenever the coefficient is zero.

9. The latter is also measured directly, but is never significant.

10. Geneva is entirely French speaking and Ticino is entirely Italian speaking. The region Espace Mittelland has German- and French-speaking parts.

11. One reason why they are significant for log(earnings+1) and not for levels may be that the variance of the log specification is less effected by some large values of the earnings variable.

REFERENCES

Bauman, A., E. Adrian, J.F. Sallis, D.A. Dzewaltowski and N. Owen (2002), 'Toward a better understanding of the influences on physical activity: the role of determinants, correlates, causal variables, mediators, moderators, and confounders', *American Journal of Preventive Medicine*, **23** (2S), 5–14.

Becker S., T. Klein and S. Schneider (2006), 'Sportaktivität in Deutschland im 10-Jahres-Vergleich: Veränderungen und soziale Unterschiede', *Deutsche Zeitschrift für Sportmedizin*, **57** (9), 226–32.

Charness, G. and U. Gneezy, (2009), 'Incentives to exercise', *Econometrica*, **77**, 909–31.

Cornelißen, T. and C. Pfeifer (2008), 'Sport und Arbeitseinkommen: Individuelle Ertragsraten von Sportaktivitäten in Deutschland', mimeo.

Downward, P. (2007), 'Exploring the economic choice to participate in sport: results from the 2002 General Household Survey', *International Review of Applied Economics*, **21**, 633–53.

Drygas, W., M. Kwasniewska, D. Kaleta, M. Pikala, W. Bielecki, J. Gluszek, T. Zdrojewski, A. Pajak, K. Kozakiewicz and G. Broda (2009), 'Epidemiology of physical inactivity in Poland: prevalence and determinants in a former communist country in socioeconomic transition', *Public Health*, **123**, 592–7.

Eisenberg, D. and E. Okeke (2009), 'Too cold for a jog? Weather, exercise, and socioeconomic status', *The B.E. Journal of Economic Analysis & Policy*, 9 (1), art 25. Available at: www.bepress.com/bcjcap/vol9/iss1/art25 (accessed 17 January 2011)

Farrell, L. and M.A. Shields (2002), 'Investigating the economic and demographic determinants of sporting participation in England', *Journal of the Royal Statistical Society* A, **165**, 335–48.

Gomez-Pinilla, F. (2008), 'The influences of diet and exercise on mental health through hormensis', *Aging Research Review*, 7, 49–62.

Grossman, M. (1972), 'On the concept of health capital and the demand for health', *The Journal of Political Economy*, **80**, 223–55.

Han M.A., K.S. Kim, J. Park, M.G. Kang and S.Y. Ryu (2009), 'Association between levels of physical activity and poor self-rated health in Korean adults: the Third Korea National Health and Nutrition Examination Survey (KNHANES), 2005', *Public Health*, **123**, 665–9.

Hollmann, W., R. Rost, H. Liesen, B. Doufaux, H. Heck and A. Mader (1981), 'Assessment of different forms of physical activity with respect to preventive and rehabilitative cardiology', *International Journal of Sports Medicine*, **2**, 67.

Lamprecht, M., Fischer, A. and Stamm, H.P. (2008), *Sport Schweiz 2008: Das Sportverhalten der Schweizer Bevölkerung*, Magglingen: Bundesamt für Sport, BASPO.

Lechner, M. (2009), 'Long-run labour market and health effects of individual sports activities', *The Journal of Health Economics*, **28**, 839–54.

Lüschen, G., T. Abel, W. Cockerham and G. Kunz (1993), 'Kausalbeziehungen und sozio-kulturelle Kontexte zwischen Sport und Gesundheit', *Sportwissenschaft*, **23**, 175–86.

Rasciute, S. and P. Downward (2010), 'Health or happiness? What is the impact of physical activity on the individual?', *Kyklos*, **63**, 256–70.

Rashad, I. (2007), 'Cycling: an increasingly untouched source of physical and mental health', NBER working paper No. 12929.

Rooth, D. (2010), 'Work out or out of work: the labor market return to physical fitness and leisure sport activities', IZA discussion paper No. 4684.

Scheerder, J., M. Thomis, B. Vanreusel, J. Lefevre, R. Renson, B. Vanden Eynde and G.P. Beunen (2006), 'Sports participation among females from adolescence to adulthood: a longitudinal study', *International Review for the Sociology of Sport*, **41** (3–4), 413–30.

Scheerder J., B. Vanreusel and M. Taks (2005), 'Stratification patterns of active sport involvement among adults: social change and persistence', *International Review for the Sociology of Sport*, **40** (2), 139–62.

Schneider S. and S. Becker (2005), 'Prevalence of physical activity among the working population and correlation with work-related factors. Results from the first German National Health Survey', *Journal of Occupational Health*, **47**, 414–23.

Xiong, H. (2007), 'The evolution of urban society and social changes in sports: participation at the grassroots in China', *International Review for the Sociology of Sport*, **42** (14), 441–71.

APPENDIX 5A: DATA SOURCES

5A.1   The Swiss Sports Study

The study is based on computer-aided telephone interviews (CATI) which have been conducted in the first half of 2007 (in Italian, French and German). The sample is representative for the population of Switzerland which could be reached with a non-mobile telephone connection and which is able to speak German, French or Italian. For further information see Lamprecht et al. (2008).

5A.2   The Swiss Household Panel (SHP)

5A.2.1   General

The following description is quoted from the website of the SHP (www. swisspanel.ch/shpdata/design.php?lang=en, accessed 10 April 2010). The reader is referred to this source for more details on response rates and so on.

> Sample: The SHP sample is a stratified random sample of private house-holds whose members represent the non-institutional population resident in Switzerland. In 1999, the methodology section of the Swiss Federal Statistical Office drew a first random sample (SHP_I) in each of the seven major statistical regions of Switzerland (Lake Geneva, Mittelland, North-Western Switzerland, Zürich, Eastern-Switzerland, Central Switzerland and Tessin) on the basis of the Swiss telephone directory (SRH – Stichprobenregister für Haushalterhebungen), which covers over 95% of all private households. In 2004, the SHP_II refreshment sample of about 2,500 newly recruited house-holds was added. These households and their individual members have been interviewed yearly since then.
>
> Questionnaire content: The 'Living in Switzerland' survey is a comprehensive survey covering a broad range of social fields and topics. The questionnaires are designed to collect both 'objective' data (resources, living conditions, life events, social position, participation, etc.) and 'subjective' data (attitudes, perceptions, satisfaction with various life domains, values, etc.).
>
> A broad range of themes are covered, including:
>
> ● education and labour market participation
> ● income and financial situation
> ● housing and geographical mobility
> ● psychological and physical health
> ● social origin and residence in Switzerland
> ● organisation of the household, division of tasks
> ● social networks and social support
> ● life events and quality of life

- partnership and family life
- social participation, religion and leisure
- political opinions, values and attitudes

Fieldwork: Since the first wave in 1999, the data collection is carried out by the Institute M.I.S. Trend (Lausanne and Bern) by the means of CATI (Computer Assisted Telephone Interviewing). Interviews are carried out in French, German and Italian. In every household a reference person is appointed who completes a grid questionnaire collecting information on the composition of the household. A household questionnaire is then administered, collecting information on the household situation. The reference person and all other household members of 14 years and older are interviewed individually. For household members below 14 years old and for those with whom an individual interview is not possible proxy interviews are conducted with the reference person. The household interviews last 15 minutes on average, with the individual ones lasting 35 minutes. In addition to the telephone interviews, SHP_I respondents completed, in 2001 and 2002, a biography questionnaire (paper and pencil). The aim of this biography questionnaire was to collect retrospective data on professional development and family life.

5A.2.2 Selection of sample

Table 5A.1 Sample selection

Selection step		Number of individuals	Share of men
1	*Full Sample*	*22 000*	*49.3%*
	Full personal interview in 1999	7 799	43.8%
	Full personal interview in 2000	7 073	44.8%
	Full personal interview in 2001	6 601	44.5%
	Full personal interview in 2002	5 700	44.5%
	Full personal interview in 2003	5 220	44.6%
	Full personal interview in 2004	8 067	44.7%
	Full personal interview in 2005	6 537	44.6%
	Full personal interview in 2006	6 659	44.3%
	Full personal interview in 2007	6 980	44.4%
	Full personal interview in 2008	6 904	43.9%
2	Filter: answered all questionnaires	2 060	40.1%
3	Filter: age in 2000 between 18 and 55	6 539	48.8%
2 & 3	All questionnaires answered + age filter	1 467	39.7%
4	Filter: exclude remaining retirees etc.	3 101	47.7%
2 & 3 & 4	*Final Sample*	*1 325*	*39.9%*

(Subgroups — rows for full personal interviews 1999 to 2008)

Table 5A.2   Questions and answers about activity levels in the SHP

Abbreviation	Question	Answer
Sports activity level	I am now going to list a number of leisure activities. How frequently do you practise them? Practising an individual or team sport (for example fitness, jogging, football, volley ball, tennis)	Daily/At least once a week/At least once a month/Less than once a month/Never
Activity at all	Now, let's talk about physical activities, which make you slightly breathless, for example: walking quickly, dancing, gardening or other types of sporting activities. Do you currently practise physical activities, which make you slightly breathless?	Yes/No
Activity days per week	At present, how many days a week do you practise for half an hour minimum a physical activity which makes you slightly breathless? These 30 minutes of daily activity can be divided up in three sessions of 10 minutes each. The week = 7 days (weekend included)	Number of days (available from 2000 onwards)

Source: Swiss Household Panel, questionnaires 1999 and 2000.

APPENDIX 5B: FURTHER DESCRIPTIVE INFORMATION AND RESULTS

Table 5B.1   Activity levels for SHP cohort

	1999	2000	2001	2002	2003	2004	2005	2006	2007	2008
Sports activity level in %					Women					
Daily	10	6	9	5	5	6	7	6	6	7
Weekly	54	62	62	64	66	67	68	66	67	64
Monthly	8	9	7	7	7	5	5	7	5	6
Less than monthly	3	4	4	3	4	2	2	2	2	3
No sports	25	19	18	20	18	19	18	19	19	20
Active at all (in %)	74	71	71	73	73	73	78	75	78	76
Days per week	n.a.	2.0	2.0	2.1	2.1	2.2	2.4	2.3	2.4	2.4
Sports activity level in %					Men					
Daily	8	5	5	3	4	4	6	5	6	5
Weekly	52	56	57	61	62	59	59	60	61	60
Monthly	13	14	12	13	11	10	10	10	8	12
Less than monthly	6	4	5	6	4	5	5	5	4	3
No sports	21	22	21	17	19	21	20	20	20	20
Active at all (in %)	72	69	67	70	66	68	71	72	76	75
Days per week	n.a.	1.9	1.7	1.8	1.7	1.9	2.0	2.1	2.1	2.1

Note: Own computations.

Source: Swiss Household Panel.

Table 5B.2   Correlates with sports activity (some sports)

Variable	Women			Men		
	2000	2004	2008	2000	2004	2008
Sports-related activities						
Efforts to remain healthy (0–10)	*3.0*	*1.9*	*2.7*	*4.2*	*4.1*	*4.2*
Voluntary work	3.9	**7.6**	**8.5**	−0.2	−2.3	**7.2**
p-value of Wald test in %	*0.0*	*0.0*	*0.0*	*0.0*	*0.0*	*0.0*
Age						
Age in years	*−0.5*	−0.1	0.2	−0.7	*−0.7*	−0.3
Age indicator: 25 or younger	−9.1	–	–	−23.1	–	–
Age indicator: 25 to 30	*−14.7*	–	–	−4.3	–	–
Age indicator: 30 or younger	–	0.7	14.3	–	−7.3	13.3
Age indicator: 50 to 55	–	−4.1	−3.9	–	−1.0	4.7
Age indicator: 56 or older	–	−5.5	1.2	–	−4.8	−0.4
p-value of Wald test in %	1.2	56.0	40.0	49.0	**1.4**	6.7
Family						
Single	*13.0*	2.0	3.6	7.0	−1.5	5.4
Kids < 3 years in household	−5.9	1.2	−3.1	−1.6	−1.7	−4.9
Kids 3–6 years in household	0.8	−1.6	1.0	1.6	0.8	−9.9
p-value of Wald test in %	*0.2*	89.0	80.0	48.0	46.0	29.0
Social background and education						
Financial problems in youth	*−7.1*	0.2	−1.0	−3.4	−2.5	−2.6
Basic education	−4.4	−1.8	−3.6	−8.0	2.0	−7.6
University education	4.3	*−13.7*	*−14.0*	*9.7*	−6.0	−3.7
p-value of Wald test in %	*3.2*	*2.8*	*1.7*	17.0	40.0	50.0
Employment (and wealth indicator)						
Full time employment	**7.5**	*7.3*	3.3	−2.2	−7.2	4.8
Not working	−0.4	8.6	1.5	9.7	–	–
Job position: Upper management	4.2	−7.6	5.7	1.9	**12.8**	**13.9**
Lower management	−6.1	−7.4	0.1	8.2	6.1	*17.8*
Skilled worker	−6.2	−3.7	1.4	2.7	*11.6*	**13.7**
Renting home	**−6.3**	*−3.7*	−5.2	−2.6	3.8	1.8
Clerks (isco)	2.8	−0.4	−2.6	−4.7	10.4	1.8
Service workers, sales person (isco)	*−10.0*	**−9.4**	−1.9	3.1	−4.3	1.8
Craft, construction, machine op. (isco)	−0.1	*−19.8*	−7.4	−1.0	−6.2	1.6
Gross yearly earnings in kCHF	−9.4	**0.2**	0.1	0.0	*0.2*	0.0
Zero earnings	−8.5	2.2	−3.2	−8.2	6.9	4.6
Nonzero annual earnings < 30kCHF	4.8	8.1	5.8	1.1	8.9	−23.8
Annual earnings > 90kCHF	−10.0	−8.0	4.3	*9.6*	*−8.3*	5.6
p-value of Wald test in %	**3.5**	*0.2*	7.4	34.0	*0.0*	*0.1*
Health (objective indicators)						
No bad back or lower back problems (last month)	−5.2	−3.6	2.5	1.4	−5.9	0.2

Table 5B.2   (continued)

Variable	Women			Men		
	2000	2004	2008	2000	2004	2008
No general weakness, weariness, lack of energy	−3.3	−2.0	**5.8**	−5.6	4.3	5.2
No difficulty in sleeping, or insomnia (last month)	2.0	*6.7*	−1.7	2.1	−4.9	*6.0*
No headaches or facial pains (last month)	2.0	0.1	*−4.7*	−3.7	−3.3	**7.8**
Health no impediment for daily work	−2.4	**6.1**	−4.0	*6.8*	−3.1	−1.5
Not in hospital (last 12 months)	1.4	−3.8	0.0	−0.0	7.6	0.0
Accident leading to at least 10 days out of work	−9.8	*−10.4*	−2.2	*5.0*	0.6	10.6
Chronic disease	2.7	–	0.9	−1.6	–	−0.7
Number of doctor visits (last 12 months)	0.1	0.0	−0.0	0.0	0.5	−0.1
p-value of Wald test in %	46.0	*8.8*	40.0	34.0	21.0	**4.0**
Subjective health						
Subjective health: very good	*15.8*	6.3	*14.9*	5.5	**15.6**	2.5
good	**9.4**	2.3	*14.9*	0.9	**14.2**	−4.2
p-value of Wald test in %	*0.1*	38.0	0.2	50.0	7.4	27.0
Regional indicators						
Canton of Geneva	*−12.8*	*−9.6*	**−7.6**	−5.8	*−13.0*	**−10.4**
Espace Mittelland	*−10.1*	−1.1	3.6	−4.6	−5.4	**−9.4**
Ticino	*−29.5*	*−16.5*	*−19.1*	*−31.4*	*−24.1*	*−11.5*
Type of agglomeration: Centres	−3.8	−0.3	−2.7	−4.4	2.7	−3.8
Industrial and tertiary sector communes	1.5	6.5	−2.2	2.0	−3.6	−5.5
Rural commuter communes	0.1	0.5	−5.0	−1.8	0.9	1.6
Agricultural communes	1.5	3.0	−3.6	−4.4	−1.2	−4.9
p-value of Wald test in %	*0.0*	**2.5**	**2.1**	**4.4**	**2.0**	**4.1**
Sample size (active/non-active)	641/155	581/215	638/158	414/115	333/196	424/105

Notes:
Own calculations from probit model.
Dependent variable is binary indicating at least some sports activities.
Independent variables are measured in the year prior to the measurement of the dependent variable.
Marginal effects are averaged over the sample.
Discrete effects are given for the binary regressors.
Constant term included as additional regressor in all estimations.
***Bold and italic*/bold/*italic*: coefficient significant at 1 per cent, 5 per cent, 10 per cent level, respectively.

Source: Swiss Household Panel.

Table 5B.3   Correlates with physical activity

Variable	Women			Men		
	2000	2004	2008	2000	2004	2008
Sports-related activities						
Efforts to remain healthy (0–10)	*3.1*	*3.3*	*2.8*	*5.8*	*4.1*	*3.2*
Voluntary work	*11.2*	−0.1	*7.5*	−5.0	−3.9	**6.3**
p-value of Wald test in %	*0.0*	*0.0*	*0.0*	*0.0*	*0.0*	**0.0**
Age						
Age in years	−0.3	−0.1	0.2	−0.5	**−0.9**	−0.3
Age indicator: 25 or younger	−10.6	–	–	*−21.9*	–	–
Age indicator: 25 to 30	−1.4	–	–	4.1	–	–
Age indicator: 30 or younger	–	*−11.6*	4.2	–	−0.1	3.3
Age indicator: 50 to 55	–	6.3	−5.7	–	6.9	5.6
Age indicator: 56 or older	–	−11.3	−5.8	–	27.5	−1.3
p-value of Wald test in %	50.0	**1.4**	89.0	*5.4*	6.2	41.0
Family						
Single	**10.8**	*9.8*	5.5	0.8	1.4	8.6
Kids < 3 years in household	−7.8	−5.0	4.0	−9.2	−1.5	−2.9
Kids 3–6 years in household	0.7	−5.6	3.0	−8.0	*10.6*	**−13.7**
p-value of Wald test in %	**2.5**	15.0	49.0	22.0	21.0	*6.7*
Social background and education						
Financial problems in youth	−0.1	0.8	−2.6	−1.1	0.2	2.0
Basic education	−3.5	−6.2	−6.0	1.7	6.3	−1.2
University education	**−10.0**	−1.2	2.9	6.9	−2.9	2.5
p-value of Wald test in %	*24.0*	51.0	41.0	65.0	70.0	91.0
Employment (and wealth indicator)						
Full time employment	**11.3**	*9.3*	6.6	−2.4	−0.7	−0.5
Not working	0.9	5.2	0.8	1.6	–	–
Job position: Upper management	−12.9	−7.4	−8.1	−5.5	8.7	*14.1*
Lower management	−11.7	−6.2	−7.5	4.5	8.6	**13.6**
Skilled worker	−8.0	−5.9	−8.4	2.7	*12.4*	7.0
Renting home	*−11.4*	**−7.4**	*−11.5*	−1.3	**−8.3**	−0.9
Clerks (isco)	*−14.8*	−2.5	−3.4	*−15.5*	**−21.7**	−0.6
Service workers, sales person (isco)	−3.9	−4.8	0.1	−12.8	−5.7	−4.7
Craft, construction, machine op. (isco)	−14.5	−9.9	−5.1	−2.2	−1.2	0.8
Gross yearly earnings in kCHF	0.1	0.0	0.0	0.0	0.0	−0.0
Zero earnings	3.2	−4.9	−4.4	−2.3	1.1	0.2
Nonzero annual earnings < 30kCHF	1.0	−4.4	0.4	10.6	12.2	−9.5
Annual earnings > 90kCHF	2.6	−8.6	1.2	9.7	2.2	**12.8**
p-value of Wald test in %	*0.1*	12.0	11.0	13.0	*5.9*	*5.2*
Health (objective indicators)						
No bad back or lower back problems (last month)	−1.2	*−5.5*	2.0	−1.8	−1.6	5.5
No general weakness, weariness, lack of energy	−2.3	−4.0	3.2	*−7.7*	4.2	3.8

Table 5B.3   (continued)

Variable	Women			Men		
	2000	2004	2008	2000	2004	2008
No difficulty in sleeping, or insomnia (last month)	2.4	*6.8*	3.9	3.7	−6.1	*13.5*
No headaches or facial pains (last month)	4.9	2.0	−3.8	−0.6	**−10.6**	7.5
Health no impediment for daily work	4.6	2.7	0.7	0.5	−0.6	−1.3
Not in hospital (last 12 months)	0.5	−1.9	*−0.9*	*10.1*	3.4	0.0
Accident leading to at least 10 days out of work	−11.3	−8.2	***−19.9***	7.2	−2.1	3.2
Chronic disease	−0.6	–	−4.2	7.2	–	3.4
Number of doctor visits (last 12 months)	−0.3	0.0	0.0	−0.2	0.2	0.2
p-value of Wald test in %	24	29	*0.5*	38.0	32.0	*0.1*
Subjective health						
Subjective health: very good	*10.6*	***18.8***	−2.1	**17.0**	***19.2***	8.5
good	*9.4*	***12.0***	−2.4	7.6	*15.8*	1.2
p-value of Wald test in %	12	*0.2*	89.0	**2.1**	10.0	34.0
Regional indicators						
Canton of Geneva	***−15.1***	***−20.9***	***−12.0***	***−16.0***	***−29.5***	***−17.6***
Espace Mittelland	***−13.5***	***−10.3***	***−9.0***	***−9.2***	***−19.4***	***−11.5***
Ticino	***−20.7***	***−33.8***	***−29.3***	***−23.0***	***−33.4***	***−28.2***
Type of agglomeration: Centres	0.1	2.6	5.2	−1.6	2.2	0.8
Industrial and tertiary sector communes	−2.2	−5.1	−0.7	5.3	5.9	−0.5
Rural commuter communes	0.2	−6.8	−4.5	0.7	2.4	−2.2
Agricultural communes	−4.0	*9.1*	1.0	−2.8	−2.4	10.7
p-value of Wald test in %	***0.0***	***0.0***	***0.0***	**2.6**	***0.0***	*0.1*
Sample size (active/non-active)	565/231	580/216	604/192	367/162	358/171	399/130

Notes:
Own calculations from probit model.
Dependent variable is binary indicating at least some activities.
Independent variables are measured in the year prior to the measurement of the dependent variable.
Marginal effects are averaged over the sample.
Discrete effects are given for the binary regressors.
Constant term included as additional regressor in all estimations.
***Bold and italic*/bold/*italic*: coefficient significant at 1 per cent, 5 per cent, 10 per cent level, respectively.

Source: Swiss Household Panel.

6. Do sporty people have access to higher job quality?*

Charlotte Cabane

1. INTRODUCTION

In their study on the General Educational Development (GED) Testing Program,[1] Heckman and Rubinstein (2001) demonstrate the importance of non-cognitive skills on life success and come to three conclusions. First, the traditional evaluations of the education efficiency are only based on measures of cognitive skills, whereas they prove that success in education is closely related to individual's endowment in non-cognitive skills (such as self-discipline and motivation). They also conclude that if cognitive skills have to be acquired in the early stages of life, non-cognitive skills can be learned over a longer period of time even after the usual period of studies. Finally, they point out that the GED send out a mixed signal that they are not able to be precise in terms of specific non-cognitive skills.

An explanation of the lack of interest in non-cognitive skills returns is the difficulty of measuring them. If cognitive skills are estimated via educational level and diploma, there is no objective measure of non-cognitive skills. Furthermore, since they can be learned even after the traditional educational period, there is no ideal moment to measure it. Also, a lot of individual's characteristics are considered as non-cognitive skills which complicates the measure: tenacity and perseverance, but also motivation, trustworthiness and self-discipline, among others.

There is no specific class which fosters non-cognitive skills formation, but extracurricular activities are commonly considered as such. Our aim is to demonstrate how an extracurricular activity can favour – through individuals' non-cognitive skills endowment and signalization – life success. Our analysis is focused on one component of life success: individuals' position on the labour market. We choose sports participation as our extracurricular activity for three reasons. On the one hand, sports can be practised almost all along individuals' life which allows taking into account the fact that non-cognitive skills can be acquired during a very long period. On the other hand, by choosing a specific extracurricular activity we reduce the number of associated non-cognitive skills. Also, sports participation does not require any specific skills (unlike artistic activities for example) and it is relatively accessible.[2]

De facto, the impact of sports practice on the labour market has received significant recognition in the USA (Barron et al., 2000, Ewing, 1998) for decades. Further, sports practice is a part of the educational system. Conversely, in Europe, sports participation is an extracurricular activity often considered as an obstacle to educational success. However, it is beginning to be recognized in the European business world. Firms seem to appreciate applicants with sporting achievements and they organize seminars led by former athletes. As an example, we can find in management teams former athletes who have good communication skills. Furthermore, common advice when writing curriculum vitae is to include two sports (an individual sport and a team sport) in the 'personal interest' section. The scarcity of academic studies analysing this topic using European data leads us to explore this topic.

Non-cognitive skills affect individual's position and evolution on the labour market at several levels (career evolution, wage, level of responsibility, type of work, and so on). We decided to centre our analysis on labour market integration and more particularly on job quality of people who came back to work after a period of unemployment. Our hypothesis is that sporty people get higher-quality jobs. This assumption relies on firms' and individuals' behaviours. On the one hand, we assume that firms believe that sporty people are persistent, responsible, independent, and so on. This assumption relies on the signalling effect (Spence, 1973). Then, employers are able to value a part of the non-cognitive skills during the hiring interview. On the other hand, we consider that sporty people have been more unremitting as they were looking for a job. The way they search a job and how they behave during the interviews is determinant. They also have better connections on the labour market (networking effect).

However, sports practice is not sufficient by itself to favour labour market integration. Being sporty and unemployed does not necessarily send a positive signal; therefore the influence of sports participation is positive only under specific conditions. We expect different effects with respect to level of education, age and the gender, but also with respect to individual's health and wealth. This means that we have to control for all an individual's characteristics which affect sports participation and labour market integration. In addition, we want to make sure that the effect of sports participation cannot be granted to any other leisure activity.

We studied two related aspects of job quality: hourly wage and level of autonomy at work. We found a robust positive impact of sports participation at the wage level. And being sporty and having a high school level of education are complementary. With respect to level of autonomy, the relation is weaker and more difficult to pinpoint. However, the two estimations cannot be compared because they do not reflect the same level of job quality.

This chapter focuses on the influence of being sporty on the quality of the job held after a break in working activity in Germany. In section 2, we review the literature before posing our problem and presenting our econometrics procedure (section 3). The data are presented in section 4. The results are reported in section 5, and then we conclude in section 6.

2.   THEORETICAL BACKGROUND

Cognitive, Non-cognitive Skills and Success in Education

Becker (1964) measures human capital by using indicators of level of education. Spence (1973) developed a concept which allows the use of education in order to signal unobservable ability but, again, it is about cognitive skills. The wage equation of Mincer (1974) only considers returns of education (and traditional labour market indicators) to explain the wages level. Therefore almost all the studies on human capital and labour market are focused on cognitive skills. But, as underlined by Heckman (2000), non-cognitive skills are necessary even for the learning process of cognitive skills.

Jacob (2002) explains the gender difference in returns to college by demonstrating that women have greater non-cognitive skills than men. He builds four measures of non-cognitive skills based on student behaviours at school. Two of these rely on disciplinary incidents, on retention in grade (during elementary school) and the two others measure effort and achievement in school. For each of these indicators, women score higher than men. In a similar way, one cannot expect the same impact of sports practice on men and women. First, firms/we credit men and women with specific soft-skills: women are supposed to be consensual when men are supposed to have more competitive spirit, for example.

Non-cognitive skills can be learned through a lot of ways: family or peer education, participation in an extracurricular activity, cultural heritage. Furthermore, this apprenticeship is informal in most cases because there is no evaluation of people's non-cognitive skills endowment. Therefore, people tend to improve non-cognitive skills they already have. For instance, if a person has a great ability for teamwork, he or she will enjoy doing team sports. But a person who likes competition can decide to join a volley-ball club and *there* learn team spirit. This means that the specific endowment of non-cognitive skills by sporty people does not necessarily result from sports practice. Also the positive impact of being sporty on the labour market can be explained by at least two different mechanisms: the signalling effect and the 'human capital effect' (increase of the human capital).

Pfeifer and Cornelißen (2010) measure the impact of sports practice on graduation, using the German Socio-Economic Panel (SOEP). Sporty students seem to improve their productivity at school by being healthier, and by having soft skills (and character) appreciated as qualities at school. The non-cognitive skills associated with sporty students are self-esteem, competitive spirit, tenacity, motivation, discipline and responsibility. They underline a larger effect for the girls and justify it pointing out their original difference. They assume that girls are by nature less competitive and have less self-esteem. Therefore they have more to learn about competition than boys.

Sports Participation and Labour Market Success: The Channel of Education

Most of the studies on this topic are American; they analyse the impact of sports participation in a cross-section framework. They have access to very detailed databases (NCAA, HBS, NELS and NLSY[3]) with accurate information especially on sports practice. The most recent studies underline the positive effect of sports participation while in school (at university) on graduation and on wages (higher for sporty people by 4 to 32 per cent). There is no study on sports participation and labour market integration. Long and Caudill (1991) found a strong positive effect for sporty people on graduation for men and women, and higher wages for men, but they only take into account athletes with good performance. They explain their results based on the signalling effect, the reputation effect and the effect due to the increase of the human capital.

The signalling effect (Spence, 1973) is based on the idea that some observable characteristics are used as a signal to select people who have some unobservable specific characteristics. In the study by Long and Caudill (1991), individuals who did sports at college and graduate well are seen as people who have a high capacity for concentration (high ability). Moreover, they could have slept (or any other non-positive 'activity') instead of practising sports. Then, if we consider that sporty people do sports because it is easy for them, it implies that they have already the soft skills and qualities that they need in order to do so (in addition to the fact that they are healthy). For example, someone who has a great team spirit would like taking part in a team sport. Thus, firms who want people with good team spirit (or any other soft skill which improves productivity) hire people who do or who have done team sports. In this case firms make a sizeable assumption about the transferability of these soft skills: they expect that sporty people will behave in the professional area as they do in the sports area. Finally, sporty people are – or are supposed to be – healthier by practising sports. Therefore, they work more efficiently and are less often absent.

The next assumption was that sports practice enhances the acquisition of non-cognitive skills (leadership, performing in a regulated system, and so on) and in this way increases workers' productivity (by increasing the human capital).

Also, there is the reputation effect which depends on the public image of the athlete. A firm would hire a former athlete because of the image he or she can give of the company (Z. Zidane for Danone, T. Woods for Nike).

Barron et al. (2000) argue that sporty people hold positions where they are paid comparative to their productivity. Since sporty people are competitive and persistent, they choose this type of jobs and, hence, they earn more. The authors maintain that sports practice is not equivalent, but better than, any other extracurricular activity.

Anderson (2001) points out the divergence of the impact of sports practice on minorities. She notices a negative influence on minorities due to an overinvestment in sports education (because an athlete would be guaranteed upward social mobility) and therefore an underinvestment in studies.

Sports Participation and Labour Market Success: Other Channels

Ewing (1998) showed that sporty people earn more. It is justified by three facts: sporty people hold jobs where the wage greatly depends on their productivity, and where they lead people (job with responsibilities). Also, they are often union members. These statements confirm the idea that sporty people behave differently: they choose specific jobs (and succeed in getting them). However, we do not know the causality. Do they behave differently because they did sports at university and they learned something from that experience? Or did they practise sports because they were already different at the university as they still are today?

A study in experimental economics, by Eber (2002), focuses on students' – with different sports practice – behaviours. Eber conducted his own survey (and database) comparing sports science students (STAPS) with others students. He found that the two groups are different and that, within the group studying sports science, girls and boys answered differently. Girls look more for equality and boys look more for competition. Eber does not control for the type of sports people practice. A priori girls and boys do not choose the same sports so differences in individual's behaviour can be enhanced by the sports they practice. One expects that men prefer team sports and women tend to practise more individual sports. Furthermore, independent of their preferences, sports opportunity differs by gender, which means even if they have the same preferences, the distribution of men and women by type of sports would not be equal. Therefore men and women do not practice the same sport, and their 'original' differences in terms of characteristics evolve with respect to the sports they practice. In his study, Eber demonstrate that sporty people are different and how different they are. However, he cannot infer the causality. Obviously the influence goes both ways but the question is to what extent?

These two studies point out the fact that sporty people behave differently from non-sporty people. And the way they behave is appreciated by firms on the labour market, which justifies the fact that they are more successful than non-sporty people.

Lechner (2009) analyses the returns of sports participation on the German labour market in terms of earnings and wages. He defines three transmission channels. First, people who practice sports are healthier and, as a consequence, they are more productive and less absent. Second, firms suppose that sporty people are more motivated and in a sense happier, which would increase their productivity. Third, sporty people can have the same unobservable characteristics as people who earn more;[4] this is the auto-selection process. He calculates that being sporty is the equivalent of an additional year of schooling in terms of return on labour market long-term outcomes.

Rooth (2010) made a double analysis in order to value the impact of practising leisure sports on labour market outcomes in Sweden. A part of his study relies on experimental economics and the hiring process. People who declare practising sports (as leisure) in their CV are more likely to get an interview. Rooth compares this to 1.5 additional years of work experience. This part of his paper clearly demonstrates the existence of a positive signalling effect for sporty people. He also estimates the impact of a variation of physical fitness on earnings and finds a positive effect (4 per cent). Unlike the previous impact, this is less easy to link to a specific effect.

To sum up, as we know for centuries: *Mens sana in corpore sano*! Being sporty positively impacts individual's productivity by improving components of his or her human capital: level of education, non-cognitive skills endowment and health. It is also used as a signal of ability by firms. One relevant issue without any clear answer remains: do sporty people actually learn to be different thanks to participation in sports or are these differences innate?

Determinants of Sports Participation

The decision to practice sports has often been investigated. There are traditionally three sets of explicative variables for sports participation: individual determinants (gender, age, marital status, number of children and health), social determinants (ethnicity and education) and economic determinants (income, worked hours, employment status). The studies highlight a positive impact of the amount of the income and the level of education on the sports practice. Conversly, the number of worked hours and the age of the individual have a negative effect. Then according to the authors, indicators about the region (Downward, 2007), about other types of leisure (Downward, 2007) and variables of interaction (Farrell and Shields, 2002) are also included in the estimations.

Humphreys and Ruseski (2009) made a double analysis: they observed people who practise sports and how long they practise it. An increase in income raises the probability of practising sports (but has no large effect on the time spent practising sports). They find a large and positive impact of the level of education on the time spent in physical activities. They assign this effect to the income effect: people who have a high educational level tend to earn more money than people with a lower educational level. Therefore people with higher educational level also have a higher opportunity cost of time. However, they spend more time doing sports which means the income effect is higher than the substitution effect (when the opportunity cost of time increases). Also sports practice is highly and not simply related to individuals' economic conditions.

This means that, on the one hand, we have to control for all the individuals' characteristics affecting sports participation and labour market integration. Healthy people, for example, are more able to practise sport and to have a standard job, whereas unhealthy people tend to be non-sporty and to get a low-quality job. Individual health is a part of human capital (which determines individual productivity), so being healthy is an advantage for being hired. The story is the same if we consider wealthy people: they have more money to spend on sports practice and they have better access to higher-quality jobs (because of their social position and network or, indirectly, thanks to the academic education they received, for example).

3.   PROBLEM AND FORMALIZED APPROACH

We are interested in sports practice as an indicator of non-cognitive skills or as a non-cognitive skills amplifier on the labour market. Therefore, our aim is to measure the effect of being sporty net of other effects, such as the increase of human capital due to health improvement or success in education (due to self-discipline and motivation). According to the literature, positive effects occur through the signalling effect, the reputation effect, the networking effect, the effect of increasing human capital, educational success, health improvement and self-selection (unobservable characteristics). Since there is already a literature on labour market success through education, we decide to leave aside this subject. This means that we control for the level of education but we focus on another effect. The reputation effect is much more common in the USA because it depends on the public image of the athlete. In Europe only athletes at national level are known to the overall population. Therefore, since we are interested in non-professional sports participation (using German data), we will not observe any effect of reputation. We focus on non-cognitive skills so we also isolate our effect from the impact of health. Consequently, the remaining effects are the signalling effect, the effect of increasing human capital, the networking effect and the effect of auto-selection.

We are not able to determine precisely which effect is operating. However, by choosing a specific individual situation on the labour market we can isolate some or part of the effects. We decide to focus our analysis on people who 'have started up with paid employment again after not having been employed for a while'.[5] We need to observe people integration on the labour market in order to capture the signalling effect. The signalling effect only matters in situations when firms cannot observe individuals' productivity. As soon as the individual works in the firm, he or she is evaluated directly on his or her work. Dealing with people who return to work is relevant because we want to discount as much as possible the impact of education. The labour market integration of people who have worked before depends at least as much on their working experience or unemployment experience as on their education level.

In this chapter we choose to focus on the quality of the job people get in t, our hypothesis becoming: sporty people have higher job quality. This quality depends on how people were looking for a job and how firms perceived them in $t - 1$. On the individuals' side, we expect sporty people to be more intense in their job search, to behave differently during the hiring interviews (to appear more motivated) and to have more connections (networking effect). On the firm's side, the most important impact comes from the signalling effect and then from the impression individuals make after the hiring interviews.

Our individuals 'have started up with paid employment again after not having been employed for a while', hence, the signals they sent out by practising sports are interpreted in a very specific way. A period of unpaid activity leads to a destruction of human capital which means a loss of individual productivity. However, one can expect that someone who did sport suffers less from this phenomenon than an 'inactive person', in two different ways. First, these people have been physically active so they are supposed to be healthier, which may increase their productivity at work and they should be absent less. Second, if they practised sports, they did it instead of another activity, which means they have a lower preference for other leisure (sleeping, hanging around, partying, and so on).

Furthermore, someone who is sporty, although whereas he is not employed, will be seen as someone who does not give up, which is a very attractive quality for firms (tenacity, perseverance). Besides sending out a positive signal, some of the sporty people actually have the expected (signalled) qualities. In this case, finding a high-quality job is a result of effort and persistence (among others things).

We assume that job quality can be determined by a set of individuals' traditional characteristics $X_{i,j}$. We take into account the past situation of each individual on the labour market (worked experience, unemployment and past household income) as well as the global situation on the labour market (year, region). $X_{i,j}$ also contains the level of education of the individual, as well as his nationality, his age and his family situation (married, number of children). We expect all these variables to have the same impact as usual. In addition, we introduce our variable of interest: *sportyi*. We assume that being sporty has a positive impact on the job quality people find, hence $\delta 1$ is positive.

$$\text{Job Quality}i = \Phi \ (sportyi, X_{i,j})$$

$$\text{Job Quality}i = \delta 0 + \delta 1 \ sportyi + \delta j \ X_{i,j} + \varepsilon i$$

As we mentioned before, we are not able to tackle the problem of unobservable characteristics (such as 'motivation') which would positively impact sports participation and labour market re-insertion. However, we choose to observe sports participation only the year before people start again to work. We have to use this information at least in $t - 1$ in order to capture the signalling effect. This way we also avoid part of the endogeneity problem: sports participation in $t - 1$ cannot be influenced by individuals' situation on the labour market (wages). Using only one point in the time as a measure of 'being sporty' allows us to work on a relative heterogeneous sample. Indeed, our sporty sample is made of regular sporty people (they are sporty each year) and occasional sporty people (they were sporty maybe only this year). Therefore, our sample is heterogeneous: we have people with unobservable characteristics positively related to labour market success (regular sporty people) and we have regular people (occasional sporty people).

As we have already explained, we do not consider that being sporty is an advantage regardless of the individuals' other characteristics. If we compare two individuals having exactly the same characteristics except for their sports activity, the sporty person has an advantage on the labour market. However, we do not know if for a different level of education, being sporty has the same impact. The question would be the same with respect to different levels of health, or income, but also with respect to the gender. Therefore, we use interaction terms in order to refine our relationship. We also add specific variables in order to control as much as possible for individuals characteristics which impact on being sporty *and* having a high-quality job. Then, as we focus our analysis on sports practice, we have to be sure that only sports participation impacts on labour market integration. If sports participation is just a way to select motivated people, for example, there is no reason why these people would not do other extracurricular activities such as music or painting. We check the robustness of our estimations by adding other extracurricular activities. Differences in the results will allow us to infer that, on the one hand, it is not just about motivation and, on the other hand, by analysing more precisely the coefficient, we will be able to precise which type of non-cognitive skills are valued.

4. DATA

We use the German Socio-Economic Panel Data (GSOEP)[6] which is a 'representative longitudinal study of private households in the entire Federal Republic of Germany'[7] from 1984 to date. One can follow the individuals during 24 years but we choose to work on the period 1991–2007 in order to have people from the united Germany. All the considerations below concern our sample, which includes only people who 'have started up with paid employment again after not having been employed for a while'. We also restrict our sample to people who are between 16 and 55 years old.

Variables of Interest: Sports Participation

Concerning the sports practice, there is only one question in the GSOEP which is asked of the whole sample:

> Which of the following activities do you take part in during your free time? Please check off how often you do each activity: at least once a week, at least once a month, less often, never.

Doing Sports Yourself

We construct a dummy (*sporty*)[8] which corresponds to 'practicing sports at least once a week' because we consider this answer as the only one qualifying sporty people. According to our definition of a sporty person, almost one-third of our sample is sporty, with a higher proportion among the youngest.

A statistical analysis by gender reveals very different sports behaviours for men and women. On average, men are sportier than women (31 per cent versus 26 per cent respectively) but each group has its own evolution with respect to individuals' age. Young men are sportier than young women (46 per cent versus 22 per cent respectively) but when people get older women are sportier (33 per cent versus 23 per cent respectively). Women's sports participation increases with age, whereas men's sports participation decreases. Obviously, men's and women's motivations to practise sports are not the same, thus we differentiate sports participation by gender. We explain men's sports participation by considering that they think of sport as leisure (that is, as a way to relax). Therefore, they enjoy practising sports which require high levels of physical capacities. As they get older their physical condition decreases and sometimes they also have more responsibilities (which means less time) and they give up on sports. For example, young men like to play football or basketball, sports that they do not appreciate in the same way when they are over 30.[9] Conversely, as women get older, they tend to practise more sports in spite of their physical capacity decreasing with age. We conclude that women choose[10] sports which help to maintain their physical condition or which help them to get back in shape (fitness for example).

Sports practice enables individuals to stay healthy, improving their productivity; however, we are interested in another transmission channel: non-cognitive skills' transmission channel. Therefore we should not retain people who are practising sports in order to keep in shape. There is no information of the type of sports people practise in the SOEP data but our statistical analysis lead us to consider that we can characterize the type of sports by gender. This is one reason to restrict our sample to men only.

Dependent Variable: Job Quality

As mentioned above we, consider only people who 'have started up with paid employment again after not having been employed for a while'. We choose to exclude women from our sample in order to lay aside the specificity of their career path. Their labour market reintegration cannot be compared to men's reintegration due to the reason for their leave and legislation. Since we already had another reason[11] to treat women separately, we decided to exclude them from our sample in this chapter. Therefore, our sample is constituted by men – coming from anywhere in Germany – who are between 16 and 55 years old, between 1991 and 2007, and who have been working again for less than a year.

As underlined by Clark et al. (2005), job quality cannot only be defined as income level per hour. It also depends on level of autonomy, on future prospects, on stress and on interpersonal relationships. Therefore, we decided to focus on two objective measures of job quality: level of autonomy and the hourly wage.

An objective measure of the level of autonomy is available in the GSOEP. It has been constructed by using accurate information about individuals' working position. It is an ordered discrete variable from 0 to 5, 0 being an apprentice. According to our research question, we decided not to take into account apprentices, so in our sample people have a level of autonomy set between 1 and 5. The distribution of the sample into these five levels is not well balanced: more than 80 per cent of the whole sample has a level of autonomy equal to 2,[12] so we aggregate the five levels in two categories. The dummy variable we obtain is equal to 0 if the level of autonomy is lower than 2 and equal to 1 if the level of autonomy is higher (equal to 3, 4 or 5). This means that we estimate the probability of having a really high level of job quality. We already observe a difference between the whole sample and the sporty sample: sporty people are almost twice more represented at higher levels of autonomy than the others.

The other job quality indicator we use is the wage people received from their main job. Since we have information on the number of months and working hours people work per week, we are able to calculate the hourly wage of each individual. We use the logarithm of this variable as dependent variable. Therefore, we can estimate a continuous variable, in opposition to our first job quality indicator (the variable of autonomy). We find a positive correlation of 0.32 (significant at a level of 1 per cent) between sport practice frequency and the dependent variable of wage.

The two variables we construct to measure job quality are, as expected, statistically positively linked to sports participation.

Independent Variables

We use a set of variables which are traditionally used in the wage equation of Mincer (1974): individuals' characteristics, indicators of the level of education and information about their situation on the labour market.

The individuals' characteristics we retain are age, nationality, marital status, number of children and region where living. The age is a discrete variable (from 17 to 55) named *Age* in our tables. For the nationality we choose to construct a dummy (*german*) which is equal to 1 if the individual is German and equal to 0 otherwise. The marital status is also a dummy variable (*married*) equal to 1 if people are married and equal to 0 otherwise. We choose to take into account only the number of children who are living in the household and who are less than 15 years old. The variable *nb children* is a discrete variable. Finally, we include the information (*West*) with respect to the region where people are living. We have to differentiate former East German from former West German because their socio-economic situations were very different in the 1990s and these differences partly remain today. As we mentioned above, individual's socio-economic characteristics does matter to labour market integration as well as to the decision to practise sport or not. Furthermore, the former East Germans were pro-professional sport but they did not focus on sports for everyone. Therefore, the availability of sports infrastructure is better in the 'West' than in the 'East'. The variable is a dummy equal to 1 if people are living in the former West Germany and equal to 0 otherwise. One-third of the people who are living in the former West Germany are sporty, whereas the proportion is one-quarter in the former East Germany. And the difference with respect to the quality of job people hold in t goes the same way: 27 per cent of the people who are living in the former West Germany have a high level of autonomy at work versus less than 20 per cent (for people who are living in the former East Germany).

The indicator of the level of education we choose is based on the high school level. It is a discrete variable equal to 1 if the individual has less education than high school level, equal to 2 if the individual has exactly the high school level and equal to 3 if he has more than the high school level. Instead of using this discrete variable, we construct three dummies (one for each level) so as to ease the interpretation. In our sample, sporty people are overrepresented at the highest level of education. The ratio of sporty people in the whole sample is one to three but it reaches almost one to two for people who have more than the high school level. This result complies with the theoretical framework.

People's position in the labour market is characterized by work experience as well as unemployment experience (discrete variables). For the work experience (*exp*), we summed the full-time work experience and the part-time work experience.

People for whom $t - 1$ was the first experience of unemployment have a higher probability to get a higher-quality job in t than people who were already unemployed several times. In order to control for individuals' history on the labour market, we introduce the variable *exp unemployment*. This is a discrete variable which is the sum of the years passed as unemployed.

To capture other parameters which could favour access to the job of higher quality, we include the logarithm of the net income the household earned in $t - 1$. This variable is a proxy of individuals' access to network and position on the labour market and in the society.

As mentioned in the literature review, the socio-economic situation of the individuals has a relevant impact on their sports participation as well as on their labour market integration. Since we are looking for an impact of sports practice through the possession of non-cognitive skills (innate or acquired), we filter out every other transmission channel. We already have a variable which reflect the level of education, and the variable *household income* allows to control for the income effect[13] and a part of the networking effect too. As we already know, health being an important factor, we add a variable on people health (*health status*). This is a discrete variable equal to 1 if people consider themselves healthy and equal to 5 if they consider themselves unhealthy.

5. RESULTS

Our objective is to measure how being sporty impacts people's job quality when they were 'unemployed' for a while. We use two correlated measures of the job quality (0.57 significant at a level of 1 per cent): the level of autonomy and the level of wage. This double estimation allows more precise and robust conclusions for at least two reasons. First, they do not measure exactly the same thing. The level of autonomy is 0 for 80 per cent of our sample which means that we estimate the probability of being one among the 20 per cent remaining. Conversely, everyone has his own level of wage and there is no barrier between people. Then, the variable of autonomy is a dummy and the variable of wage is continuous. Therefore, it allows two different specifications, meaning that we are more flexible on our hypothesis linking sports practice to job quality.

The level of autonomy is a dummy variable. Accordingly we have to use a probit model ($X_{i, t-1}$ being a vector of control variables):

$$autonomy_{i, t} = \alpha_1 + \alpha_2 X_{i, t-1} + \alpha_3 sporty_{i, t-1} + \varepsilon_{i, t} \qquad (6.1)$$

We use the logarithmic form for the hourly wage and run a simple ordinary least squares (OLS) ($X_{i, t-1}$ being a vector of control variables):

$$w_{i,t} = \beta_1 + \beta_2 X_{i,t-1} + \beta_3 sporty_{i,t-1} + \mu_{i,t} \qquad (6.2)$$

First, we estimate each of our dependent variables without any indication of sports participation. This way we test the accuracy of the variable we choose in order to explain job quality. Our outcome is an indicator of the job quality people who 'have started up with paid employment again after not having been employed for a while' have in t. This means that firms have chosen to hire them in $t - 1$. Therefore, some of the individuals' characteristics used in the estimation are the one people had in $t - 1$. Indeed we report the health status, the marital status, the household level of income, the number of children and the sports participation people have in $t - 1$. The characteristics which automatically increase for a year every year (such as age) and characteristics which are stable (such as education in our sample) are the one people have in t. The results[14] appear in Table 6.1[15] and 6.2,[16] next to the results of the estimation once sports participation (*sporty*) has been added. Both of the two estimations have a great power of explanation of the job quality. The traditional variables have the expected impact when they are significant. And the most important effect is due to the same two variables: *west* and *education: more than high school*. People substantially increase their chance to get a high-quality job[17] if they have a level of education higher than the high school level and if they live in the former West Germany. However, we are already able to confirm that the two job quality indicators do not exactly reflect the same idea. Wage variations are closely related to labour market indicators, whereas the level of autonomy depends widely on individuals' characteristics. Other variables do matter, but in a smaller proportion.

In a second step we add our indicator of sports participation *sporty* (columns 2 and 3 of the tables). To control for the impact of sports participation on job quality through the channel of the health, we add simultaneously an indicator of individuals' health status. In both estimations, the impact of the traditional variables is quite stable except with respect to the level of education. Education lost some of its importance, which can be explained by the duality of skills it used to represent before the addition of an extracurricular activity. Also, the probability of having a high level of autonomy at work is now independent from the household income. As expected, we observe an upward relationship between being sporty and our indicators of job quality. Being sporty raises the hourly wage by 8.3 per cent and increases the probability of having a higher-quality job by 1.1 point of percentage. Being healthy also positively affects job quality, and in almost the same proportion than being sporty. The fact that both estimations have a higher power of explanation and that the variables *health*

Table 6.1   Effect of sports practice on the hourly wage

	Hourly wage		
	(1)	(2)	(3)
Being sporty		0.083	−0.103
		(2.67)***	(1.36)
Being sporty & HS			0.221
			(2.03)**
Being sporty & sup HS			0.207
			(1.46)
Age	−0.002	0.002	0.003
	(0.37)	(0.42)	(0.44)
West Germany	0.377	0.376	0.373
	(12.84)***	(11.87)***	(11.77)***
German	0.051	0.061	0.055
	(1.24)	(1.39)	(1.27)
Married	0.086	0.094	0.096
	(2.59)***	(2.60)***	(2.67)***
Nb of children	−0.023	−0.022	−0.021
	(1.30)	(1.19)	(1.15)
Education: high school (HS)	0.112	0.082	0.028
	(2.74)***	(1.92)*	(0.55)
Education: more than high school (sup HS)	0.378	0.325	0.274
	(5.55)***	(4.42)***	(2.75)***
Experience	0.027	0.028	0.027
	(3.51)***	(3.30)***	(3.15)***
Experience squared	−0.001	−0.001	−0.001
	(4.09)***	(4.17)***	(4.00)***
Exp unemployment	−0.015	−0.022	−0.024
	(1.69)*	(2.22)**	(2.43)**
Household income	0.078	0.061	0.059
	(3.42)***	(2.37)**	(2.29)**
Health: bad		−0.034	−0.039
		(0.61)	(0.70)
Health: good		0.064	0.054
		(1.84)*	(1.52)
Constant	0.955	0.927	1.003
	(3.41)***	(2.94)***	(3.17)***
Observations	5088	4933	4933
R-squared	0.38	0.41	0.41

Notes: Robust z statistics in parentheses.
* Significant at 10 per cent; ** significant at 5 per cent; *** significant at 1 per cent.

Table 6.2   Effect of sports practice on autonomy at work

	Autonomy		
	(A1)	(A2)	(A3)
Being sporty		0.011	−0.002
		(2.03)**	(0.14)
Being sporty & HS			0.017
			(0.034)
Being sporty & sup HS			0.013
			(0.024)
Age	0.004	0.003	0.003
	(4.15)***	(4.11)***	(4.10)***
West Germany	0.167	0.166	0.165
	(11.63)***	(11.31)***	(11.29)***
German	0.021	0.017	0.017
	(4.26)***	(4.12)***	(4.19)***
Married	0.031	0.027	0.027
	(3.87)***	(3.56)***	(3.62)***
Nb of children	−0.011	−0.009	−0.009
	(3.12)***	(2.74)***	(2.72)***
Education: high school (HS)	0.014	0.011	0.008
	(2.56)**	(2.22)**	(1.27)
Education: more than high school (sup HS)	0.394	0.336	0.315
	(9.52)***	(8.38)***	(6.49)***
Experience	−0.001	−0.000	−0.000
	(0.84)	(0.24)	(0.24)
Experience squared	−0.000	−0.000	−0.000
	(2.56)**	(2.70)***	(2.68)***
Exp unemployment	−0.013	−0.012	−0.012
	(7.15)***	(6.75)***	(6.74)***
Household income	0.011	0.007	0.007
	(2.35)**	(1.57)	(1.57)
Health: bad		0.001	0.001
		(0.13)	(0.11)
Health: good		0.012	0.012
		(1.93)*	(1.86)*
Observations	5498	5288	5288
(pseudo) R-squared	0.47	0.49	0.49

Notes: Robust z statistics in parentheses.
* Significant at 10 per cent; ** significant at 5 per cent; *** significant at 1 per cent.

and *sporty* are significant and positive allows us to consider that sports practice does have an impact on job quality even once we have controlled for health.

As we have already outlined, sports practice is not supposed to be an advantage whatever the individuals' characteristics are. The positive impact of being sporty should depend on level of education. Firms would not grant non-cognitive skills to someone who cannot give proof of cognitive skills. We include a term of interaction between the level of education and the sports characteristics. The results are interesting: being sporty does not have an impact unless individuals have a level of education equal to high school. However, being sporty and having high school level education increases the hourly wage by 22 per cent, these characteristics are complementary. This means that being sporty only matters for people who have the high school level; it does not have any impact for the others. With respect to the probability of having a high level of autonomy at work, the addition of the interaction term cancels out any effect of being sporty. This result is quite coherent with our previous results because our estimation is, 'which is the probability to find a job with a very high level of autonomy?' We found earlier that being sporty has an effect only for people who have a level of education equal to the high school level. People who have continued their studies do not need sports participation to get higher wages in our specific situation. These people are the ones who could reach positions with a high level of autonomy. Therefore, the most important characteristics people should have in order to get a high-quality job are the traditional ones. At that level and just after having been unemployed for a while, being sporty (as we defined it) is not relevant.

Signal influences hiring decisions when firms cannot base their judgement on individuals' work experience and productive value. Therefore, we would expect a lesser effect of sports participation for people who already have ten years of work experience than for people who have only one year of work experience. We introduce an interaction term between sports participation and years of work experience in order to test this hypothesis. The addition of this term does not change the previous results. The interaction term is not significant and being sporty only has a significant effect if the individual has exactly the high school level. There is no relation of synergy or substitution between being sporty and the number of years of work experience. The addition of an interaction terms between sports participation and health status is not relevant: the coefficient stays the same as well as if we add an interaction term between *age* and *sporty*. Also, older people who are sporty do not send any specific signal to the employers, as we could expect.

Finally, we demonstrate that the positive effect of sports participation does not result from the fact that people are participating in some extracurricular activity. The successive addition of others activities such as artistic activities, political commitment or working as a volunteer in an association allows us to observe the robustness of our effect. We previously defined each involvement as we defined sports involvement, which means we consider only people who say they take part in the activity at least once a week during the year before they found their job.[18] We observe (statistically) that people who are sporty tend to have more extracurricular activities than the others. Therefore, their particularity could be that they get more involved than the others. This characteristic can be accorded to a lot of other extracurricular activities, and it is relevant here as to precisely why sporty people are preferred.

The results appear in Table 6.3. The information about the participation of artistic activities is available only for three waves, which explains the substantial reduction of the sample. But this activity does not have any impact on the hourly wage. This is also the case for people who are volunteer workers. This result is very surprising because we expected a high positive impact. It is well known that firms value personal commitment. However, our individuals did not have any paid activities in $t - 1$ and it might be that firms consider that volunteer work is too far from 'paid work'. Participating in political activities has a considerable negative impact. One explanation is that firms consider that political activists protest too much to have access to high-quality jobs. They are expected to cause trouble within the firm. With respect to the level of autonomy, participating in an artistic activity increases the probability of having a high level of autonomy at work from 0.028. This impact is greater than the one obtained from being sporty but it does not cancel it out. Practising artistic activities is a plus. However, as we already notice, the sample is twice smaller, which moderates the interpretation. The other extracurricular activities do not have any significant effect on the level of autonomy.

6.   CONCLUSION

Our aim was to measure the impact of sports participation on the job quality of people who came back to work for less than a year. We found a positive effect on both of our job quality indicators after having controlled for individuals' health and wealth. Furthermore, the introduction of other extracurricular activities (even 'being a volunteer worker') does not weaken our results. Therefore, we are able to say that the effect we found cannot be accorded to any other extracurricular activity.

Table 6.3   Robustness checks of the effect of sports practice on the hourly wage and on autonomy at work

	Hourly wage			Autonomy		
Being sporty	0.090	0.087	0.082	0.011	0.011	0.013
	(1.74)*	(2.80)***	(2.62)***	(1.86)*	(2.03)**	(2.19)**
Age	−0.006	0.003	0.002	0.002	0.003	0.003
	(0.57)	(0.56)	(0.30)	(2.04)**	(4.04)***	(3.98)***
West Germany	0.326	0.373	0.373	0.087	0.163	0.162
	(6.42)***	(11.79)***	(11.04)***	(6.11)***	(11.18)***	(10.92)***
German	0.144	0.062	0.061	0.006	0.017	0.017
	(1.50)	(1.41)	(1.37)	(0.91)	(4.11)***	(4.00)***
Married	0.071	0.100	0.099	0.040	0.027	0.027
	(1.14)	(2.77)***	(2.74)***	(3.29)***	(3.63)***	(3.64)***
Nb of children	−0.033	−0.023	−0.024	−0.015	−0.009	−0.009
	(1.03)	(1.25)	(1.24)	(3.79)***	(2.83)***	(2.79)***
Education: high school	0.020	0.080	0.076	0.008	0.011	0.012
	(0.21)	(1.87)*	(1.76)*	(1.44)	(2.15)**	(2.45)**
Education: more than high school	0.370	0.320	0.325	0.230	0.329	0.348
	(2.63)***	(4.32)***	(4.40)***	(4.46)***	(8.22)***	(8.49)***
Experience	0.034	0.026	0.029	0.000	−0.000	−0.000
	(2.11)**	(3.15)***	(3.41)***	(0.33)	(0.17)	(0.07)
Experience squared	−0.001	−0.001	−0.001	−0.000	−0.000	−0.000
	(1.63)	(4.20)***	(4.28)***	(1.53)	(2.74)***	(2.77)***
Exp unemployment	−0.019	−0.023	−0.022	−0.009	−0.011	−0.011
	(1.22)	(2.35)**	(2.20)**	(4.58)***	(6.67)***	(6.56)***
Household income	0.084	0.062	0.059	−0.001	0.006	0.006
	(1.98)**	(2.39)**	(2.27)**	(0.23)	(1.49)	(1.47)
Health: bad	0.075	−0.025	−0.035	0.002	0.000	0.002
	(0.63)	(0.45)	(0.62)	(0.17)	(0.03)	(0.16)
Health: good	0.032	0.066	0.062	−0.003	0.012	0.012
	(0.55)	(1.89)*	(1.76)*	(0.56)	(1.89)*	(1.93)*
Artistic activity	0.008			0.028		
	(0.08)			(1.87)*		
Political activity		−0.482			0.055	
		(2.90)***			(1.09)	
Volunteer worker			0.009			−0.004
			(0.18)			(0.61)
Constant	0.809	0.907	0.761			
	(1.51)	(2.86)***	(2.45)**			
Observations	2327	4926	4924	2455	5280	5275
(pseudo) R-squared	0.37	0.41	0.41	0.54	0.49	0.49

Notes: Robust t-statistics in parentheses.
* Significant at 10 per cent; ** significant at 5 per cent; *** significant at 1 per cent.

Our analysis is more accurate with respect to the impact on the hourly wage. Being sporty is relevant only for men who have completed high school (neither more, nor less) and these men need to be sporty in order to value their educational level. Sports participation and high school level are complementary. Therefore, men who have this specific level of education should be encouraged to practise sports in order to better integrate themselves into the labour market. Furthermore, owing to their level of education, they will not benefit from a large career evolution. Consequently, it is really important for them to integrate into the labour market at the highest level they can. The results concerning the level of autonomy are less impressive. But as we have already mentioned, people who reach a high level of autonomy (after having been unemployed for a while) may have much more than sports participation to signal.

Age, health status or work experience do not have more impact than the traditional characteristics whether the individual is sporty or not. There is no effect of synergy or of substitution.

As expected, practising sports has a positive effect on the individuals' labour market reintegration because it is associated with non-cognitive skills. Our variable is defined only on the sports participation people had the year before their labour market reintegration. This means that we are sure to catch the signalling effect in our results. However, we cannot infer that everyone should be sporty because we do not know by which other mechanisms the effect occurs. Part of the reason is that people behave differently; thus, we still have to determine if they do so because of their sports practice or because they are different from the beginning.

We already have several subjects for further research. First, we have to replicate our analysis on a sample of women. We would take into account their very specific career path and their sports participation. Second, it would be interesting to find out if sports participation (and for how long[19]) reduces the job search duration. Third, since we observe only people who were out of the labour market for a while, we underestimate the impact of sports participation on labour market outcomes. People who are working 'for a while'[20] are more likely to be sporty than the others (because of their wages, among other things) and they have a greater position on the labour market. Therefore, we should also analyse the impact of being sporty on a sample of regular workers.

NOTES

*   We thank Wladimir Andreff, the participants of the V Gijon Conference on Sports Economics and Thomas Barré for helpful comments and discussions.

1. The General Educational Development Testing Program is 'a second-chance program that administers a battery of cognitive tests to self-selected high-school dropouts to determine whether or not they are the academic equivalents of high-school graduates', Heckman and Rubinstein (2001: 146).
2. If the infrastructures are available.
3. National Collegiate Athletics Association, High School and Beyond, National Education Longitudinal Survey and National Longitudinal Surveys of Youth.
4. This explanation is the same as that suggested by Ewing (1998).
5. This is the expression as used in the survey.
6. The data used in the presentation were extracted using the Add-On package PanelWhiz v2.0 (November 2007) for Stata. PanelWhiz was written by Dr John P. Haisken-DeNew (john@panelwhiz.eu). The PanelWhiz generated DO files to retrieve the SOEP data used here and any Panelwhiz Plugins are available upon request. Any data or computational errors in this paper are my own. Haisken-DeNew and Hahn (2006) describe PanelWhiz in detail.
7. http://www.diw.de/english/soep/soepoverview/27908.html (accessed May 2009).
8. Descriptive statistics for all the variables we use are presented in Table 6A.1 in the Appendix.
9. Because of a lack of time and physical condition.
10. Or, as we already mentioned, 'have to choose' because the supply is limited.
11. We observe significant differences by gender in sports participation.
12. This is perfectly normal considering that we only have people who came back to work for less than a year.
13. Wealthier people have a better access to extracurricular activities such as sports.
14. The statistical and econometric work has been done by using STATA and PanelWhiz.
15. Each estimation contains a dummy for each year in order to control for the economic conjuncture but it does not appear in the table of results for lack of clarity.
16. The coefficients which appear for the probit estimation are the marginal effects.
17. With respect to our criteria: hourly wage and level of autonomy at work.
18. The question is the same as the one about sports participation; we only have information on the frequency.
19. Is perseverance in being sporty rewarded?
20. In opposition to people who have been unemployed 'for a while'.

REFERENCES

Anderson, D.J. (2001), '"If you let me play": the effects of participation in high school athletics on students' educational and analyse market success', University of Arizona, working paper.

Barron, J., Ewing, B. and Waddell, G. (2000), 'The effects of high school athletic participation on education and labor market outcomes', *Review of Economics and Statistics*, **82**, 409–21.

Becker, G. (1964), *Human Capital: A Theoretical and Empirical Analysis with Special Reference to Education*, New York: Columbia University Press.

Clark, A., Bazen, S., Lucifora, C. and Salverda, W. (2005), 'What makes a good job? Evidence from OECD countries', in S. Bazen, C. Lucifora and W. Salverda (eds), *Job Quality and Employer Behaviour*, Basingstoke, UK: Palgrave Macmillan, pp. 11–30.

Downward, P. (2007), 'Exploring the economic choice to participate in sport: results from the 2002 General Household Survey', *International Review of Applied Economics*, **21** (5), 633–53.

Eber, N. (2002), 'La pratique sportive comme facteur de capital humain', *Revue juridique et économique du sport*, **65**, 55–68.

Ewing, B. (1998), 'Athletes and work', *Economics Letters*, **59**, 113–17.

Farrell, L. and Shields, M.A. (2002), 'Investigating the economic and demographic determinants of sporting participation in England', *Journal of Royal Statistics Society*, **165** (2), 335–48.

Haisken-DeNew, J.P. and Hahn, M. (2006), 'PanelWhiz: a flexible modularized stata interface for accessing large scale panel data sets', mimeo, available at: www.panelwhiz.eu (accessed May 2009).

Heckman, J.J. (2000), 'Policies to foster human capital', *Research in Economics*, **54** (1), 3–56.

Heckman, J.J. and Rubinstein, Y. (2001), 'The importance of noncognitive skills: lessons from the GED Program', *The American Economic Review*, **91** (2), 145–9.

Humphreys, B.R. and Ruseski, J.E. (2009), 'The economics of participation and time spent in physical activity', University of Alberta working paper No. 2009-09.

Jacob, B.A. (2002), 'Where the boys aren't: non-cognitive skills, returns to school and the gender gap in higher education', *Economics of Education Review*, **21**, 586–98.

Lechner, M. (2009), 'Long-run labour market and health effects of individual sports activities', *Journal of Health Economics*, **28** (4), 839–54.

Long, J. and Caudill, S. (1991), 'The impact of participation in intercollegiate athletics on income and graduation', *Review of Economics and Statistics*, **73**, 525–31.

Mincer, J. (1974), *Schooling, Experience, and Earnings*, New York: NBER Press.

Pfeifer, C. and Cornelißen, T. (2010), 'The impact of participation in sports on educational attainment: new evidence from Germany', *Economics of Education Review*, **29** (1), 94–103.

Rooth, D.-O. (2010), 'Work out or out of work: the labor market return to physical fitness and leisure sport activities', IZA Discussion Paper No. 4684.

Spence, A.M. (1973), 'Job market signaling', *Quarterly Journal of Economics*, **87** (3), 355–74.

APPENDIX

Table 6A.1   Summary statistics

Variable	Obs	Mean	Std. dev.	Min.	Max.
Wage	6312	2.06754	.4590483	−.465925	4.778326
Autonomy	6823	0.2164737	0.411871	0	1
Age	6823	37.2666	9.810474	17	55
West	6823	0.2386047	0.4262618	0	1
german	6822	0.9413662	0.2349553	0	1
married	5556	0.287977	0.4528611	0	1
nb children	5593	0.6754872	0.8449134	0	5
educ_HS	6753	2.108989	0.4843193	1	3
sporty	5422	0.2760974	0.4471068	0	1
exp	6784	13.32552	10.07519	0	37.2
exp²	6784	279.0638	345.1539	0	1383.84
exp unemployment	6784	1.075059	1.587119	0	20.3
household income	5591	10.23373	0.5099638	4.339771	12.88173
health status	5475	2.791416	0.8375326	1	5
year	6823	2002.079	4.287573	1994	2007

Source: GSOEP author calculation.

Table 6A.2   Summary statistics with respect to the level of education

Education	Freq.	Percentage	Cum.
less than high school	464	6.87	6.87
high school	5089	75.36	82.23
more than high school	12	17.77	100.00
Total	6753	100.00	

Source: GSOEP author calculation.

Table 6A.3   Sample year distribution

Years	Freq.	Percentage	Cum.
1994	93	1.36	1.36
1995	1075	15.76	17.12
1996	95	1.39	18.51
1997	91	1.33	19.84
1998	137	2.01	21.85
1999	119	1.74	23.60
2000	1146	16.80	40.39
2001	174	2.55	42.94
2002	158	2.32	45.26
2003	161	2.36	47.62
2004	1124	16.47	64.09
2005	158	2.32	66.41
2006	1141	16.72	83.13
2007	1151	16.87	100.00
Total	6823	100.00	

Source: GSOEP author calculation.

7. Team success, productivity and economic impact

Michael C. Davis and Christian M. End

1. INTRODUCTION

Professional football in the United States is a big-time leisure activity with millions of fans fervently anticipating the games of their favorite teams every Sunday in the fall. Unlike the other quintessential American game, baseball, which is described as a marathon with the possibility of redemption the next day, each football game is seemingly the 'most important game of the year' with fans forced to wait a week before their favorite teams compete again. The win and/or conversations highlighting the previous victory may induce an emotional high that could make getting through the following workweek tolerable, and maybe even pleasant. Perhaps even an increase in productivity at work could follow a win the proceeding weekend? This chapter hopes to show a link between the success of the local National Football League (NFL) team and worker productivity in the local metropolitan area.

It is possible that simply being the hometown of the NFL team is beneficial. However, the economics literature has extensively shown that the construction of stadiums, the presence of teams or the hosting of major events does not have a positive impact on the local economies (see Coates and Humphreys, 2008, for a comprehensive summary). Examining those papers specifically related to football, Baade and Dye (1990), Coates and Humphreys (1999, 2001) and Gius and Johnson (2001) found little evidence in support of a positive effect of having an NFL team in the city on the per capita income of the cities. Lertwachara and Cochrane (2007) found that the entrance of an NFL team into a metropolitan area does not have a positive impact on income. Miller (2002) found that the construction of the Trans World Dome, primarily for the NFL St. Louis Rams, had no significant impact on construction employment in St. Louis. Coates and Humphreys (2008) and Matheson (2008) summarized the major findings that mega events also have little impact on the local economies. The major mega event associated with the NFL is the Super Bowl.

151

Studies have shown no discernable impact of hosting the Super Bowl on the local economy for either income (Baade and Matheson, 2006; Coates and Humphreys, 2002) or employment (Baade and Matheson, 2000). Studies of taxes have generally found no impact of hosting the Super Bowl (Baade et al., 2008; Porter, 1999), though Coates (2007) did find a positive impact for Houston's tax receipts after the 2004 Super Bowl. Baumann et al. (2009) found a fairly negligible impact (equivalent to 8000 additional people) on tourism in Hawaii of hosting the Pro Bowl, the NFL's all-star game at the end of the season.

While the evidence in favor of an economic impact directly from the sport is minimal, that does not mean that sports are unrelated to a city's overall well-being. There is a reason that the newspaper, *USA Today*, has one of its four sections devoted to sports. This finding is particularly true of football in the United States. Fenn and Crooker (2008), using contingent valuation methodology, found a point estimate of a value of $756 million to Minnesotans of having the Vikings in the Minneapolis area. Carlino and Coulson (2004, 2006) using hedonic wage modeling found that people are willing to pay more to live in cities with NFL franchises. While Johnson et al. (2007) found a lower expected contingent value for the Jacksonville Jaguars and Coates et al. (2006) offered a compelling critique of Carlino and Coulson, there is substantial evidence that football is important to many Americans.

Fans' interest in football suggests another direction to explain the impact that sports have on the local economies of cities with teams. Davis and End (2010) and Coates and Humphreys (2002) suggest that the improved mood of the fans of winning teams may increase the income of the local economies associated with those teams. Both studies test for an impact across the NFL, National Basketball Association (NBA) and Major League Baseball (MLB) but only find the effect is important for the NFL. Coates and Humphreys found evidence of a higher income for cities with Super Bowl winning teams, while Matheson (2006) showed evidence contradicting the results in their paper. Davis and End (2010) extended the results to an examination of winning percentage.

This chapter plans to extend Davis and End (2010) to address a couple of minor limitations of that paper. Davis and End suggest, and support with evidence from psychological studies, two theoretical processes that could account for the impact of team success on economic activity. In both cases the team success leads to an improvement in mood of the fans. The first explanation is that improved mood leads fans to spend more. The second explanation speculates that economic gains are the result of an increase in productivity at work, again stimulated by mood gains. We will focus more closely on the productivity explanation by making use of studies in economics, organization theory and psychology. While we will not develop a formal model of the impact of team success on personal income, we will show a more complete process of the steps by which the logical progression from winning to higher income would proceed.

Another critique of Davis and End is the inclusion of many sports related variables including winning parentages, stadium size, team entrance and departure for the NBA, NFL and MLB. While the inclusion of so many variables in the model does not necessarily bias the results, it does add difficulty to the task of trying to disentangle the actual importance of having a football team and the winning percentage of that team. This chapter will only focus on the winning percentages of the NFL teams. One additional change will be to update the data more to the present, extending the data set from 2001 to 2007.

2. THEORETICAL BASIS

Multiple explanations for how improvements in mood might account for increases in productivity and, ultimately, to higher incomes exist. Staw et al. (1994) suggest three ways that improved mood could lead to higher worker productivity: greater self-motivation, greater responsiveness to co-workers, and greater responsiveness of co-workers to the employee. Tsai et al. (2007) found evidence that improved mood led to higher worker productivity through an increased likelihood of helping co-workers and from greater task persistence. While the greater individual production through increased effort and being more diligent at work is just as important, we will only detail the relationship between mood and cooperation in the workplace, the latter two effects listed above.

Coffey et al. (2009) suggest that sports could affect productivity, through greater interaction at work with colleagues. While they referred mostly to the effect of people just talking with each other at work in general, even if the conversation was simply about the game, it is possible that colleagues' improved moods (post-victory) may be the source of the greater interaction and eventual productivity.

The path of the logic is that the team success leads to an improvement in mood, which leads to greater social interaction and cooperation among employees. The interaction and cooperation between employees leads to an increase in productivity, ultimately leading to greater output and income. A single study showing the full range of this development would be quite daunting. However, empirical support for the individual steps of this process has been found by researchers across a number of disciplines.

Psychologists have shown that there is a positive relationship between team success and fan mood (Hirt et al., 1992; Wann and Branscombe, 1992; Wann et al., 1994) and a relationship between improved mood and workplace cooperation (Hertel et al., 2000). There is also literature showing that there is an association between mood and productivity, specifically through increased social interactions (Tsai et al., 2007). Lastly, there has been a considerable amount of interest in the economic literature about the link between productivity and output or income (Kydland and Prescott, 1982; Solow 1956).

Inferring causation from the results summarized above can be problematic due to what is commonly known as 'the directionality problem', as well as the presence of confounding variables. For example, the correlation between mood and productivity may be spurious as an increase in happiness because of team success may also limit productivity because it also causes a distraction in the workplace. It would therefore be optimal if we could find the links between the earlier effects, like mood, and the later outcomes, like productivity. For instance, the economics literature has shown a link between team success and productivity (Coffey et al., 2009) and team success and income (Coates and Humphreys, 2002; Davis and End, 2010). There are a number of studies from the psychology literature (Hertel et al., 2000; Tsai et al., 2007), and more recently economics (Oswald et al., 2009), showing a link between improved mood and productivity. Economists have studied the relationship between cooperation and economic output (for instance Francois and Zabojnik, 2005), though most of this literature examines long-term social capital formation which is not particularly applicable to the short-term effects associated with year-to-year changes in NFL team success. There has been considerable study of the relationship between economic output and happiness (see Frey and Stutzer, 2002, for a survey) but almost all of the analysis is based on output increases leading to greater happiness and not the reverse ('the directionality problem'). As far as the authors know, there are no studies specifically examining the relationship between sport team success and cooperation in the workplace. However, in a study of a different type of cooperation, End et al. (2009) have shown that romantic partners of sports fans report less enjoyment interacting with their partners after a loss by a favorite team. Additionally, End (2001) found that fans of teams communicate with each other on the Internet more after a victory than a loss, though that result might suggest less workplace productivity rather than more if the surfing is taking place at work.

3.　DATA

The per capita personal income and population come from the Bureau of Economic Activity website (bea.gov). The first dependent variable is the per capita personal income deflated by the CPI (RPCPI). The second is the growth rate of the real per capita personal income (RPCPIG). The winning percentage data comes from Rod Fort's website (www.rodneyfort.com).

We have two sets of data. The first uses the general metropolitan statistical areas (MSAs) for the 50 largest metropolitan areas in the country. The second approach uses the metropolitan divisions for the cities for which those are available and the MSAs for the others. In this sample we include every city that had a MLB, NBA, NFL or National Hockey League (NHL) team during the sample period. These two approaches roughly correspond to the approaches of Matheson (2006) and Coates and Humphreys (2002) as described in Davis and End (2010). The advantages of the first approach are that it is less ad hoc and keeps all of the metropolitan area definitions the same. For the second, it actually looks at the relevant possible markets for the NFL (those with a major-league team) and includes more NFL winning percentage data (by separating the 49ers from the Raiders in the San Francisco Bay Area and including the Green Bay Packers).

The intent of this study is to keep the model as reduced-form as possible, so we limit the number of additional variables that are included. Yearly dummy variables are necessary to account for the national economy in a given year. We also include individual city time trends and the population growth of the city. Many of the control variables for special non-sports occurrences as suggested by Matheson (2006) are excluded. However, there are two events in recent years that had such strong effects on the local economy of a region that their inclusion is absolutely necessary. The technology boom in the San-Francisco Bay Area caused a large spike in incomes in 1999 and 2000, and Hurricane Katrina in 2005 caused a large drop in incomes in New Orleans. Six dummy variables are included to account for these two events (see Table 7.1).

4.　METHODOLOGY

We estimate the following panel model:

$$y_{it} = \alpha + y_{i,t-1}\gamma + x_{it}\beta_i + \eta_i + \varepsilon_{it} \qquad (7.1)$$

Table 7.1   Indicator variables for key events

Indicator variable	Cities	Year
Tech Boom 1	San Francisco, San Jose	1999
Tech Boom 2	San Francisco, San Jose	2000
Tech Bust 1	San Francisco, San Jose	2001
Tech Bust 2	San Francisco, San Jose	2002
Katrina 1	New Orleans	2005
Katrina 2	New Orleans	2006

where x_{it} is a series of explanatory variables that are included in the model and y_{it} is the real per capita income for each city i in year t. The explanatory variables in the model are the ones mentioned in the section on data. The lagged dependent variable is included if the dependent variable is RPCPI but not if it is RPCPIG, since the latter is a growth rate.

The inclusion of the lagged dependent variable makes the model a dynamic panel model. Davis and End (2010) dealt with this problem by using the methodology of Arellano and Bond (1991). However, Judson and Owen (1999) have shown that the bias associated with a dynamic panel decreases with increases in the amount of data along the time dimension. Since we have an additional nine years of data, the bias should have been reduced, and the gains from using a more complicated methodology lessened.

5.   RESULTS

The results for the first data sample, the one with the 50-largest MSAs, can be found in Table 7.2. The first two columns show a negligible impact of an NFL team winning on RPCPI and RPCPIG. This result is quite different from the finding of Davis and End (2010). There are three possibilities for the discrepancy: a diminishing of the effect; a change due to the reduced-form model; or a change in the data from the BEA. To examine this first possibility, we re-estimate the model using only the data through 1998 (the same as the Davis and End data sample). We find that the winning effect does seem to exist with the shorter data set, suggesting that, according to this sample, the effect has dissipated over the last decade.

The results from the second data sample, which only includes the major-league cities and uses the smallest divisions of those metropolitan areas can be found in Table 7.3. These results show a much stronger effect for

Table 7.2   50 largest metropolitan area data

Dependent variable	RPCPI	RPCPIG	RPCPI	RPCPIG
Years	1970–2007	1970–2007	1970–98	1970–98
RPCPI (−1)	0.864***	NA	0.827***	NA
	(0.013)		(0.014)	
NFL	−29.07	−0.00212	−70.35*	−0.00467
	(38.85)	(0.00256)	(39.57)	(0.00300)
NFL Win %	11.39	0.00273	74.78*	0.00686**
	(41.24)	(0.00279)	(43.52)	(0.00329)
Population	4893.03***	0.105**	5513.44***	0.0871*
growth	(711.77)	(0.0437)	(709.36)	(0.0488)
Katrina 1	−6904.43***	−0.420***	NA	NA
	(238.66)	(0.0157)		
Katrina 2	11137.01***	1.166***	NA	NA
	(293.87)	(0.0192)		
Tech Boom 1	1216.82***	0.049***	NA	NA
	(167.10)	(0.0110)		
Tech Boom 2	3181.99***	0.109***	NA	NA
	(168.72)	(0.0110)		
Tech Bust 1	−1884.61***	−0.0817***	NA	NA
	(178.69)	(0.0111)		
Tech Bust 2	−1555.28***	−0.0663***	NA	NA
	(172.27)	(0.0111)		
Constant	1473.69***	0.00676**	1903.15***	0.00840***
	(138.31)	(0.00251)	(155.88)	(0.00264)

Notes: Standard errors in parentheses.
*** Significant at 1 per cent level, ** significant at 5 per cent level and * significant at 10 per cent level.
Variables for the year and individual city time trends are not shown.

winning on RPCPI and RPCPIG, but even here the results are weaker than for the earlier sample used by Davis and End.

The decrease in the effect can be explained by either a diminishing of the importance of winning on the economic outcomes or by the inclusion of more data eliminating a false-positive. However, one other possibility is that the economic situation of the country changed in such a way that the NFL winning percentage effects are being overwhelmed by more important and unaccounted for economic impacts. We attempted to account for Hurricane Katrina and the Tech Boom and Bust, but a simple examination of the data from the last decade shows a considerable amount of fluctuation in incomes in cities with a high degree of influence from technology

Table 7.3   Metropolitan areas with an NBA, NFL or MLB team

Dependent variable	RPCPI	RPCPIG	RPCPI	RPCPIG
Years	1970–2007	1970–2007	1970–98	1970–98
RPCPI (−1)	0.895***	NA	0.835***	NA
	(0.013)		(0.015)	
NFL	−26.17	−0.00337	−54.05	−0.00530**
	(35.69)	(0.00224)	(35.91)	(0.00262)
NFL Win %	43.87	0.00506*	110.33**	0.00879***
	(42.21)	(0.00265)	(42.73)	(0.00312)
Population growth	5120.54***	0.179***	5717.01***	0.154***
	(830.43)	(0.0503)	(825.17)	(0.0574)
Katrina 1	−6876.09***	−0.417***	NA	NA
	(248.99)	(0.0157)		
Katrina 2	11367.06***	1.183***	NA	NA
	(323.56)	(0.0203)		
Tech Boom 1	1512.59***	0.057***	NA	NA
	(174.76)	(0.0110)		
Tech Boom 2	3459.09***	0.110***	NA	NA
	(177.17)	(0.0110)		
Tech Bust 1	−2290.01***	−0.0861***	NA	NA
	(190.48)	(0.0111)		
Tech Bust 2	−2040.14***	−0.0740***	NA	NA
	(181.48)	(0.0111)		
Constant	1157.94***	0.00665***	1834.73***	0.00817***
	(144.07)	(0.00264)	(163.20)	(0.00277)

Notes: Standard errors in parentheses.
*** Significant at 1 per cent level, ** significant at 5 per cent level and * significant at 10 per cent level.
Variables for the year and individual city time trends are not shown.

sectors. Since there is no good way to account for a whole decade of fluctuations, we re-estimate the model excluding the three metropolitan areas that seem to have been influenced the most: San Francisco, San Jose and Seattle. The results for the same models as in Table 7.3 are presented in Table 7.4. The results are striking. There is a substantial increase in the importance of winning percentage across the entire sample compared to when those three cities are included, and the winning percentage variable in the RPCPI regression becomes significant. When compared to the earlier sample, the winning percentage still seems to have lost some of its strength, but the loss is not as great as compared to the case when the technology sector is included.

Table 7.4   *Metropolitan areas with a NBA, NFL or MLB team excluding San Francisco, San Jose and Seattle*

Dependent variable	RPCPI	RPCPIG	RPCPI	RPCPIG
Years	1970–2007	1970–2007	1970–98	1970–98
RPCPI (−1)	0.891***	NA	0.842***	NA
	(0.013)		(0.014)	
NFL	−36.35	−0.00402*	−53.78	−0.00570**
	(33.64)	(0.00224)	(41.58)	(0.00265)
NFL Win %	82.25**	0.00622**	120.33***	0.00991***
	(40.09)	(0.00268)	(41.58)	(0.00317)
Population	5196.31***	0.169***	5731.73***	0.155***
growth	(797.94)	(0.0506)	(808.62)	(0.0586)
Katrina 1	−6861.38***	−0.417***	NA	NA
	(226.94)	(0.0152)		
Katrina 2	11390.07***	1.181***	NA	NA
	(299.11)	(0.0199)		
Tech Boom 1	NA	NA	NA	NA
Tech Boom 2	NA	NA	NA	NA
Tech Bust 1	NA	NA	NA	NA
Tech Bust 2	NA	NA	NA	NA
Constant	1199.86***	0.00839***	1743.18***	0.00961***
	(139.93)	(0.00267)	(155.59)	(0.00284)

Notes: Standard errors in parentheses.
*** Significant at 1 per cent level, ** significant at 5 per cent level and * significant at 10 per cent level.
Variables for the year and individual city time trends are not shown.

6.   CONCLUSION

The results here are not as definitive in finding a relationship between NFL team success and income of the local metropolitan area as the results in Davis and End (2010). However, there is some support for the hypothesis, depending on which model is valid. If they all showed the same effect, it would not be important to distinguish between them, but since they are different we will attempt to determine the most correct model. The more restrictive version of what constitutes the metropolitan area may be the correct model to use because psychologists have shown that many of the psychological advantages associated with being a sports fan are only for those fans of local teams (Wann, 2006). Therefore, we would only want those areas that are strongly associated with a particular NFL team to be included. The geographically larger metropolitan areas may start to extend out of the local team's fan base. This particular problem would be particularly acute when San Francisco and Oakland are combined in one metropolitan area as they are in the 50-largest metropolitan area sample.

Additional work should examine the time-series aspects of this econometric model. More advanced models capable of handling some more troubling aspects of the data should be used for further examination. In particular, there are some concerns about a unit root in the dependent variable, which would suggest focusing on the results for the growth in real per capita income as opposed to the level.

While the results here are not necessarily conclusive in one direction or another, the likely best model when considering the issues of how far a fan base extends, the possible unit root issue and the concerns about the overwhelming of the NFL winning percentage variable by the technology sector is the model for the growth rate of real per capita personal income while excluding San Francisco, San Jose and Seattle. This model supports the findings of Davis and End (2010) and Coates and Humphreys (2002) that a successful NFL team can have a positive effect on the local economy. However, regardless of the model chosen, the effect seems weaker than those found in Davis and End. Also, since the presence of an NFL team coefficient is negative, we cannot conclude that having a team has a net positive impact.

Additional work should extend the analysis to include additional variables that might predict mood, and in turn economic outcomes. One possibility would be to extend whether unexpected success (or failure) increases (or decreases) income more than predictable results. Another extension would be to examine additional countries and their most popular sports (Davis and End, 2010), such as hockey in Canada or soccer in European countries.

REFERENCES

Arellano, M. and Bond, S. (1991), 'Some tests of specification for panel data: Monte Carlo evidence and application to employment equations', *Review of Economic Studies*, **58**, 277–97.

Baade, R.A. and Dye, R.E. (1990), 'The impact of stadiums and professional sports on metropolitan area development', *Growth and Change*, **21** (2), 1–14.

Baade, R.A. and Matheson, V.A. (2000), 'An assessment of the economic impact of the American Football League Championship, the Super Bowl on host communities', *Reflets et Perspectives*, **34** (2–3), 35–46.

Baade, R.A. and Matheson, V.A. (2006), 'Padding required: assessing the economic impact of the Super Bowl', *European Sport Management Quarterly*, **6** (4), 353–74.

Baade, R.A., Baumann, R.W. and Matheson, V.A. (2008), 'Selling the game: estimating the economic impact of professional sports through taxable sales', *Southern Economic Journal*, **74** (3), 794–810.

Baumann, R.W., Matheson, V.A. and Muroi, C. (2009), 'Bowling in Hawaii: examining the effectiveness of sports-based tourism strategies', *Journal of Sports Economics*, **10** (1), 107–23.

Carlino, G. and Coulson, N.E. (2004), 'Compensating differentials and the social benefits of the NFL', *Journal of Urban Economics*, **58**, 25–50.

Carlino, G. and Coulson, N.E. (2006), 'Compensating differentials and the social benefit of the NFL: reply', *Journal of Urban Economics*, **60**, 132–8.

Coates, D. (2007), 'The tax benefits of hosting the Super Bowl and the MLB All-Star game: the Houston experience', *International Journal of Sport Finance*, **1** (4), 239–52.

Coates, D. and Humphreys, B.R. (1999), 'The growth effects of sport franchises, stadia, and arenas', *Journal of Policy Analysis and Management*, **18** (4), 601–24.

Coates, D. and Humphreys, B.R. (2001), 'The economic consequences of professional sports strikes and lockouts', *Southern Economic Journal*, **67** (3), 737–47.

Coates, D. and Humphreys, B.R. (2002), 'The economic impact of postseason play in professional sports', *Journal of Sports Economics*, **3** (3), 291–9.

Coates, D. and Humphreys, B.R. (2008), 'Do economists reach a conclusion on subsidies for sports franchises, stadiums, and mega events?', *Economic Journal Watch*, **5** (3), 294–315.

Coates, D., Humphreys, B.R. and Zimbalist, A.S. (2006), 'Compensating differentials and the social benefits of the NFL: a comment', *Journal of Urban Economics*, **60**, 124–31.

Coffey, B., McLaughlin, P.A. and Tollison, R.D. (2009), 'Regulators and redskins', unpublished manuscript.

Davis, M.C. and End, C.M. (2010), 'A winning proposition: the economic impact of successful National Football League franchises', *Economic Inquiry*, **48** (1), 39–50.

End, C.M. (2001), 'An examination of NFL fans' computer mediated BIRGing', *Journal of Sport Behavior*, **24** (2), 162–81.

End, C.M., Worthman, S., Foster, N.J. and Vandemark, A.P. (2009), 'Sport and relationships: the influence of game outcome on romantic relationships', *North American Journal of Psychology*, **11** (1), 37–48.

Fenn, A.J. and Crooker, J.R. (2008), 'Estimating local welfare generated by an NFL team under credible threat of relocation', *Southern Economic Journal*, **76** (1), 198–223.

Francois, P. and Zabojnik, J. (2005), 'Trust, social capital, and economic development', *Journal of the European Economic Association*, **3** (1), 51–94.

Frey, B.S. and Stutzer, A. (2002), 'What can economists learn from happiness research', *Journal of Economic Literature*, **40** (2), 402–35.

Gius, M. and Johnson, D. (2001), 'An empirical estimation of the economic impact of major league sports teams on cities', *The Journal of Business and Economic Studies*, **7** (1), 32–8.

Hertel, G., Neuhof, J., Theuer, T. and Kerr, N.L. (2000), 'Mood effects on cooperation in small groups: does positive mood simply lead to more cooperation?', *Cognition and Emotion*, **14** (4), 441–72.

Hirt, E.R., Zillmann, D., Erickson, G.A. and Kennedy, C. (1992), 'Costs and benefits of allegiance: changes in fans' self-ascribed competencies after team victory versus defeat', *Journal of Personality and Social Psychology*, **63** (5), 724–38.

Johnson, B.K, Mondello, M.J. and Whitehead, J.C. (2007), 'The value of public goods generated by a National Football League team', *Journal of Sport Management*, **21** (1), 123–36.

Judson, R.A. and Owen, A.L. (1999), 'Estimating dynamic panel data models: a guide for macroeconomists', *Economics Letters*, **65** (1), 9–15.

Kydland, F.E. and Prescott, E.C. (1982), 'Time to build and aggregate fluctuations', *Econometrica*, **50**, 1345–71.

Lertwachara, K. and Cochran, J.J. (2007), 'An event study of the economic impact of professional sport franchises on local U.S. economies', *Journal of Sports Economics*, **8** (3), 244–54.

Matheson, V.A. (2006), 'Contrary evidence on the economic effect of the Super Bowl on a victorious city', *Journal of Sports Economics*, **6** (4), 420–28.

Matheson, V.A. (2008), 'Mega-events: the effect of the world's biggest sporting events on local, regional, and national economies', in B.R. Humphreys and D.R. Howard (eds), *The Business of Sports*, Vol. 1: *Perspectives of the Sports Industry*, Westport, CT: Praeger, pp. 81–99.

Miller, P.A. (2002), 'The economic impact of sports stadium construction: the case of the construction industry in St. Louis, MO', *Journal of Urban Affairs*, **24** (2), 159–73.

Oswald, A.J., Proto, E. and Sgroi, D. (2009), 'Happiness and productivity', IZA discussion paper No. 4645.

Porter, P.K. (1999), 'Mega-sports events as municipal investments: a critique of impact analysis', in J. Fizel, E. Gustafson and L. Hadley (eds), *Sports Economics: Current Research*, Westport, CT: Praeger, pp. 61–74.

Solow, R.M. (1956), 'A contribution to the theory of economic growth', *The Quarterly Journal of Economics*, **70** (1), 65–94.

Staw, B.M., Sutton, R.I. and Pelled, L.H. (1994), 'Employee positive emotion and favorable outcomes at the workplace', *Organization Science*, **5** (1), 51–71.

Tsai, W.-C., Chen, C.-C. and Liu, H.-L. (2007), 'Test of a model linking employee positive moods and task performance', *Journal of Applied Psychology*, **92** (6), 1570–83.

Wann, D.L. (2006), 'Understanding the positive social psychological benefits of sport team identification: the team identification – social psychological health model', *Group Dynamics: Theory, Research, and Practice*, **10**, 272–96.

Wann, D.L. and Branscombe, N.R. (1992), 'Emotional responses to the sports page', *Journal of Sport and Social Issues*, **16** (1), 49–64.

Wann, D.L., Dolan, T.J., McGeorge, K.K. and Allison, J.A. (1994), 'Relationships between spectator identification and spectators' perceptions of influence, spectators' emotions, and competition outcome', *Journal of Sport and Exercise Psychology*, **16** (4), 347–64.

8. Sports participation and happiness: evidence from US micro data

Haifang Huang and Brad R. Humphreys

1. INTRODUCTION

How does participation in physical activity benefit society? Policy makers around the world have implemented programs to increase participation in physical activity in order to promote health, fight rising obesity, deter crime, impart important life skills to youth, and achieve other important societal goals over the past few decades (Schoppe et al., 2004). This wide-scale adoption of policies and broad range of outcomes highlights the importance of physical activity in modern society. In this chapter, we address a question that has received relatively little attention to date: does participation in physical activity and sports enhance quality of life? Some previous research hints at an answer. Both exercise and sports have been identified as a cause of joy (Argyle and Martin, 1991). Experiments on American and Italian teenagers showed they tended to be the happiest when engaging in sports and games (Csikszentmihalyi and Wong, 1991[1]). Does the happiness generated from sport participation extend beyond the duration of the activity? There are good reasons to expect it does. Physical activity promotes health, which is important for a happier life. Furthermore, participation in sport provides opportunities for socialization and helps develop communication and cooperation skills, all of which may lead to a more fruitful life. It is thus possible that participating in sports produces not just transitory, but long-lasting, happiness.

Prior research using micro-level data suggests a positive correlation between sports participation and self-reported quality of life (Fox, 1999). The interpretation of this correlative relationship, however, is not straightforward: individuals choose to participate in physical activity; those who choose to do so may be naturally healthier, more active and sociable, and therefore happier even without participating in physical activity. It is difficult to firmly establish a causal link between sport participation and quality of life using only micro-level data.

One way to overcome this problem is to combine micro-level data with information describing the proximal environment surrounding individuals. Differences in environmental factors such as access to sports facilities and peer influence may affect participation in sport and, in turn, affect happiness. If there is no reason to suspect a causal link between the presence of nearby sports facilities and self-reported well-being, and these two factors exhibit statistical correlation, then the correlation likely arises via participation in sport and physical activity. Existing research has taken this approach. One example is Forrest and McHale's (2009) analysis of participation in physical activity and happiness in British adults. The environmental factor they exploit is proximity to a sports facility, defined as the ability to travel to such a facility from home within 20 minutes. They find that British females who have such access are more likely to participate in sports, and report a higher level of happiness.

In this chapter, we adopt a similar approach and apply it to micro data from the US. We focus on two research questions: does participating in sports lead to a higher reported quality of life, and, if so, what mechanisms convey this effect? We combine data from a nationally representative survey of individual Americans with a data set that describes the local sports environment in US counties. We use the Centers for Disease Control and Prevention's (CDC) Behavioral Risk Factor Surveillance System (BRFSS) survey data for the years 2005 through to 2008. In these four years, the BRFSS sampled more than 1 million respondents and contained questions on both self-reported life satisfaction and detailed information on participation in physical activity and exercise. The environmental factor we exploit to establish a causal relationship between participation in sport and happiness is the number of sports establishments per person in the county of residence. We collected data on the number of sports establishments from the 2007 US County Business Patterns data and merged this with the BRFSS survey data based on geographic descriptors in both surveys. The combined data set has a usable sample of 1.2 million individuals living in 2297 US counties. There are large differences in the number of sports establishments per person across counties in the sample, ranging from .02 per thousand to 3.7 per thousand. Such differences in the availability of sports facilities likely reflect differences in population, demographics, sports culture and government provision of sports facilities. We posit that, for individuals, these environmental differences, either in terms of access to facilities or in peer influence, are exogenous to individuals' tendency to participate in physical activity and to their well-being; thus the number of local sports facilities can be used as an instrument to explain observed participation in sport and analyse the causal relationship between sport participation and self-reported happiness. Our empirical analysis also includes an extensive list of demographic and personal control variables, as well as county-level characteristics.

We show that individuals, despite having similar demographic and personal backgrounds, participate more actively in sports and physical activity if they live in counties that have a larger number of sports establishments per resident. These physically active individuals also report higher levels of life satisfaction. Since the number of sports establishments is unlikely to affect well-being directly, we interpret its influence on well-being as due to sports participation.

The second research question addresses the mechanism through which participation in sports and physical activity affects self-reported well-being. We find that the number of sports establishments in a county is significantly correlated with the self-reported health status in the BRFSS. Based on this result, we interpret causation as running from sports to health. If we control for health status in the empirical equation explaining well-being, the instrumental variable for participation in physical activity loses half of its coefficient size. This suggests that most of the well-being benefit from participation in physical activity arises from the latter's ability to promote physical health, or at least the feeling of being healthy.

2. THE LITERATURE ON SPORTS AND HAPPINESS

Research on happiness has exploded in recent years, especially in psychology and economics. Little attention has been given to the relationship between sport participation and happiness. A large literature indicating that participation in physical activity has a positive effect on mental well-being exists; Fox (1999) surveyed this literature and found that exercise improves mental well-being through improved mood and self-perception and is an effective treatment for clinical depression and anxiety. If exercise enhances mental well being and mitigates the effects of depression and anxiety, then it could also affect happiness.

Economists have recently begun to explore the economic determinants of happiness, proceeding from the central role of utility, a concept closely related to happiness, in neoclassical economic theory. Dolan et al. (2008) reviewed the economic literature on happiness and identified the effect of exercise on happiness as an important area for future research. Relatively little economic research has focused on the relationship between physical activity and happiness. Ferrer-i-Carbonell and Gowdy (2007) found that gardening, which can be a physical activity and is listed among the categories of physical activity in the BRFSS, was associated with greater self-reported happiness in a reduced-form regression model using data from the British Household Panel Survey. Forrest and McHale (2009) found that women who participated in sport reported higher well-being than women with similar characteristics who did not participate in sport, using data from the National Survey of Culture, Leisure and Sport in the UK in 2005–06. Forrest and McHale's (2009) evidence comes from a structural instrumental variables model that identifies sport participation using proximity to sports facilities as an instrument, and thus represents causal evidence about the relationship between sport participation and happiness.

Kavetsos and Szymanski (2010) investigated the effect of hosting major sporting events, such as the Olympic Games, the FIFA World Cup, and the UEFA European Football championship, on self-reported happiness in 12 European countries over the period 1974–2004. The data used by Kavetsos and Szymanski (2010) came from the Eurobarometer Survey Series conducted biannually by the European Commission. While hosting major sporting events differs from individual participation in sport, many host countries conduct programs aimed at increasing sport participation in conjunction with hosting major sporting events, and the ability to view major sporting events live may have some effect on sport participation. Kavetsos and Szymanski (2010) found that hosting the FIFA and UEFA championships increased happiness in the host countries, but national success in these events had no effect on reported happiness.

Clearly, research on the relationship between sport and happiness has just begun. The existing evidence comes primarily from Europe and only a handful of studies have been done. Given the expanding number of large secondary data sets containing both happiness data and data on participation in physical activity, this literature will likely expand. The key issue for empirical analysis of the relationship between happiness and participation in physical activity is econometric identification of participation in sport in order to eliminate the possibility of reverse causality from happiness to participation in physical activity and the other associated econometric problems associated with reverse causality. Like Forrest and McHale (2009) we use proximity to sports facilities to indentify participation in physical activity in a large survey of US residents.

3.   DATA AND EMPIRICAL ANALYSIS

3.1   Data

Our data source is the CDC's Behavioral Risk Factor Surveillance System (BRFSS). The BRFSS is a state-based system of surveys that collect information on health risk behaviors, preventive health practices and health care access in the United States. The Centers for Disease Control and Prevention is responsible for conducting these random digit dial telephone surveys. The BRFSS contains information from more than 350000 American adults (age 18 and over) each year. The survey includes a question on self-reported life satisfaction beginning in 2005. In the four years since this question was added, the BRFSS has collected survey information from 1.4 million Americans. The BRFSS survey data are publicly available from the CDC website. Life satisfaction in the BRFSS is measured on a standard four-step scale. The survey asks: 'In general, how satisfied are you with your life?' Respondents choose one of the following four answers: very satisfied, satisfied, dissatisfied or very dissatisfied. Oswald and Wu (2010: 576) used these data to look for objective confirmation of subjective measures of human well-being; they concluded: '[a]cross America, people's answers trace out the same pattern of quality of life as previously estimated, from solely nonsubjective data . . . There is a state-by-state match ($r = 0.6$, $P < 0.001$) between subjective and objective well-being.'

Table 8.1 contains the descriptive statistics from the 2005–08 BRFSS sample. After dropping observations with missing values, the final sample contains data on 1.2 million respondents out of the total of 1.4 million in the BRFSS universe. All the summary statistics reported in Table 8.1 use the BRFSS sample weights, because the survey is unbalanced in its unweighted form (for example, it heavily samples from females).

In the weighted sample, 1 per cent of the respondents reported they were 'very dissatisfied', 4.3 per cent reported they were 'dissatisfied', 49.4 per cent reported they were 'satisfied' and 45.3 per cent reported they were 'very satisfied'. The survey also provides information related to sports participation. Unlike some previous year's surveys, the BRFSS from 2005 to 2008 did not ask detailed questions about participation in physical activity and sport. We use a proxy, based on a question on leisure-time physical activity or exercise: 'During the past month, other than your regular job, did you participate in any physical activities or exercises such as running, calisthenics, golf, gardening, or walking for exercise?' The responses are yes, no, or refused to answer; almost all responded yes or no. About 76 per cent of respondents said they participated in physical activities or exercised in the past month. While more detail on the nature of participation in physical activity would be ideal, we believe this question contains sufficient information about participation in physical activity and sport for our purpose.

The county-level sports establishment data come from the 2007 County Business Patterns (CBP) report from the US Census Bureau. The CBP report 'contains data covering establishments with paid employees . . . in more than 3,100 counties' in the United States.[2] The CBP defines an

Table 8.1   Summary statistics, BRFSS data

Variable	Mean
Self-reported satisfaction: Very dissatisfied	0.010
Self-reported satisfaction: Dissatisfied	0.043
Self-reported satisfaction: Satisfied	0.494
Self-reported satisfaction: Very satisfied	0.453
Participated in physical activity	0.765
Self-reported health: Excellent	0.040
Self-reported health: Very good	0.114
Self-reported health: Good	0.298
Self-reported health: Fair	0.336
Self-reported health: Poor	0.211
Annual household income less than $10 000	0.040
Annual household income $10 001 to $15 000	0.042
Annual household income $15 001 to $20 000	0.059
Annual household income $20 001 to $25 000	0.073
Annual household income $25 001 to $35 000	0.101
Annual household income $35 001 to $50 000	0.134
Annual household income $50 001 to $75 000	0.156
Annual household income more than $75 000	0.280
Annual household income not reported	0.114
Male	0.486
Age	45.88
High school education or less	0.385
College or university degree	0.348
Married	0.643
Self-employed	0.087
Long-term unemployed	0.020
Recently unemployed	0.032
Limitation on activity	0.191
Race: black only, non-Hispanic	0.098
Other race, non-Hispanic	0.051
Multiracial, non-Hispanic	0.015
Race: Hispanic	0.138

establishment as a 'single physical location at which business is conducted or services or industrial operations are performed'. The CBP reports the number of establishments for most of the 1100 industries identified in the North American Industrial Classification System (NAICS). From the NAICS we identify all those industries that are related to sports. We ignore two, marinas and skiing facilities, because their specific geographic demands (mountains and water) make them relatively rare in

Table 8.2   Summary statistics – county level data

Variable	Mean	SD	Minimum	Maximum
County: median household income	53516.9	13261.7	20999.0	107200.0
County: population per square mile land	1934.4	6450.4	1.0	66951.0
County: percentage pop. in urban areas	0.820	0.217	0.000	1.000
County: percentage owner-occupied housing	0.663	0.108	0.195	0.894
County: percentage black population	0.117	0.122	0.000	0.847
County: percentage Hispanic population	0.127	0.149	0.000	0.981
County: percentage all minority	0.304	0.204	0.006	0.984
Sports establishments per 1000: category 1	0.082	0.055	0.000	2.085
Sports establishments per 1000: category 2	0.016	0.021	0.000	0.685
Sports establishments per 1000: category 3	0.203	0.079	0.000	1.453
Sports establishments per 1000: category 4	0.021	0.021	0.000	0.326
Sports establishments per 1000: all categories	0.323	0.130	0.016	3.656

most counties. We classify the rest into four establishment categories. Category 1 is sporting goods stores, based on NAICS classification 451110 'Sporting Goods Stores'. Category 2 is spectator sports establishments. It includes NAICS classifications 711211 'Sports Teams and Clubs', 711212 'Racetracks' and 711219 'Other Spectator Sports'. Category 3 is sports facilities and instruction providers. It includes 713910 'Golf Courses and Country Clubs', 713940 'Fitness and Recreational Sports Centers', 713950 'Bowling Centers' and 611620 'Sports and Recreation Instruction'. Category 4 is sports promoters. It includes 711310 'Promoters of Performing Arts, Sports, and Similar Events with Facilities' and 711320 'Promoters of Performing Arts, Sports, and Similar Events without Facilities'. We are not able to remove the performing arts from this category because of data limitations.

Table 8.2 contains descriptive statistics for the county level data. We express all establishment counts in terms of number of establishments per 1000 residents in the county. The national mean is 0.32 sports related establishments per 1000 county residents; the standard deviation is 0.13. The most important category of establishments, in absolute magnitude and in term of cross-county variation, is sports facilities and instruction providers. Its mean is 0.20 per 1000 county residents and its standard deviation is 0.08.

We mentioned above that our empirical work is not limited by the fact that the BRFSS question on leisure-time physical activity is broader than sports. This is because we focus on the correlation between responses to these questions and the number of sports establishments in the county of residence. To the extent that such correlation exists, it most likely reflects exogenous sports-related activity, and not unobservable individual specific factors. Of course, there is potential for spurious correlation. Differences in the availability of sports facilities may reflect differences in population density, urbanization, population composition, neighborhood amenities and other factors. For this reason, we include in our empirical work an extensive list of controls at the county level.

Our use of the CBP data is inspired by Rupasingha et al. (2006), who used CBP data to construct a county-level database of social capital. Our data, however, differs from what they have made available online. We use a recent CBP release, the 2007 report, to better match the period of our BRFSS data; we also expanded the selection of sports-related establishments to a broader definition.

3.2 Empirical Strategy and Results

Our empirical analysis contains four steps. In step one we estimate a reduced-form regression model explaining observed variation in self-reported life satisfaction; we regress self-reported life satisfaction on the number of sports establishments in the county and a vector of other covariates typically included in happiness regressions. Once we establish the existence of reduced-form conditional correlation, we proceed to a structural approach in order to identify causality. In step two we show that the establishment count correlates positively with the probability of participation in physical activity and sport. In the third step, we use a two-stage instrumental variables approach, like that used by Forrest and McHale (2009), to examine the well-being effect of participation in physical activity. Specifically, we use county establishment counts to predict the probability of participation in physical activity and sport in the first stage, and use the fitted values from this first stage as an instrumental variable for participation in the second stage. Finally, we explore health benefits as a channel through which participation in physical activity and sports affects well-being. Together these four steps provide answers to our two primary research questions: does participation in physical activity and sport raise well-being, and, if so, what mechanism is at work?

3.2.1 Reduced-form regression analysis

Here we ask if an individual who is living in a county that has a higher number of sports establishments per resident is happier in life. We will control for both personal differences and cross-county differences in important aspects. The reduced form regression model is:

$$WB_{i,j} = X_i\alpha + Z_j\gamma + \beta E_j + u_i \tag{8.1}$$

where the dependent variable $WB_{i,j}$ is self-reported well-being for individual i in county j. The right-hand side of the model includes a vector of demographic and personal control variables X_i, and a vector of county-level controls Z_j. The sports-establishment count in county j is E_j.

Again, the well-being measure is the answer to a standard four-response life satisfaction question in the BRFSS. We reversed the original order of the BRFSS responses, so that 1 indicates the least satisfied response and 4 indicates the most satisfied response. The four-step responses strictly speaking are not cardinal measures of happiness. But such responses are often treated as cardinal in happiness research, thus ordinary least squares (OLS) or similar methods are used. Examples include Di Tella et al. (2001), who use responses to a 4-step life satisfaction question from the Euro-Barometer survey to study preferences over inflation and unemployment. Ferrer-i-Carbonell and Frijters (2004) find that the choice of probit versus OLS makes virtually no differences in detecting the relation between happiness and key right-hand side variables. Helliwell and Huang (2008) use an ordered probit approach to estimate compensating differentials for workplace environments, and report that probit and the linear probability model give similar results, because changing regression methods tends to affect the estimated coefficients on right-hand side variables proportionally. The compensating differential measure used is the ratio of coefficients, which remains robust to different regression methods. We make similar comparisons. Based on OLS estimates of equation (8.1), the estimated coefficient on the sports-establishment variable (the sum of all categories per 1000) is 71 per cent of the impact of moving an individual from the sixth income bracket to the seventh bracket. The ratio is 73 per cent if we switch to ordered probit estimation. Because the size of the estimated coefficients in well-being models does not have an easy interpretation, either using OLS or probit, an interpretation based on ratios of coefficients appears to be sensible. Since the choice of OLS and probit models make little difference on such ratios, we use OLS, following Oswald and Wu (2010), who use the same self-reported life satisfaction question responses from the BRFSS.

The demographic and individual control vector, X_i, includes age, age squared, gender, marital status, educational attainment, household income, racial/ethnicity indicators and detailed employment status variables, commonly used explanatory variables in happiness research. Oswald and Wu (2010) use the same vector of explanatory variables. We expand the vector of explanatory variables to include a dummy variable derived from the response to the BRFSS question, 'Are you limited in any way in any activities because of physical, mental, or emotional problems?', because activity limitation likely affects participation in sports; later we will use the same set of individual covariates to model participation, so it is useful to include it here. In our sample 20 per cent of Americans said they have activity limitations. Another variable in X_i reflects activity limitation, the employment status 'unable to work'; 4 per cent of the sample reported they were unable to work.

The county-level vector of control variables, Z_j, contains the log of the county population density, the percentage of the county population living in urban areas, the racial compositions of the county, the percentage of owner-occupied housing (to measure the stability of population) in the county, the log of median household income (to measure economic conditions), and state dummy variables to capture unobservable state specific factors that affect sport participation like climate. All of the county-level control variables come from the year 2000 census profile except for median household income, which is from the 2007 USA Counties data file. It is particularly important to control for population density in this setting. Higher population density is correlated with a smaller number of sports facilities per capita. But it probably also correlates with lack of other facilities and low provision of public services that may adversely affect well-being. Existing literature has already shown a negative relationship between population density and well-being (Dolan et al., 2008). By controlling for population density, we reduce the chance that the correlation between sports facilities and well-being is spurious. We experimented with the population density in linear, logarithmic and quadratic forms. The logged transformation minimizes the size and t-statistics of the coefficient on sports establishments.

All regressions allow the errors term to cluster at the county level, and use the overall weighting variable in the BRFSS, which allows us to draw conclusions about the entire population of the US.

Table 8.3 contains the regression results for the reduced form model. The parameter estimate on the count of sports establishments in the

Table 8.3   Reduced-form regression results

Variable	Parameter	SE	p-value
Sports establishments per 1000: all categories	0.043	0.014	0.003
Annual household income less than $10000	−0.137	0.010	<0.001
Annual household income $10001 to $15000	−0.109	0.013	<0.001
Annual household income $15001 to $20000	−0.096	0.005	<0.001
Annual household income $20001 to $25000	−0.073	0.006	<0.001
Annual household income $25001 to $35000	−0.038	0.006	<0.001
Annual household income $50001 to $75000	0.060	0.004	<0.001
Annual household income more than $750000	0.150	0.004	<0.001
Male	−0.025	0.003	<0.001
Age	−0.008	0.000	<0.001
Age squared	0.000	0.000	<0.001
High school education or less	−0.024	0.004	<0.001
College or university degree	0.067	0.003	<0.001
Married	0.148	0.005	<0.001
Divorced/separated/widowed	−0.017	0.005	<0.001
Self-employed	0.014	0.004	0.001
Long-term unemployed	−0.221	0.010	<0.001
Recently unemployed	−0.185	0.008	<0.001
Unable to work	−0.208	0.007	<0.001
Limitation on activity	−0.239	0.003	<0.001
Black	−0.020	0.005	<0.001
Other, non-Hispanic	−0.063	0.011	<0.001
Hispanic	0.009	0.006	0.183
County: log median household income	−0.030	0.010	0.002
County: log pop. per square mile	−0.010	0.002	<0.001
Number of counties	2297		
Number of observations	1 209 740		
R-squared	0.128		

county has a positive and statistically significant coefficient. We define the establishment count as the sum of all four types of establishments. This result is robust to narrower definitions of sports establishments, for example, by removing sports stores, promoters and spectator sports, thus leaving behind only the sum of bowling center, fitness facilities, sports instructors and golf courses. In that case, the coefficient is still positive with a p-value of 2.7 per cent.

Table 8.3 contains results for selected explanatory variables; the model contains state indicator variables and the standard errors are corrected for clustering at the county level. The other parameter estimates are similar to those found in happiness research. Self-reported life satisfaction increases with income and education. The employed report more satisfaction than the unemployed. Whites report higher happiness than minorities. Next, we turn to an analysis of participation in physical activity and sport.

3.2.2 Sports establishments and participation in physical activity

In this section, we further explore the relationship between the presence and number of sports establishments and participation in physical activity and sport. We hypothesize that the establishments affect well-being primarily by encouraging individual residents to participate in physical activity and sports. A larger number of sports establishments implies easier access to facilities and/or more importance placed on sports and exercise in the community. We again emphasize our exogeneity assumption. At the aggregate level, the number of sports establishments is not exogenous to features of a population. A county that has higher percentages of young, male and affluent residents naturally has greater demand for sports. The supply will respond and the number of sports establishments rises. But at the individual level, these environmental differences are exogenous to an individual's incentive to participate, controlling for their own demographic and personal differences such as age, gender, income, race and activity limitations.

Are establishment counts and participation in physical activity and sport correlated? To answer this question, we estimate the following linear probability model:

$$P_{i,j} = X_i\alpha + Z_j\gamma + \beta E_j + v_i \qquad (8.2)$$

The dependent variable in equation (8.2), $P_{i,j}$, is a dummy variable that indicates the response to the BRFSS question: 'During the past month, other than your regular job, did you participate in any physical activities or exercises such as running, calisthenics, golf, gardening, or walking for exercise?'

The right-hand side variables are the same as those in the reduced-form well-being equation, equation (8.1). The demographic and personal controls are contained in X_i, which includes age, gender, marital status educational, income, racial/ethnicity, employment status and limitation on activity. The vector of county-level control variables, Z_j, includes logged population density, an urbanization indicator, population racial composition variables, county home ownership rate, the log of median county household income and state dummy variables. The establishment count at the county level is E_j. The use of total establishment counts assumes that different types of sports establishments have the same influence on sport participation and intensity of participation.

Table 8.4   Linear probability model results, first stage regression

Variable	Parameter	SE
Annual household income less than $10 000	−0.075***	[0.006]
Annual household income $10 001 to $15 000	−0.075***	[0.005]
Annual household income $15 001 to $20 000	−0.061***	[0.005]
Annual household income $20 001 to $25 000	−0.050***	[0.004]
Annual household income $25 001 to $35 000	−0.022***	[0.004]
Annual household income $50 001 to $75 000	0.022***	[0.003]
Annual household income more than $75 000	0.053***	[0.002]
Male	0.032***	[0.002]
Age	−0.001	[0.000]
Age squared	−0.000***	[0.000]
High school education or less	−0.079***	[0.002]
College or university degree	0.047***	[0.002]
Married	−0.018***	[0.003]
Divorced/separated/widowed	−0.024***	[0.003]
Self-employed	0.030***	[0.003]
Long-term unemployed	−0.005	[0.009]
Recently unemployed	0.013**	[0.006]
Unable to work	−0.122***	[0.005]
Limitation on activity	−0.117***	[0.002]
Black	−0.050***	[0.004]
Other, non-Hispanic	−0.063***	[0.005]
Hispanic	−0.081***	[0.004]
County: median household income	0.007	[0.006]
County: population per square mile land	0.000	[0.001]
County: percentage pop. in urban areas	0.013	[0.007]
County: percentage owner-occupied housing	−0.012	[0.018]
Sports establishments per 1000 population	0.063***	[0.008]
N	1 208 697	
R-squared	0.101	
F Statistic, excluding establishment count	58.32	

Notes: Dependent variable = 1 if individual participated in physical activity. Standard errors in brackets; *** p<0.01, ** p<0.05.

Table 8.4 contains the parameter estimates from equation (8.2). These results show that the greater the number of sports establishments in a county, the higher the probability that an individual will participate in physical activity or sport. In equation (8.2), the coefficient estimate on the total establishment count is positive and significantly different from zero at the 1 per cent level. The F statistic for excluding the establishment count variable is 58, indicating that this variable provides a good exclusion restriction for the IV estimator used in the next section. The coefficient on the establishment count variable is rather small. An increase of one establishment for every 10000 residents, about a standard deviation, is associated with about 0.6 per cent higher probability of participation.

The estimated parameters on the other variables in equation (8.2) are consistent with results in other research on the economic determinants of participation in physical activity (Humphreys and Ruseski, 2007, 2009). Participation in physical activity rises with income and education and falls with age; males participate more than females, and whites participate more than minorities.

The results from this model form the basis of a structural approach to examining the relationship between participation in physical activity and happiness in the following section. The fitted values from this regression will be used as an instrument in a second-stage regression of the determination of self-reported happiness.

3.2.3   Participation in physical activity and subjective well-being: IV results

In this step we use a two-stage instrumental variable (IV) approach to estimate the effect of participation in physical activity on well-being. We use the IV approach to identify the participation in physical activity promoted by environmental factors exogenous to unobservable individual-specific factors affecting participation. Specifically, we use the predicted participation probability from estimates of equation (8.2) as a right-hand side variable to explain self-reported well-being. The coefficient on the fitted probability of participating in physical activity can be interpreted as the estimated effect of participation on well-being. The consistency of this estimate hinges on two factors: exogenous environmental factors do not affect well-being directly, and do affect individuals' participation in physical activity and sport.

The second-stage regression model is

$$WB_{i,j} = X_i\alpha + Z_j\gamma + \beta\hat{P}_{i,j} + u_i \tag{8.3}$$

where the fitted values from the first stage regression are P_{ji}-hat, which comes from equation (8.2). The vector of variables X_i, contains demographic and personal covariates including age, gender, marital status, educational, income, racial/ethnicity, employment status and limitation on activity. The vector of county-level control variables, Z_j, includes logged population density, an urbanization indicator, population racial composition variables, county home ownership rate, the log of median county household income and state dummy variables. Standard errors have been corrected for clustering at the county level.

Table 8.5 contains selected results from the second stage regression model; full results are available from the authors on request. The contribution to self-reported well-being from participating in sports is 0.68. The estimated coefficient is three times as big as the coefficient of being unemployed and is comparable in size to the effect reported by Forrest and McHale (2009) for British females. Forrest and McHale's (2009) estimated contribution from participation in physical activity is twice the size of the coefficient on being unemployed. We also performed the IV regression separately for males and females. These results are in the last two columns on Table 8.5. The male subsample had 455 849 observations and the female subsample had 752 848. Our findings regarding gender differ from those in Forrest and McHale (2009). We find that both genders benefit from participating in sports; both samples produce positive and significant coefficients on the participation variable. Furthermore, male Americans appear to gain more happiness from participating in physical activity than females.

The other parameter estimates on Table 8.5 are similar to the reduced-form estimates from equation (8.1) reported in Table 8.3. Happiness rises with income and education, and falls with age. Married people report being happier than singles, and the employed report being happier than the unemployed. Whites report being happier than minorities. Note that people living in higher-income counties are not as happy as people living in lower-income counties, holding individual income constant. This result is consistent with the idea that relative income affects happiness. In counties with a higher median income, an individual is more likely to observe or interact with someone who earns more than they do, reducing the individual's happiness. Dolan et al. (2008) review the evidence on the effect of relative income on reported happiness.

3.2.4 Health benefits as transmission mechanism

Here we address our second research question: how does participating in physical activity and sports affect self reported well-being? One hypothesis is that the participation improves the quality of life by improving health. It is well accepted that active lifestyles are conductive toward better physical health. At the individual level, participation in physical activity and health status are positively correlated, although such association may arise from common factors; it is also likely that the causation flows from unobserved physical capability of participation in physical activity. As a result, it is not easy to interpret the simple conditional correlation between physical activity and health. Again, we believe that exploring differences in the external sports environment overcomes such difficulty. In this section, we proceed in two steps: first, we determine if the presence of sports establishments in

Table 8.5   *IV estimates, self-reported happiness and participation in physical activity*

Variable	Pooled	Male	Female
Participation in physical activity (instrumented)	0.677*** [0.228]	0.986** [0.410]	0.464** [0.182]
Annual household income less than $10000	−0.086*** [0.020]	−0.043 [0.036]	−0.116*** [0.015]
Annual household income $10001 to $15000	−0.059*** [0.021]	−0.004 [0.039]	−0.099*** [0.016]
Annual household income $15001 to $20000	−0.055*** [0.015]	−0.023 [0.024]	−0.084*** [0.014]
Annual household income $20001 to $25000	−0.039*** [0.012]	−0.012 [0.021]	−0.064*** [0.011]
Annual household income $25001 to $35000	−0.022*** [0.007]	−0.008 [0.013]	−0.035*** [0.007]
Annual household income $50001 to $75000	0.045*** [0.007]	0.034*** [0.013]	0.053*** [0.006]
Annual household income more than $750000	0.114*** [0.013]	0.092*** [0.027]	0.129*** [0.010]
Age	−0.008*** [0.001]	−0.007*** [0.002]	−0.007*** [0.001]
Age squared	0.000*** [0.000]	0.000*** [0.000]	0.000*** [0.000]
High school education or less	0.03 [0.018]	0.048 [0.030]	0.014 [0.016]
College or university degree	0.035*** [0.011]	0.013 [0.021]	0.050*** [0.009]
Married	0.160*** [0.007]	0.194*** [0.011]	0.125*** [0.007]
Divorced/separated/widowed	−0.001 [0.007]	0.019 [0.016]	−0.021*** [0.006]
Self-employed	−0.006 [0.008]	−0.01 [0.010]	0.007 [0.012]
Recently unemployed	−0.194*** [0.009]	−0.205*** [0.015]	−0.183*** [0.012]
Unable to work	−0.124*** [0.029]	−0.096* [0.051]	−0.142*** [0.024]
Limitation on activity	−0.160*** [0.027]	−0.122*** [0.042]	−0.193*** [0.025]
Black	0.015 [0.012]	0.014 [0.012]	0.002 [0.014]
Hispanic	0.064*** [0.020]	0.102*** [0.032]	0.026 [0.019]

Table 8.5   (continued)

Variable	Pooled	Male	Female
County: log median household income	−0.034*** [0.011]	−0.026* [0.015]	−0.041*** [0.012]
County: log population per square mile	−0.011*** [0.002]	−0.011** [0.004]	−0.010*** [0.002]

Notes: Standard errors in brackets; *** p<0.01, ** p<0.05.

a county is correlated with individuals' self-reported health status; second, we add the health status to the second-stage well-being equation, equation (8.3), to see if doing so reduces the importance of the instrumental variable for participation in physical activity and sport.

A reduced form regression model explores the relationship between the sports environment and self-reported health status:

$$H_{i,j} = X_i\alpha + Z_j\gamma + \beta E_j + u_i. \tag{8.4}$$

The dependent variable is self-reported health status, derived from the response to the BRFSS question: 'Would you say that in general your health is: Excellent, Very good, Good, Fair, or Poor?' We assign the five responses values from 1 to 5 in an ascending order. We treat it as cardinal; treating them as ordinal and using ordered probit generated similar positive and significant coefficient estimates on the sports establishment count variable. The regression model controls for the same sets of individual and county level factors as used above. These controls include age, gender, activity limitation, race, income of the individual, among others, and median income and logged population density at the county level, among others.

We are interested in estimates of β, the coefficient on the county-level establishment count variable. A positive estimate of β suggests that, despite similar backgrounds, people tend to say they are healthier if they live in an area that has more sports establishments. How does the causation run in this case? We interpret the causation as flowing from sports establishments, via sports participation, to self-reported health. The reverse causality interpretation, where causality flows from individual health to the county sports environment, requires that individuals' unobservable health characteristics, independent of their age, gender, income, activity limitation, race and others, somehow tend to live together and have greater demand for local sports facilities. We regard such an interpretation as implausible, especially after controlling for county-level differences in income, population composition, population density, and unobservable state-specific effects.

The parameter estimates of equation (8.4) are not reported, but they are available from the authors on request. The results show that the coefficient on the sports establishment count variable is positive and significantly different from zero with a p value lower than 1 per cent and an F-statistic that exceeds 56. The estimates from equation (8.4) indicate a statistically significant link between participation in physical activity and sport and self-reported health status. In addition to these results, we looked for evidence linking participation in physical activity and health at the aggregate level. The Robert Wood Johnson Foundation and the University of Wisconsin Population Health Institute published US County Health Rankings in 2010. They measured health outcomes based on premature deaths, birth outcomes and health-related quality of life (the latter is from the same BRFSS data as we use here). We found that the county-level sports establishment count per person is a strong predictor of cross-county differences in the ranking of health outcomes as reported in this ranking. Such analysis at the aggregate level suffers from the fact that population compositions differ across counties: a younger population is healthier and also demands more sports facilities. This contrasts to the approach we use here; we overcome the confounding effects of county population composition by focusing on similar individuals and exploit differences in proximity to sports facilities. Taken together, these results suggest that health plays an important role in the relationship between participation in physical activity and sport, and suggests an important area for future research on this topic.

4.   CONCLUSIONS

We initially posed two research questions: does participating in physical activity and sports improve happiness, and, if so, what is the underlying transmission mechanism? Obtaining causal evidence to help answer the first question takes some care. Simply regressing individuals' reported happiness on an indicator of participation in physical activity suffers from endogeneity problems and possible reverse causality. We addressed this problem by exploiting differences in proximal environmental factors that influence participation in physical activity to statistically identify participation. Specifically we used the number of sports establishments per-capita in the county of residence as an instrument in an IV model of the determination of happiness and participation in physical activity. The results of this IV estimation indicate that otherwise-similar individuals are more likely to participate in physical activity and sport if she or he lives in a county that has greater access to sports establishments; those individuals also report higher life satisfaction. The estimated contribution of participation in physical activity on happiness is three times the size of the increased happiness associated with the status of being employed. Both men and women gain happiness from participating in physical activity, and men appear to benefit more. Our results control for demographic and personal characteristics including age, gender, education, income, marital status, limitation on physical activity, races and employment status. We also control for cross-county differences in income, density, urbanization, population stability, and population's racial composition. We also develop evidence that the relationship between participation in physical activity and happiness relates to the effect of physical activity on health.

Our results suggest that the effects of increased participation in physical activity extend well beyond previous boundaries; in addition to previously documented reductions in obesity and improvements in health, participation in physical activity also appears to increase happiness in the general population. This broader impact of physical activity provides additional evidence supporting government policies to increase physical activity. In addition, our results suggest that policy discussion regarding policies designed to increase participation in physical activity should not be isolated from the discussion on spending on public health. The key role played by access to establishments related to physical activity and sport also highlights the importance of the supply of sports facilities in any policy intervention designed to increase participation in physical activity, and implies that additional research should focus on this poorly understood topic.

Our results differ in several important ways from existing studies in this area, suggesting several important avenues for future research. We find that both men and women in the US gain additional happiness from participating in physical activity, while Forrest and McHale (2009) in a similar study using data from the UK find that only females gain additional happiness from participation. This difference in the effect of physical activity on happiness in two similar populations suggests that important economic, cultural or environmental differences may exist between the US and the UK. Understanding the role these differences play would move the happiness literature forward in an important way. Also, we present evidence that the relationship between participation in physical activity and happiness is mediated by health. This result suggests that physical activity may play a role in the production of health, and also be related to happiness. Models of health production, and the related empirical research on health production, would appear to be a good jumping-off point for additional research in this area.

NOTES

1. Csikszentmihalyi and Wong's (1991) measurement of happiness is 'based on repeated self-reports of happiness that each respondent provides eight times each day, whenever signaled by an electronic pager, for one week'.
2. Press release, US Census Bureau News, 'U.S. business employers add 100,000 establishments in 2007, Census Bureau Reports', Thursday, 30 July 2009, available at: www.census.gov/Press-Release/www/releases/archives/county_business_patterns/014105.html (accessed 30 June 2010).

REFERENCES

Argyle, M. and Martin, M. (1991), 'The psychological causes of unhappiness', in F. Strack, M. Argyle and N. Schwarz (eds), *Subjective Well-Being: An Interdisciplinary Perspective*, Oxford: Pergamon Press, p. 77.

Csikszentmihalyi, M. and Wong, M.M. (1991), 'The situational and personal correlates of happiness: a cross-national comparison', in F. Strack, M. Argyle and N. Schwarz (ed.), *Subjective Well-being: An Interdisciplinary Perspective*, Elmsford, NY: Pergamon Press, pp. 193–212.

Di Tella, R., MacCulloch, R.J. and Oswald, A.J. (2001), 'Preferences over inflation and underemployment: evidence from surveys of happiness', *American Economic Review*, **91**, 335–41.

Dolan, P., Peasgood, T. and White, M. (2008), 'Do we really know what makes us happy? A review of the economic literature on the factors associated with subjective well-being', *Journal of Economic Psychology*, **29**, 94–122.

Ferrer-i-Carbonell, A. and Frijters, P. (2004), 'How important is methodology for the estimates of the determinants of happiness', *The Economic Journal*, **114**, 641–59.

Ferrer-i-Carbonell, A. and Gowdy, J.M. (2007), 'Environmental degradation and happiness', *Ecological Economics*, **60** (3), 509–16.

Forrest, D. and McHale, I.G. (2009), 'Public policy, sport and happiness: an empirical study', working paper, Salford University.

Fox, K.R. (1999), 'The influence of physical activity on mental well-being', *Public Health Nutrition*, **2**, 411–18.

Helliwell, J.F. and Huang, H. (2010), 'How's the job? Well-being and social capital in the workplace', *Industrial and Labor Relations Review*, **63** (2), 205–27.

Humphreys, B.R. and Ruseski, J.E. (2007), 'Participation in physical activity and government spending on parks and recreation', *Contemporary Economic Policy*, **25**, 538–52.

Humphreys, B.R. and Ruseski, J.E. (2009), 'The economics of participation and time spent in physical activity', working paper 2009-9, University of Alberta, Department of Economics.

Kavetsos, G. and Szymanski, S. (2010), 'National well-being and international sports events', *Journal of Economic Psychology*, **31** (2), 158–71.

Oswald, A. and Wu, S. (2010), 'Objective confirmation of subjective measures of human well-being: evidence from the USA', *Science*, **327**, 576–8.

Rupasingha, A., Goetz, S.J. and Freshwater, D. (2006), 'The production of social capital in US counties', *The Journal of Socio-Economics*, **35** (1), 83–101.

Schoppe, S., Bauman, A. and Bull, F. (2004), 'International review of national physical activity policy: a literature review', Centre for Physical Activity and Health, report no. CPAH04-0002.

9. Subjective well-being and engagement in sport: evidence from England

David Forrest and Ian G. McHale

1. INTRODUCTION

One bishop in the nineteenth-century Anglican Church, whenever asked to say Grace before a public dinner, was wont to pronounce: 'For this food, for our friendship and for all the happiness cricket brings to the World, Thank God.' Implicitly, the Bishop was hypothesizing that subjective well-being is a function of engagement in sport, and it is this possibility that we address in this chapter.

The issue perhaps has more relevance to public policy now than it did back then in the nineteenth century. In Britain, as in many European countries, the contemporary state takes a major part of the responsibility for providing sports facilities: even where it is private clubs, rather than municipalities, that own and operate the centres and complexes, they are often in receipt of grants from lottery funds or quasi-governmental organizations. This steady stream of revenue underpins access to sport in many areas. But, undoubtedly, it is threatened by the current crisis of government debt. Where public expenditure has to be scaled down, sports budgets represent a 'soft' target, partly because it is hard to measure what benefits flow from the subsidies. It therefore appears to us timely to investigate the question of whether people's lives are enhanced by participating in sport and whether it is possible to quantify the benefit.

We take a direct approach. It is argued, for example by Layard (2005), that increasing happiness should be the overriding role of government and, moreover, that this principle provides a practical framework for informing policy decisions because happiness can be measured in a meaningful way by collecting people's happiness scores. Now routinely included in datasets from many social surveys worldwide, happiness scores, often on a 1 to 10 scale, are respondents' answers to a question about how happy their lives are. Patterns of responses to such a question are remarkably similar across countries (Peiró, 2006) and intuitively appealing (in the sense that things like health and living with a partner are consistently found to be the most important factors contributing to a sense of individual well-being). This has generated increasing confidence among economists that it is legitimate to treat happiness scores as direct measures of the elusive concept of utility and, in examining the association between happiness scores and playing sport, we therefore seek to answer the question of whether government facilitation of participation in sport raises the utility of those who answer the call to play.

Happiness studies is a sub-discipline with a large literature (for a survey from the perspective of economics, see Dolan et al., 2008) but its application to sport, at least through formal econometric analysis, has been very limited. Kavetos and Szymanski (2010) looked at the impact on happiness not of participation but of national team success. Huang and Humphreys (Chapter 8 in this volume) attempt to quantify the causal impact of exercise on self-reported life satisfaction in the USA. Otherwise, there appear to be no prior or contemporaneous studies to report.

2. THE DATA

Taking Part is an annual survey of the use of leisure time by adults (defined as 16 or over) in England. It is commissioned by the UK government's Department for Culture, Media and Sport in conjunction with stakeholder organizations, such as Sport England. We exploit data from the largest-scale edition of this survey, carried out in the 16 months period up to October, 2006. It collected happiness scores from 27989 adults in England (not Scotland, Wales or Northern Ireland), along with considerable detail on their leisure activities and a range of information on demographic and socio-economic variables. All interviews were conducted face to face and had a median length in excess of half an hour. Fieldwork was by the British Market Research Bureau. The core sample was deemed representative of the adult population (Williams, 2006) but there was also a booster sample of ethnic minority communities to ensure adequate numbers for meaningful analysis of participation in cultural life by race. Data from *Taking Part* are lodged in the UK Data Archive (www.data-archive.ac.uk).

The happiness question posed was similar to others used internationally in general social surveys: 'Taking all things together how happy would you say you are? On a scale of 1–10, 10 = extremely happy, 1 = extremely unhappy.' The phrase 'taking all things together' was intended to encourage respondents to consider not their level of contentment that moment or that day but rather their satisfaction with life more generally. As such,

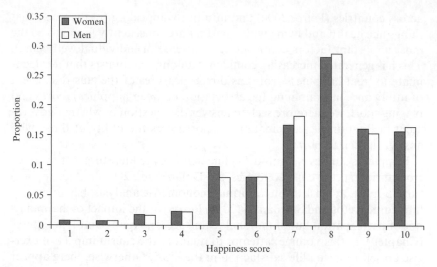

Figure 9.1   Distribution of happiness scores in the sample

answers will be used below not to investigate whether playing sport makes them feel happy on game day (losers of course may not!) but whether there is a more durable effect, in short whether it makes them 'happier people'.

Fortunately for our purpose, the survey asked not only a happiness question (the distribution of the answers to which are illustrated in Figure 9.1) but also whether subjects had participated in active recreational activities in the four weeks preceding the date of the interview. They were shown a list of 60 activities ranging almost from A to Z (American football to yoga) and were also prompted to mention any others in which they had participated that were not on the list (this uncovered a further eight categories such as frisbee and pilates).

Our focus was to be on sport, so we defined our focus variable *sports player* by reference only to those activities which would conventionally be regarded as sports, as opposed to pastimes or exercise. Of course, a precise definition of sport is hard to formulate (see, for example, Farrell and Shields, 2002) and necessarily involves an element of subjectivity. Nevertheless, we decided that partitioning off 'sports' from 'exercise' was still appropriate. Sport is a distinctive activity that offers a bundle of characteristics of which exercise is only one: competition (which involves social interaction as well) and skill are other elements which are invariably features of a sport but are not necessarily components of an exercise activity such as jogging. Since they offer different experiences, the relationship between well-being and sport might be misrepresented by examining the relationship between well-being and an aggregation of sports and exercise activities.

From the list of activities in the survey, many, such as badminton and baseball, cricket and curling, were self-evidently sports. Other pursuits, such as hill trekking and attendance at the gym, we regarded as exercise rather than sport because they lack the element of competition. But a number of cases, including swimming, were ambiguous because they are practised by some participants as keep-fit and by others competitively. Our criterion with these was to treat as 'sport' only those which we judged to be more commonly practised in the context of a contest (the score is kept) than for pure recreation. Accordingly, our final list of 'sports' to be used to construct the indicator variable *sports player* excluded pastimes such as fishing, skiing, swimming and yachting. On our narrow definition, 47.9 per cent of respondents had engaged in sport in the preceding four weeks (a similar order of magnitude to the sports participation rate of 44.5 per cent reported by Farrell and Shields, 2002, from a data-set collected in 1997). Engagement was significantly more common among men (54.9 per cent) than among women (42.3 per cent).

3. ARE SPORTS PEOPLE HAPPY PEOPLE?

Mean happiness scores for sports and non-sports players are displayed in Table 9.1. Of course, in calculating means we are implicitly treating the data as cardinal rather than ordinal. But it is not obvious that this is legitimate because the gap in happiness implied by a happiness score of 9 as opposed to 8 might not be equivalent to, say, the gap between 5 and 4. On the other hand, Ferrer-i-Carbonell and Frijters (2004) reviewed evidence

Table 9.1   Sample happiness scores

	Mean happiness score	Standard deviation	Sample size
Whole sample	7.60	1.83	27989
Males	7.63	1.81	12493
Females	7.57	1.85	15496
All sports players	7.73	1.69	13432
All non-sports players	7.48	1.95	14557
Male sports players	7.74	1.69	6871
Male non-sports players	7.50	1.95	5622
Female sports players	7.73	1.70	6561
Female non-sports players	7.46	1.95	8935

consistent with respondents typically answering as if the scale were cardinal. They attributed this to evolution having given people a common understanding of how numbers are used to convey information concerning their feelings, such that they treat the choice of numbers 'much as they interpret weights in the supermarket'. Fortunately, Ferrer-i-Carbonell and Frijters went on to demonstrate that, in practice, it makes little difference which approach is adopted in studying determinants of happiness, since similar patterns emerged from each when they applied them in turn to major happiness data-sets. Here, we treat the data as cardinal but note that no substantive difference in qualitative findings emerged when we modelled happiness scores employing methods appropriate to ordinal data. We prefer to present 'cardinal' results throughout because of their ease of interpretation.

The raw data in Table 9.1 point to sports people being happier on average than non-sports people. The difference of very close to one-quarter of a point is virtually exactly the same whether one considers both genders together or only men or only women. Of incidental interest in Table 9.1 is that the mean and variance of happiness scores of men and women are so close. Here, England may have followed the same path as the USA where the once significant gap in happiness scores (in favour of women) has now entirely disappeared, according to three decades of experience of happiness scores in the *General Social Survey* (Stevenson and Wolfers, 2008).

That the part of the population playing sport self-reports higher happiness than the rest is not in itself very interesting since the difference might be due merely to the composition of the two groups. For example, sports people may also be financially better off and in better health on average than non-sports people. What is interesting is to ask whether there is any difference in happiness score between otherwise similar people according to whether or not they participate. The answer to this question is most conveniently conveyed through ordinary least squares regression.

Table 9.2 presents results from regressing happiness score on the indicator variable *sports player* and a set of control variables selected to reflect gender, age, self-identified ethnicity, labour force status, religious practice, educational qualification, marital status, the presence of children in the household, own evaluation of state of health, income and type of neighbourhood. Most of the variables are self-explanatory (for the groups of indicator variables, the excluded, or reference, categories are *female, white British, employed or not seeking a job, does not practise religion, single, no children present in the household, fair health* and *other type of neighbourhood*).[1] However, a few require explanation.

Table 9.2   Ordinary least squares regression results

Dependent variable	Happiness score	$|t|$
male	−0.011	0.41
age	−0.025	6.42
age squared	0.0003	8.48
Asian	−0.222	5.06
black	−0.070	1.37
Chinese	−0.513	5.37
mixed race	−0.303	6.33
white other	−0.214	3.91
retired	0.218	5.40
unemployed	−0.460	7.33
student with job	0.297	3.91
student, no job	0.143	2.09
off sick	−0.296	5.28
practises a religion	0.166	5.66
degree	−0.133	5.78
A level	−0.140	3.46
GCSE	0.130	4.20
other qualification	−0.147	2.71
married	0.674	19.60
cohabiting	0.503	11.30
separated	−0.161	2.55
divorced	−0.053	1.16
widowed	−0.264	5.31
child(ren) aged 8 or below	−0.108	2.96
child(ren) aged 9 to 12	−0.003	0.07
teenager(s)	−0.115	2.52
child(ren) aged 8 or below* male	0.106	1.93
child(ren) aged 9 to 12* male	−0.039	0.57
teenager(s)* male	−0.001	0.02
very good health	1.013	33.05
good health	0.530	18.61
bad health	−0.561	11.48
very bad health	−1.103	5.11
income if reference person	0.003	2.70
not reference person	0.141	2.96
neighbourhood: 'wealthy achievers'	−0.337	1.82
neighbourhood: 'urban prosperity'	−0.449	2.40
neighbourhood: 'comfortably off'	−0.262	1.42
neighbourhood: 'moderate means'	−0.376	2.02
neighbourhood: 'hard pressed'	−0.301	1.62
sports player	**0.115**	**5.07**
constant	7.393	35.48

Table 9.2 (continued)

Dependent variable	Happiness score	$|t|$
Adjusted R-squared	0.139	
Number of observations	27989	

Note: The specification also included a series of indicator variables to represent missing information on age/health/ethnicity/religious practice/reference person income; there was also an indicator variable for where income was in the top band.

On the magnitude and significance of most of the control predictor variables, there is a strong consensus across studies irrespective of when and where they were conducted. But there have been mixed findings on whether the subjective wellbeing of adults is affected by the presence of children in the household, for example Alesina et al. (2004) found a negative impact. Here we focus on the age rather than the number of children present in the household by including indicator variables to capture the presence or not of one or more children in the young, 9–12 and teenager age groups respectively. Given the possibility that childcare responsibilities press more heavily on women, we also include slope dummy variables (for example, *young child* is multiplied by *male*)[2] to allow us to show any difference between men and women in how children influence self-reported well-being.

Whether income appears to be an important factor has also varied across studies (for a survey of the relevant literature, see Clark et al., 2008). One of the practical problems in testing is that the same income for an individual could signify poverty (if the level of income is low and the respondent is the breadwinner) or affluence (if the respondent is a secondary earner and can afford to take a part-time or undemanding job). Accordingly, we include income in the model only if the respondent was the 'household reference person' (HRP) (for example, if the person was responsible for paying the rent or mortgage, he or she was the HRP; if partners shared the responsibility, the one with higher income was the HRP). We deem the income of non-HRPs as probably not sufficiently well correlated with family resources to capture living standards and so non-HRPs are represented by setting an appropriate indicator variable to one in their case. It should also be noted that income was collected in the form of bands. We assigned *income*, which refers to the amount before tax received in the preceding 12 months, as the mid-point of the band. This is unlikely significantly to have distorted the results because the bands were narrow, either £2500 or £5000.[3]

The survey collected the residential postcode of each respondent and, employing Geographical Information Systems, this could potentially have given access to a rich set of variables relating to neighbourhood characteristics. But, since each UK postcode refers to a very small area (typically 50 or 100 addresses), these were excluded, for reasons of confidentiality, from the data-set released for use by researchers. However, the public data did include an ACORN (A Classification of Residential Neighbourhoods) code supplied by the commercial service CACI which assigns each postcode in the country to one of a series of neighbourhood descriptors (representing the sort of people who live there) on the basis of very micro-level Census statistics concerning the area in which the postcode is located. This was the source of our set of neighbourhood descriptor indicator variables.

Estimation results displayed in Table 9.2 present familiar patterns. Health is by far the most powerful input in the happiness production function; unemployment is associated with quite severely depressed well-being; it is better to have a partner than to be single; most ethnic minorities are less satisfied than white British; well-being is lowest among the middle aged (the turning point in the quadratic relationship between happiness score and age is at age equals 38.05); the religious report themselves happier than others (consistent with Helliwell, 2003); income is a positive factor in determining well-being; and neighbourhood variables play a role (for example, living in an affluent urban area is a negative predictor of well-being; given that the model holds income constant, this could reflect either that satisfaction with income is influenced by levels of neighbours' incomes or that high housing costs erode the amount of discretionary spending). There appears to be no difference in predicted happiness between those who hold different levels of educational qualification (suggesting that benefits from extra qualifications are only achieved through the income variable) but those with no educational qualification at all are happier (income held constant).

There are novel findings on the effect of children. Young children significantly lower happiness scores, though the impact is almost exactly cancelled out by the male slope dummy. Thus we find that the whole cost, in terms of utility, of the burden of looking after young children appears to fall on women. By contrast, both genders seem to suffer equally from a teenager living in the home.

Finally from Table 9.2, the coefficient estimate on our focus variable, *sports player*, is positive and highly significant. Thus, even after controlling for a rich set of variables relating to life circumstances, it remains true that sports players are indeed happier people than non-sports players, albeit that removing composition effects has lowered the difference to a fairly modest level (0.11 happiness points).

4. DOES SPORT MAKE SPORTS PEOPLE HAPPIER PEOPLE?

Ordinary least squares is an effective tool for describing data as it allows us to control for a large number of observed variables. But it cannot allow for the effects of non-observed or unobservable variables and that is why, in the present context, our results so far cannot reasonably be interpreted as showing causation running *from* playing sport *to* well-being: the results are only descriptive. The problem is that the status of *sports player* is not distributed randomly within the sample. Rather, sports players self-selected into that group. If they did so on the basis of non-observed or unobservable personal characteristics that also had a direct impact on happiness score, then ordinary least squares will yield a biased estimate of the *causal* impact of sport on happiness. It will yield an *overestimate* if the relevant personal characteristics that incline an individual to play sport also tend independently to raise his or her ability to achieve happiness. It will yield an *underestimate* if the independent effect of those characteristics is to tend to lower the ability to achieve happiness.

We had no priors concerning the direction of the bias. Let the decision to play sport depend in part on a set of 'unknown individual characteristics'. These may be 'favourable' in the sense of raising an individual's capacity to achieve happiness or 'unfavourable' in the sense of lowering an individual's ability to achieve happiness. If positive traits, like being tall or having an extrovert personality, dominate in the influence exerted on sports participation by the set of unknown individual characteristics, then persons playing sport will have an atypically high capacity for happiness. In ordinary least squares estimation, there will be omitted variable bias such that the influence of the non-observed or unobservable individual characteristics will be captured in an inflated coefficient estimate on *sports player*. In other words, sports people may be happier because of the sorts of people they are rather than because they play sport. The ordinary least squares coefficient estimate on *sports player* will then be biased upwards.

On the other hand, the decisions of sports people to play sport may have been strongly influenced by negative traits like aggression or over-competitiveness. In this case, those observed to play sport will have a relatively low capacity to achieve happiness and the ordinary least squares estimate will be biased downwards. Sport would be doing more for participants than was evident because sport was attracting disproportionate numbers of people with negative traits. Like the first possibility, this also would not be implausible. For example, aggressive individuals drawn to sport might then avoid behaviour that leads to lower satisfaction with life if they 'take out' their aggression on opponents in a setting where this is socially acceptable.

What is suspected here is a type of selection bias that can be addressed with an appropriate statistical model. The two-step treatment effects model (for a treatment, see Greene, 2008, pp. 889–90) was developed, within the framework of Heckman, for employment in situations such as we face here. The researcher wishes to estimate the effect of treatment (playing sport), represented by a binary variable, on outcome (happiness score). But the decision to undergo treatment is taken by the subject rather than being determined randomly. This raises the possibility of selection bias.

The model proceeds in two stages. The first is a probit to account for the decision whether or not to be treated and the second is the regression of outcome on treatment (and controls). There is selection bias if the errors at stage 1 are correlated with the errors at stage 2. In this event, information extracted at stage 1 is capable of being used at stage 2 to improve explanatory power and, if it is not, there will be omitted variable bias at stage 2. The treatment effects model adds a term, derived from the correlation (if any) between the errors, to capture the influence of selectivity and permit the coefficient estimate on treatment then to be unbiased.

Estimation is enabled to be more precise if it is possible to include exogenous variables at stage 1 which have no direct effect on outcome and can therefore be excluded from stage 2. We employed two such variables, each binary. The first is *access* which is set equal to one for respondents who answered positively to a question on whether sports facilities were available within 20 minutes travelling distance of home (the presence of neighbourhood variables reduces the chance that this will proxy neighbourhood quality). The second is *encouragement* which is set equal to one for respondents who answered positively to a question on whether, as a child, he or she had received parental encouragement to play sport. Unsurprisingly in a small, urbanized country, more than 80 per cent enjoyed *access*. More than 30 per cent had received *encouragement*. We judged that neither variable 'belonged' in stage 2 because they would be expected to influence happiness through the *sports player* variable rather than directly.

Table 9.3 displays our results. Some incidental interest attaches to the stage 1 estimates since they illustrate vividly the extent to which sports players in England have a profile that could fairly be described as privileged. Participation is correlated strongly with income, education, belonging to a white ethnic group and residing in an affluent area. Marginal effects here are large. For example, relative to a benchmark subject (defined by continuous variables set to the sample means and indicator variables set to zero), who has a .468 predicted probability of participation, a degree

Table 9.3   Treatment effects model

Dependent variable	Happiness score			
	Stage 1 probit	|t|	Stage 2	|t|
male	0.316	15.28	−0.048	1.41
age	−0.009	2.84	−0.023	5.62
age squared	−0.0001	4.18	0.0003	8.59
Asian	−0.418	12.11	−0.166	3.02
black	−0.343	8.61	−0.023	0.40
Chinese	−0.245	2.10	−0.477	3.10
mixed race	−0.143	2.33	−0.285	3.38
white other	0.009	0.21	−0.212	3.86
retired	0.134	4.14	0.209	5.11
unemployed	0.100	2.08	−0.471	7.45
student with job	0.108	1.77	0.285	3.72
student, no job	0.155	2.86	0.126	1.81
off sick	−0.243	5.25	−0.263	4.42
practises a religion	0.014	0.68	0.165	6.47
degree	0.435	15.98	−0.190	3.91
A level	0.341	13.65	−0.185	4.45
GCSE	0.214	8.88	−0.157	4.51
other qualification	0.064	1.49	−0.153	2.81
married	0.006	0.21	0.671	19.42
cohabiting	−0.074	2.15	0.510	11.38
separated	−0.029	0.59	−0.158	2.51
divorced	0.123	3.41	−0.068	1.46
widowed	0.033	0.81	−0.273	1.43
child(ren) aged 8 or below	−0.087	3.13	−0.097	2.60
child(ren) aged 9 to 12	0.072	2.20	−0.014	0.33
teenager(s)	−0.036	1.04	−0.109	2.38
child(ren) aged 8 or below male*	0.026	0.62	0.100	1.81
child(ren) aged 9 to 12 male*	0.102	1.90	−0.051	0.73
teenager(s) male*	0.039	0.71	−0.008	0.12
very good health	0.358	15.02	0.969	24.09
good health	0.217	9.74	0.503	15.53
bad health	−0.217	5.09	−0.541	10.75
very bad health	−0.350	3.79	−1.001	10.55
income if reference person	0.004	4.66	0.002	2.05
not reference person	0.078	3.52	0.131	4.49
neighbourhood: 'wealthy achievers'	0.350	2.37	−0.379	2.02

Table 9.3   (continued)

Dependent variable			Happiness score	
	stage 1 probit	$\|t\|$	stage 2	$\|t\|$
neighbourhood: 'urban prosperity'	0.238	1.57	−0.477	2.53
neighbourhood: 'comfortably off'	0.249	1.69	−0.292	1.57
neighbourhood: 'moderate means'	0.148	1.00	−0.393	2.10
neighbourhood: 'hard pressed'	0.101	0.68	−0.313	1.68
sports player			**0.467**	**2.26**
access	0.347	12.60		
encouragement	0.110	6.46		
lambda			−0.215	1.72
constant	−0.447	2.67	7.212	30.78
Pseudo R-squared	0.155			
Number of observations	27989			

Note: The specification also included a series of indicator variables to represent missing information on age/health/ethnicity/religious practice/reference person income; there was also an indicator variable for where income was in the top band.

is estimated to raise this by more than 17 percentage points, whereas membership of the Asian community lowers it by very close to 16 percentage points. Other features of the table include: that males are more likely than females to play sport; that, for a given age and income of course, the unemployed and the retired and students, provided they do not also have a job, are more likely to take part in sport (presumably they are time rich relative to the benchmark); that young children deter parents' participation but the effect is opposite for the 9–12 age group (we speculate that this is the age when parents and children can go to the sports club together); and that cohabitation lowers participation but marriage does not (our interpretation is that most cohabiters are at a stage in their relationship when they still need to be together most of the time). Encouragingly, our two 'additional' variables each appear to exert a strong impact on probability of participation with marginal effects of more than 13 and more than 4 percentage points for *access* and *encouragement* respectively.

In the stage 2 results, the estimated coefficient on the selectivity correction term is significant, though weakly so ($p = .086$), and negative. The sign

Table 9.4   Reduced-form model

Dependent variable	Happiness score	$|t|$
male	−0.005	0.20
age	−0.025	6.50
age squared	0.0003	8.40
Asian	−0.228	5.20
black	−0.073	1.42
Chinese	−0.503	3.31
mixed race	−0.305	3.66
white other	−0.206	2.76
retired	0.221	5.48
unemployed	−0.454	7.24
student with job	0.294	3.87
student, no job	0.149	2.18
off sick	−0.304	5.42
practises a religion	0.163	6.45
degree	−0.128	3.67
A level	−0.137	4.26
GCSE	−0.129	4.19
other qualification	−0.151	2.78
married	0.671	19.50
cohabiting	0.496	11.15
separated	−0.163	2.60
divorced	−0.050	1.08
widowed	−0.262	5.62
child(ren) aged 8 or below	−0.011	3.04
child(ren) aged 9 to 12	−0.0009	0.02
teenager(s)	−0.113	2.47
child(ren) aged 8 or below* male	0.108	1.97
child(ren) aged 9 to 12* male	−0.035	0.51
teenager(s)* male	−0.003	0.04
very good health	1.024	33.52
good health	0.534	18.80
bad health	−0.562	11.49
very bad health	−1.022	10.93
income if reference person	0.003	2.81
not reference person	0.143	5.04
neighbourhood: 'wealthy achievers'	−0.132	1.79
neighbourhood: 'urban prosperity'	−0.447	2.39
neighbourhood: 'comfortably off'	−0.261	1.41
neighbourhood: 'moderate means'	−0.378	2.03
neighbourhood: 'hard pressed'	−0.303	1.63
access	**0.076**	**2.29**

Table 9.4   (continued)

encouragement	0.114	2.57
constant	7.354	35.10
Adjusted R-squared	0.141	
Number of observations	27 989	

Note: The specification also included a series of indicator variables to represent missing information on age/health/ethnicity/religious practice/reference person income; there was also an indicator variable for where income was in the top band.

implies negative correlation between stage 1 and stage 2 errors and so it is suggestive of ordinary least squares giving downwardly biased estimates of the impact of playing sport. It underestimates the impact of sport because it fails to take into account that a disproportionate number of those who are sports players are endowed with unfavourable characteristics from the perspective of wanting to be happy. The point estimate on *sports player* is 0.467. This represents the *causal* impact of being a sports player on happiness score. It is a large payoff. Though not by any means as important as marriage, the estimated average effect of constraining a current player not to take part in sport is almost exactly the same as that from moving a currently employed subject into unemployment. The framework for policy debate in the near future is likely to be on closing sports facilities as a contribution to reducing the public sector deficit. Our results illustrate that participation in sport makes a significant contribution to the well-being of many people and that if closures cause them to give up or play less often, then this would imply a high social cost.

Finally, and similar to Huang and Humphreys (Chapter 8 in this volume), we estimate a reduced form model to check directly the importance of sports facilities. The underlying model is that *happiness score* depends on the value of *sports player* (which is endogenous) and the values of control variables. In turn, *sports player* is a function of the same controls and *access* and *encouragement*. The reduced form equation then has *happiness score* depends on all the exogenous variables including *access* and *encouragement*.

The point estimate on *access* in Table 9.4 suggests that maintaining the availability of a sports facility to a randomly selected individual raises the expected happiness score by 0.076 points. This could be regarded as a very strong effect indeed. For example, if a particular sports centre were the only facility serving the needs of a local population of 1000, the loss in aggregate happiness points from closing it would be roughly equivalent to that from 155 'household reference persons' across the country becoming unemployed (this takes into account both the direct impact of unemployment on happiness score and the effect from receiving the sample mean income associated with unemployment rather than the sample mean income associated with employment). As Huang and Humphreys (Chapter 8 in this volume) imply, the loss could be even greater if there is also an effect (on well-being) through health variables (which will happen if health suffers when participation in sport is reduced or terminated). The policy conclusion of our chapter is that sports infrastructure should not lightly be discarded by government.

NOTES

1. The labour force status categories were allocated from answers to questions about whether the interviewee was employed, retired or a student. There was no explicit category called 'unemployed' but we were able to construct our own *unemployed* variable, set equal to one for those respondents who had not answered 'employed' to the main economic status question (they had not done paid work in the preceding seven days) but answered 'yes' to a subsequent question about whether they had been looking for work or a place on a training scheme in the preceding four weeks. This left the reference category to include the employed and others, such as homemakers, who were neither students nor retired but who were not seeking a job.
2. *Male* of course refers to the gender of the respondent, not that of the child.
3. The top band, over £50000, was unbounded. We gave the respondents in this small category (3 per cent of the sample) the value of £55000 but, since this was arbitrary, we also included an indicator variable for this group.

REFERENCES

Alesina, A., Di Tella, R. and MacCulloch, R. (2004), 'Inequality and happiness: are Europeans and Americans different?', *Journal of Public Economics*, **88**, 2009–42.
Clark, A.E., Frijters, P. and Shields, M.A. (2008), 'Relative income, happiness and utility: an explanation for the Easterlin Paradox and other puzzles', *Journal of Economic Literature*, **46**, 95–144.
Dolan, P., Peasgood, T. and White, M. (2008), 'Do we really know what makes us happy? A review of the economic literature on the factors associated with subjective well-being', *Journal of Economic Psychology*, **29**, 94–122.
Farrell, L. and Shields, M.A. (2002), 'Investigating the economic and demographic determinants of sporting participation in England', *Journal of the Royal Statistical Society, Series A*, **165**, 335–48.
Ferrer-i-Carbonell, A. and Frijters, P. (2004), 'How important is methodology for the estimates of the determinants of happiness?', *Economic Journal*, **114**, 641–59.
Greene, W.H. (2008), *Econometric Analysis*, 6th edn, Upper Saddle River, NJ: Pearson Education.

Helliwell, J.F. (2003), 'How's life? Combining individual and national variables to explain subjective well-being', *Economic Modelling*, **20**, 331–60.
Kavetskos, G. and Szymanski, S. (2010), 'The impact of major sporting events on happiness', *Journal of Economic Psychology*, **31** (2), 158–71.
Layard, R. (2005), *Happiness: Lessons from a New Science*, London: Penguin Books.
Peiró, A. (2006), 'Happiness, satisfaction and socio-economic conditions: some international evidence', *Journal of Socio-Economics*, **35**, 348–65.
Stevenson, B. and Wolfers, J. (2008), 'Happiness inequality in the United States', *Journal of Legal Studies*, **37**, 533–79.
Williams, J. (2006), *Taking Part: The National Survey of Culture, Leisure and Sport. Final Technical Report*, London: British Market Research Bureau Ltd.

10. High school sports and teenage births*

Joseph Price and Daniel H. Simon

1. INTRODUCTION

The public generally views sports as an effective way to help youth learn life skills, stay out of trouble, finish high school and go on to college. Of particular interest is the ability of sports to help young women. For example, a recent Nike advertisement includes the following lines along with images of teenage girls playing sports: 'If you let me play, I will have more self-confidence, I will suffer less depression, I will be 60% less likely to get breast cancer, I will be more likely to leave a man who beats me, I will be less likely to get pregnant before I want to.'

A growing body of research documents a strong positive connection between participation in high school sports and the types of outcomes mentioned in this Nike advertisement. The primary challenge in testing the impact of sports participation on these type of outcomes, is that unobserved factors could influence both sports participation and the outcome of interest (yielding a spurious correlation).We provide evidence of this type of spurious correlation using data from a nationally representative dataset of youth. We find that the simple correlation between sports participation and teenage pregnancy declines by about half (and loses statistical significance) when we control for basic demographic characteristics such as race, family income and whether both parents are present in the home.

The ideal research design would be a randomized control trial where some girls are assigned to play sports and others are denied the chance to play sports. While such an experiment is unlikely, in 1972, Congress created something close to this type of experiment when it enacted Title IX of the Educational Amendments. Title IX required schools to raise girls' sports participation rates to match that of boys. As a result, there was a sharp increase in female sports participation rates in the mid-1970s with the largest increases in female sports participation rates occurred in those states that had the highest male sports participation rates before Title IX.

We use this natural experiment to test whether the states that experienced the largest increases in female sports participation rates experienced a differential change in teen birth rates.

2. EFFECTS OF SPORTS PARTICIPATION

A number of studies show that sports participation increases the likelihood that a student will finish high school, go to college and eventually have higher earnings. While the focus has primarily been on male athletes, recent research indicates that the effects on female athletes are just as large. In this chapter, we test the effect that sports participation has on the likelihood that young women experience a teen birth, an event that has a large impact on educational and labor market outcomes (Kleipenger et al., 1999; Taniguchi, 1999).

Much of the recent research is focused on the channels through which sports participation could lead to positive outcomes. For example, sports provide constructive use of after-school time where there is peer interaction and adult supervision. Athletic activity can increase self-confidence and thus enable athletes to better withstand peer pressure. Competitive athletics also provide an added motivation to stay physically fit for competition, which may discourage athletes from sexual activity and encourage the use of birth control. Finally, athletes may see sports as an opportunity to get scholarships to pay for higher education – they have relatively more to lose if their sports career is disturbed by pregnancy or the need to raise a child.

Recent research has shown a negative correlation between sports participation and various measures of sexual activity. Savage and Holcomb (1993) find that female athletes are less likely than non-athletes to engage in sexual activity, have fewer sex partners and are older when they first have sex. Miller et al. (1998) find that female athletes are less likely to report having sex (though the correlation for male athletes is just the opposite). Similarly, Pate et al. (2000) show that female athletes are less likely to report sexual activity in the previous three months.

However, Dahl and Della Vigna (2009) note that many interventions can have both an exposure effect and an effect on the time use of the participants, which may operate in opposite directions. Thus, the effects of increasing access to high school sports will depend on the activities these young women would have engaged in or the type of supervision they would have received in the absence of high school sports. The counterfactual environment for young women may differ based on their race or family background.

3.   ANALYSIS USING NELS DATA

As a starting point, we follow the approach of past studies, using data from the National Education Longitudinal Study of 1988 (NELS 1988). This is a nationally representative sample of 8th graders in 1988, which were resurveyed in both 10th grade and 12th grade. We use these data to test whether sports participation in 10th grade influences whether the female students have a child by 12th grade (we exclude girls who have had a birth by 10th grade from the analysis). The results in Table 10.1 show that 4 per cent of the non-athletes had a teen birth, compared to only 2.5 per cent of the athletes. If this difference were interpreted as a causal effect, then it would suggest that playing sports decreases the chances that a girl has a teen birth by 38 per cent.

We test the sensitivity of this estimate to the inclusion of a few additional control variables, such as the student's race, whether her family is above the median income for the sample ($35000 in 1988 dollars) and whether she lives with both parents. All of these variables were measured when the respondent was an 8th grader. The results in panel B in Table 10.1 show that 34.7 per cent of girls who do not live with both parents play sports compared to 45.6 per cent of those who live with both parents. The gap based on family income is 14.7 percentage points and the racial gap is about 7 percentage points.

The successive columns in panel A of Table 10.1 provide the change in the relationship between sports participation and having a teen birth as we include these additional controls. When we include any one of these demographic measures individually, the estimated teen birth gap between athletes and non-athletes drops to about 1.0–1.3 percentage points. When we include all three together, the gap drops to 0.8 percentage points and is no longer statistically significant at even the 10 per cent level.

These results are similar to those of Dodge and Jaccard (2002), who use data from the National Longitudinal Survey of Adolescent Health (a sample of 7th–12th graders, first interviewed in 1995). They find that girls who play sports were 35 per cent less likely to get pregnant. However, when they control for the girl's grade level, ethnicity and maternal education, the coefficient on sports participation becomes trivial and statistically insignificant.

These results highlight the role that individual characteristics play in influencing the relationship between sports participation and teen births. In the next section, we describe an alternative approach in which we exploit changes in female sports participation that are unrelated to the individual's characteristics. This method allows us to compare outcomes for otherwise similar girls who experienced large differences in their ability to play high school sports.

Table 10.1 How sensitive are OLS estimates to basic family controls?

A. Factors associated with having a baby by 12th grade:

	(1)	(2)	(3)	(4)	(5)
Plays sports	−0.015***	−0.013**	−0.010*	−0.013**	−0.008
	(0.005)	(0.005)	(0.005)	(0.005)	(0.005)
Both parents		−0.026**			−0.016*
		(0.006)			(0.006)
Higher income			−0.037**		−0.029**
			(0.005)		(0.005)
White				−0.035**	−0.027**
				(0.007)	(0.007)
Constant	0.040***	0.057**	0.055**	0.066**	0.082**
	(0.004)	(0.006)	(0.005)	(0.007)	(0.008)

B. Factors associated with playing high school sports in 10th grade:

	(1)	(2)	(3)	(4)
Both parents	0.106**			0.068**
	(0.014)			(0.014)
Higher income		0.147**		0.124**
		(0.013)		(0.014)
White			0.070**	0.033*
			(0.014)	(0.014)
Constant	0.347**	0.355**	0.365**	0.294**
	(0.011)	(0.008)	(0.012)	(0.014)

Notes:
Sample drawn from NELS female respondents.
Girls who had birth by 10th grade are excluded.
N = 7607.
Observations include weights to reflect oversampling of Asians and Hispanics and non-response rates.
*, ** and *** indicate statistical significance at the 10 per cent, 5 per cent and 1 per cent level respectively.

4. TITLE IX AS A NATURAL EXPERIMENT

The 1972 Educational Amendments to the 1964 Civil Rights Act had important implications for schools nationwide. The law stated: 'No person in the United States shall, on the basis of sex, be excluded from participation in, be denied the benefits of, or be subjected to discrimination under any education program or activity receiving Federal financial assistance.' This regulation applied to all institutions which received federal funding, and though the amendment itself does not specifically cite its applicability to sports and competition, the effect of Title IX on sports has become the public face of the legislation.

Since the amendment left matters of practical implementation in the hands of individual schools, the Ford administration drafted an interpretation of the law which would clarify the meaning of the legislation and the criteria for evaluating compliance. The provisions included a three-pronged approach which stipulated that schools should measure their compliance with Title IX based on the principles of (1) financial equity proportional to male and female participation, (2) equal access to equipment, facilities, and coaching, and (3) adequate provision of programs to accommodate the interests and abilities of each gender. Because these changes could not be made immediately, it was expected that all federally funded institutions be in compliance by 1978, six years after the original legislation was passed.

During those six years, schools increased their funding of athletics to comply with the provision for program availability according to interest and ability, which in practice meant increasing the availability of female athletic programs until participation rates and funding for women were proportionally equal to men. As a result, girls nationwide saw a significant increase in the programs available to them, and as a consequence, their participation rates increased dramatically between 1972 and 1978.

At the time the law was made, the male sports participation rates varied across states, ranging from about 0.3 in Alabama, Florida, Maryland, North Carolina and Rhode Island to over 1 in Minnesota, Nebraska and North Dakota (individuals playing in more than one sport are counted multiple times). Because the legislation required matched expenditures on male and female sports, states with high male sports participation rates had to direct relatively more resources into female sports in order to reach parity. As a result, the increase in female sports participation was largest in states with the highest levels of male participation to start with. Nationally, Stevenson (2007) documents that Title IX increased female sports participation from about 3 per cent in 1972 to 25 per cent in 1978, while male participation stayed relatively constant at about 50 per cent.

Stevenson (2010) uses the combination of the passage of Title IX and the initial differences across states in male sports participation rates to examine the impact that sports participation has on post-secondary education and employment outcomes for women. She finds that a 10 per cent increase in female sports participation leads to a .055-year increase in female educational attainment and a 1.8 per cent increase in female employment. Kaestner and Xu (2006) use a similar approach and divide states into three groups based on the change in the female sports participation rate that accompanied the passage of Title IX. They compare states in the top third (in terms of the largest change) with the bottom third and find that increased sports participation leads to increased physical activity and decreased weight and BMI for girls.

5. DATA

We use state-level measures of female sports participation from annual volumes published by the National Federation of State High School Associations that include information on the number of athletes by state, gender and sport.[1] We calculate sports participation rates in each state by dividing the total numbers of male and female athletes by high school enrollment data from the National Center of Educational Statistics (with a gender adjustment made using 1970 and 1980 IPUMS (Integrated Public Use Microdata Series) data).

We construct state-year-age specific birth rates using two approaches. The first approach is to calculate the fraction of girls ages 15–17 in the 1970 and 1980 census who report having had a child. In the 1970 census data, we pool together six different 1 per cent samples and in the 1980 census data, we pool together the 5 per cent and 1 per cent sample. We aggregate the data up to the year-state-age level (though in some analysis we also separate by race). We use 1970 as our pre-Title IX measure of teenage births and 1980 as the post-title IX measure.

We also use data from US birth certificates to measure the number of teenagers (separately by age) who give birth in each state (adjusting the count for whether the state provided a 50 per cent or 100 per cent sample[2]). We combine the birth counts with state-year-age specific population counts calculated by the SEER program at the National Cancer Institute. One advantage of this approach is that we can construct data for each year. As a result, we use the years 1969–71 as pre-Title IX period and 1978–80 as the post-Title IX period.

A major difference between the two approaches is that the census data reports whether the individual has ever had a baby (the stock of past teen births) while the natality data measures the flow of new teen births. To make the natality data comparable to the census data, we look only at first-time mothers and keep only one observation per birth event in the case of twins or triplets. We construct our birth count measures based on birth year of the mother and her age when she gives birth. For each age-year-state group, we include all of the current-year births for that age group, as well as any births that occurred to those same groups in past years. For example, the teen birth rate for 17-year-olds in 1971 is

Table 10.2   Teenage birth rates

A. Sample mean	Census	Natality
Age		
15	0.0159	0.0170
16	0.0322	0.0454
17	0.0685	0.0908
Race/ethnicity		
Non-Hispanic white	0.0257	
Black	0.1164	
Other	0.0592	
Full sample	0.0389	0.0511

B. Sample median	Census	Natality
Age		
15	0.0138	0.0142
16	0.0285	0.0413
17	0.0634	0.0874
Race/ethnicity		
Non-Hispanic white	0.0176	
Black	0.0929	
Other	0.0364	
Full sample	0.0296	0.0412

N	300	900

Notes:
The unit of observation in each dataset is the state, year, age group for girls ages 15–17.
The census data includes a 6 per cent sample from the decennial census in 1970 and 1980.
The natality data is based on data from 1969–71 and 1978–81.
Teenage birth rate refers to the fraction of girls who have had a birth by age 15, 16, or 17.
The sample mean is an unweighted average across states.

the number of births to 17-year-olds in 1971, 16-year-olds in 1970 and 15-year-olds in 1969 (we ignore any births to girls 14 years or younger, which represent only 5 per cent of births to mothers 17 years or younger).

Table 10.2 provides both the mean and median teen birth rate across states separately by age and race for each of our two datasets. Most of our analysis will focus on estimates from the census data and the average teenage birth across states for this data is 3.89 per cent. This fraction increases as girls age, from 1.59 per cent at age 15 to 6.85 per cent at age 17. Overall, black young women are more than four times more likely to have experienced a teenage birth (11.6 per cent versus 2.6 per cent).

Finally, we use data on 1247 girls, ages 14–17, from the first and second

Table 10.3   Factors associated with frequency of exercise (NHANES data)

	Full sample	Wave 1 (1971–74)	Wave 2 (1976–80)
Age	−0.058**	−0.051**	−0.065**
	(0.012)	(0.017)	(0.018)
Black	0.063	−0.002	0.162**
	(0.036)	(0.047)	(0.058)
Income > $10k	0.049	0.055	0.054
	(0.030)	(0.041)	(0.046)
Year	−0.021**	−0.021	0.014
	(0.005)	(0.022)	(0.017)
Constant	0.643**	0.656**	0.395**
	(0.035)	(0.051)	(0.122)
Observations	1247	660	587

Notes:
Data on all female respondents age 14–17 to the first and second wave of the National Health and Nutritional Examination Surveys.
The outcome variable is one if the response to the frequency of exercise was 'much exercise' and zero if it was 'moderate, little, or no exercise'.

wave of the National Health and Nutritional Examination Surveys (NHANES I and II) to examine which racial differences in the change in sports participation rates in response to Title IX. We use a question about the frequency of exercise as a proxy for sports participation. Our descriptive results in Table 10.3 indicate that 51.4 per cent of the girls report 'much exercise' (as opposed to moderate or little to no exercise). This fraction drops by 5 percentage points for each year of age and is 5 percentage points higher for families with incomes above the median for the sample. The most striking pattern is that while there is no racial difference in exercise in the first wave (1971–74), black girls in the second wave (1976–80) reported athletic participation rates 19 percentage points higher than their white counterparts. These results suggest that Title IX may have had a much larger effect on the sports participation rates of black young women.

6. RESULTS

Our first empirical approach is to regress each state's teenage birth rate on the state's level of athletic participation in that year and an indicator for whether it was the post-Title IX period. All of our regressions include age and state fixed effects. The unit of analysis is the state-year-age group,

Table 10.4   Impact of state female athletic participation rate on teenage birth rate

A. OLS results	Census	Natality
State female sports rate	0.018	0.033*
	(0.013)	(0.014)
Post-Title IX	−0.003	−0.009
	(0.004)	(0.005)

B. IV Results	Census	Natality
State female sports rate	0.038*	0.041*
	(0.016)	(0.017)
Post-Title IX	−0.008	−0.011
	(0.005)	(0.006)

C. Reduced-from results	Census	Natality
Post*male sports rate	0.015*	0.016*
	(0.006)	(0.007)
Post-Title IX	−0.006	−0.009
	(0.004)	(0.005)

N	300	900

Notes:
Unit of observation is state-year-age.
The census sample includes girls ages 15–17 in 1970 (pre) and 1980 (post).
The natality sample includes girls ages 15–17 in 1969–71 (pre) and 1978–80 (post).
All regressions include age and state of residence fixed effects.
Standard errors are clustered at the state level are reported in parenthesis.
* and ** indicate significance at the 5 per cent and 1 per cent levels respectively.

providing 300 observations (50 states, 2 years and 3 age groups) in the census data and 1200 in the natality data (50 states, 8 years, and 3 age groups). The results in panel A of Table 10.4 indicate that a 10-percentage point increase in the female sports participation rate is associated with a 0.18–0.33 percentage point increase in the teen birth rate (a 7 per cent increase).

One concern about using the female sports participation rate directly is that there might be other factors, such as state programs and policies, that influence both the provision of sports for girls and teen births. To address this problem, we instrument for the state's female sports participation rate using the male participation rate in 1971.[3] Our IV estimates indicate that a 10-percentage point increase in the female sports participation rate increases the teen birth rate by about 0.38–0.41 percentage points (a 10 per cent increase).

As a final approach, we run a reduced-form regression of teen birth rates on our instrument directly interacted with an indicator for whether it was post-Title IX period. We find that states that had a 10-percentage point higher male sports rate in 1971 had a 0.15–0.16-percentage point higher teen birth after Title-IX was in place. These results provide evidence that the change in female sports participation rates was the mechanism underlying the changing birth rates, as the states with the highest male sports participation rates prior to Title IX are the ones where we see the largest increase in female sports participation and the largest increases in teen births.

In Table 10.5, we examine our results separately by race. We find that the positive effect of sports on teen birth rates is most pronounced for non-Hispanic white students. The estimates for this group are slightly larger than those of the full sample and more precisely estimated. When we look at black students, we find that the coefficients are consistently negative, with the IV estimate indicating that a 10-percentage point increase in sports lead to a 0.8-percentage point decrease in teen birth rates for black young women, which is a 20 per cent decrease in the teen birth rate for that group. The estimated coefficient for students who are of another race are similar to those of black young women.

7. DISCUSSION

There are a lot of reasons to believe that sports produce many positive effects for young women. In fact, past research using Title IX as a natural experiment find that high school sports increases the fraction of girls who go to college, who eventually enter the labor force or who choose to enter traditionally male-dominated careers (Stevenson, 2010). Using the same natural experiment, we find that the increase in female sports participation that accompanied the passage of Title IX increased teen birth rates (though the effect appears to be largely limited to non-Hispanic whites).

This result is similar to research by Jacob and Lefgren (2003) that examines the role that schools play in preventing crime. They find that on school inservice days (when there is no school for non-holiday related reasons), property crimes go up but violent crimes go down. As such, after-school programs designed to keep youth out of trouble may actually put students together who would normally not interact outside of school. In the Jacob and Lefgren study, this increased interaction between students lead to more fights and, in our case, it appears to have led to more teen births.

Table 10.5 Impact of state female athletic participation rate on teenage pregnancy rate (census data)

A. OLS results	White	Black	Other
State female sports rate	0.025*	−0.370	−0.199
	(0.009)	(0.230)	(0.109)
Post-Title IX	−0.005	0.073	0.065*
	(0.003)	(0.047)	(0.025)

B. IV results	White	Black	Other
State female sports rate	0.040**	−0.081	−0.097
	(0.011)	(0.192)	(0.091)
Post-Title IX	−0.010**	−0.002	0.037
	(0.003)	(0.050)	(0.031)

C. Reduced-form results	White	Black	Other
Post*male sports rate	0.016**	−0.030	−0.040
	(0.004)	(0.073)	(0.037)
Post-Title IX	−0.007**	−0.007	0.032
	(0.003)	(0.040)	(0.027)

Notes:
N = 300.
Unit of observation is state-year-age.
Sample includes girls ages 15–17 in 1970 (pre) and 1980 (post).
All regressions include age and state of residence fixed effects.
Standard errors (reported in parentheses) are clustered at the state level.
* and ** indicate significance at the 5 per cent and 1 per cent levels respectively.

Our results also indicate that there may be racial difference in the effects of sports on female youth outcomes. We find a very strong and pronounced positive correlation between sports and teen births for white students, but all of our estimates (though imprecisely estimated) suggest that sports have the opposite effect on black students. This finding relates to work by Hoffmann and Xu (2002) that indicates that the effects of participating in school activities on black students differs based on the racial composition of the high school. Participating in additional school activities was associated with more delinquent behavior for black students in high-minority schools but less delinquent behavior in low-minority schools. Applying our approach to data that includes information on the racial composition of a student's school could test this particular interaction. In fact, the forced segregation policies, which also occurred in the 1970s (Guryan 2004), may even provide a type of combined natural experiment.

Finally, most past research has focused on the positive effects of high school sports with rarely any mention of unintended consequences. These studies are often used to justify the expansion of sports programs for girls. Our results are not meant to dampen the enthusiasm for the expansion of such programs since other studies document other types of positive effects of sports for girls. However, our results suggest that it might be important for future research to explore some of the mechanisms through which these effects of the expansion of high school sports for young women and teen births is operating. This may allow high school programs to be designed in a way that takes advantages of all of the benefits of sports and reduces any negative unintended effects.

NOTES

* The research in this chapter was supported by a grant from the Women's Research Institute at Brigham Young University (BYU). Excellent research assistance was provided by Greg Astill, Jason Cook, Ryan Fairchild, Kevin Moon, Angie Otteson, Kristy Parkinson and Ulya Tsolmon.
1. The high school sports data does not provide any more disaggregated data based on age or race of the participants.
2. Starting in 1971, states began moving from a 50 per cent sample of births to a 100 per cent sample of births. There were six states with 100 per cent samples in 1971 and by 1980 there were 44 states with 100 per cent samples. We adjust all of our counts of teen births to reflect these changes in reporting samples.
3. We use the male participation rate in 1971 because this provides a baseline measure of male participation prior to the enactment of Title IX in 1972.

REFERENCES

Dahl, Gordon and Stefano Della Vigna (2009), 'Does movie violence increase violent crime?', *Quarterly Journal of Economics*, **124**, 677–734.
Dodge, Tonya and James Jaccard (2002), 'Participation in athletics and female sexual risk behavior: the evaluation of four causal structures', *Journal of Adolescent Research*, **17** (1), 42–67.
Guryan, Jonathan (2004), 'Desegregation and black dropout rates', *American Economic Review*, **94** (4), 919–43.
Hoffmann, John and Jiangmin Xu (2002), 'School activities, community service, and delinquency', *Crime & Delinquency*, **48** (4), 568–91.
Jacob, Brian and Lars John Lefgren (2003), 'Are idle hands the devil's workshop? Incapacitation, concentration and juvenile crime', *American Economic Review*, **93** (5), 1560–77.
Kaestner, Robert and Xin Xu (2006), 'Effects of Title IX and sports participation

on girls' physical activity and weight', *Advances in Health Economics and Health Services Research*, **17**, 79–111.

Klepinger, Daniel, Shelly Lundberg and Robert Plotnick (1999), 'How does adolescent fertility affect the human capital and wages of young women', *The Journal of Human Resources*, **34** (3), 421–48

Miller, Kathleen, Donald Sabo, Michael Farrell, Grace Barnes and Merrill Melnick (1998), 'Athletic participation and sexual behavior in adolescents: the different worlds of boys and girls', *Journal of Health and Social Behavior*, **39** (2),108–23.

Pate, Russell, Stewart Trost, Sarah Levin and Marsha Dowda (2000), 'Sports participation and health-related behaviors among US youth', *Archives of Pediatrics and Adolescent Medicine*, **154**, 904–11.

Savage, Michael and Derek Holcomb (1999), 'Adolescent female athletes' sexual risk-taking behaviors', *Journal of Youth and Adolescence*, **28** (5), 595–602.

Stevenson, Betsey (2007), 'Title IX and the evolution of high school sports', *Contemporary Economic Policy*, **25** (4), 486–505.

Stevenson, Betsey (2010), 'Beyond the classroom: using title IX to measure the return to high school sports', *Review of Economics and Statistics*, **92** (2), 284–301.

Taniguchi, Hiromi (1999), 'The timing of childbirth and women's wages', *Journal of Marriage and the Family*, **61** (4), 1008–19.

11. Physical activity and subjective well-being: an empirical analysis

Georgios Kavetsos

1. INTRODUCTION

According to the European Commission, a substantial amount of premature death and avoidable illnesses in its member states can be directly attributed to two main factors: (1) unhealthy diets, and (2) sedentary lifestyles (Commission of the European Communities, 2005). The combined effect of these two pillars can lead to obesity; broadly defined as a body mass index (BMI = weight/height^2) exceeding 30.[1]

Active (dynamic) physical engagement is thus one of the suggested tools to combat obesity, which in turn minimizes the probability of contracting a variety of serious diseases, such as type-II diabetes, coronary heart disease, some sorts of cancer, musculoskeletal disorders, gall bladder disease and obstructive sleep apnoea. Other measures have also been proposed, including investment in physical education and information, an obesity tax and advertising regulations. These lie outside the scope of this chapter; the interested reader can refer to relevant studies by Philipson and Posner (2008), Schroeter et al. (2008), Mazzocchi et al. (2009) and Yaniv et al. (2009).

Nonetheless, wide concerns exist linking obesity to adverse psychological states and social exclusion (BHF National Centre, 2007). Additionally, beneficial mental states arguably arise through physical activity (Glenister, 1996). To some extent then, participation in some sort of physical activity promotes social cohesiveness, although it is also reasonable to assume that the latter might have an effect on participation as well.

In line with this argument, this study attempts to test the relationship between individual welfare and sports participation empirically using a recent large cross-sectional data-set. Given the findings from the existing literature, it is hypothesized that subjective well-being of individuals increases through the participation in physical activity and with the frequency of participation. The estimated results confirm this hypothesis.

2.   LITERATURE REVIEW

2.1   Tangible Effects

To date the literature has mainly focused on tangible effects of physical activity and obesity. Extensive evidence exists suggesting that sports participation is linked to career attainment. Long and Caudill (1991) find contrary evidence to the view that more time devoted for sport during college/university has adverse effects on graduation rates. In fact, they estimate that ten years following graduation males who devoted some time in athletic participation during college earn about 4 per cent more over those who did not. The corresponding effect for females, although positive, is smaller and statistically insignificant. Similar results for individuals involved in sport during high school are provided in Barron et al. (2000).

Robst and Keil (2000) study the link between Grade Point Average (GPA) scores and athletic participation. Controlling for student ability (for example, standard assessment task – SAT – scores), they find that students engaging in athletics have higher GPAs than those not engaging in athletics; a result which is again particularly true for males. Furthermore, in line with similar studies, they find that students participating in sports have higher graduation rates as well.

In a European context, Cornelissen and Pfeifer (2007) study the impact of extra-curricular sports activities on education success among Germans and find that additional involvement in sport increases the probability that the student registers in a higher ranked school and receives a university degree.

2.2   Welfare Effects

The welfare implications of weight and participation have recently attracted the interest of social scientists. Social exclusion is probably the most common psychological effect associated with obesity. This, though, is not a universal sentiment, since one adapts to a community's social norm. Put differently, it may be more acceptable to be obese in a society that is obese (Blanchflower et al., 2009).

At the extreme, obesity can potentially lead to depression (see, for example, Roberts et al., 2000). Two studies support this argument empirically using self-reported subjective well-being data. Stutzer (2007) uses a 2002 cross-sectional data-set for Switzerland to find that obesity is negatively related with well-being. Oswald and Powdthavee (2007) use the 2004 wave of the British Household Panel Survey and the 2002 wave of the German Socio-Economic Panel, suggesting that significantly negative association between life satisfaction and BMI exist in both countries. For the British case, they also provide evidence suggesting that psychological distress is positively related with BMI.

On similar grounds, physical exercise has been associated with diminution of depression, and relatively recent studies suggest that the former should be more widely used in order to treat the latter (see, for example, Pollock, 2001 and the edited volume by Biddle et al., 2000a). In a context similar to that of this chapter, Melin et al. (2003) relate participation in sport and physical activity with life satisfaction in a Swedish sample. Findings suggest that physically active individuals report higher levels of satisfaction with life, on average.

Clearly, all of the above studies cannot be used to infer causality. It might well be the case that more satisfied or happier individuals tend to participate more in sport and unhappiness leads to obesity. Nevertheless, we are aware from clinical studies that physical activity releases endorphins and serotonin in the brain, which are responsible for feelings of joy and satisfaction (Chaouloff, 1997; Hoffmann, 1997). Knowledge of this fact leads to an informal justification of the assumed direction of causality, from participation to welfare. Furthermore, substantial evidence appears to exist suggesting that 'there is . . . a causal link between physical activity and reduced clinically defined depression' (Biddle et al., 2000b: 155).

Nevertheless, to conclude on the causality issue, further investigation is required. A co-twin study is one of the most appropriate methods to resolve this, since twins share not only the same genes determining ability of participation, but socio-economic status and neighbourhood characteristics as well. The results of such a study based in the Netherlands were recently released by Stubbe et al. (2007), who argue on the possibility of an underlying factor (for example, a shared environment or a shared genetic code) impacting both physical activity and well-being.

3. DATA AND METHODOLOGY

The data used in this study comes from the International Social Survey Programme (ISSP), an annual survey performed in a number of countries across all continents. The countries included in the surveys are Argentina, Australia, Austria, Belgium (Flanders), Bulgaria, Chile, Croatia, Cyprus, the Czech Republic, the Dominican Republic, Finland, France, Germany, Great Britain, Hungary, Ireland, Israel, Japan, Latvia, Mexico, New Zealand, Norway, the Philippines, Poland, Russia, Slovakia, Slovenia,

South Africa, South Korea, Sweden, Switzerland, Taiwan, Uruguay and the USA. In total, nearly 50 000 individuals are surveyed.

The 2007 survey includes two features that are of interest here. First, it asks individuals to report their level of happiness by posing the question: 'If you were to consider your life in general these days, how happy or unhappy would you say you are, on the whole? [very happy; fairly happy; not very happy; not at all happy; can't choose]'.[2] For a relevant overview of the happiness literature, its advantages and limitations, see Dolan et al. (2008) and Kavetsos and Szymanski (2010). Second, the 2007 survey focused on sports and included the following question on frequency of participation in sports and physical: 'How often do you take part in physical activities such as sports, going to the gym, going for a walk, in your free time? [daily; several times a week; several times a month; several times a year or less often; never]'.

An ordered limited dependent variable model can then be estimated, where given the unobserved variable $Happy_{i,s}$* representing the true level of individual happiness of individual i in country s, we observe: $Happy = 1$ if $Happy^* \leq k_1$; $Happy = 2$ if $k_1 < LS^* \leq k_2$; $Happy = 3$ if $k_2 < LS^* \leq k_3$; and $Happy = 4$ if $LS^* \geq k_4$, where k are cut-off points. The estimated model is then represented by:

$$Happy_{i,s} = b_1 SP_i + b_2 DEMO_i + b_3 D_s + v_{i,s} \qquad (11.1)$$

where, $Happy$ is the ordered life satisfaction of individual i at country s; SP is a binary variable equal to unity if individual i participates in some sort of physical activity/sport; $DEMO$ is a set of personal characteristics for the individual, including age (and squared aged), gender, marital and employment status, education level, household income (derived in quartiles), and urbanicity; D_s are country dummy variables, and v represents the error term.

Taking advantage of the frequency of participation in physical activity, equation (11.1) is re-estimated by including different binary variables to account for the effects of frequency of participation:

$$Happy_{i,s} = \Sigma_{j=1\ldots4} \, b_j SPF_{i,f} + b_5 DEMO_i + b_6 D_s + v_{i,s} \qquad (11.2)$$

where, SPF represents sports participation frequency variables for j ranging from 'daily' to 'never'; 'several times a year or less often' is the reference variable.

Strictly speaking, both models estimated here account only for significant correlations between welfare and participation and not causality, as also described in the previous section.

4. RESULTS

Table 11.1 reports some descriptive statistics of the key variables of interest. In this geographically wide sample we observe that the overwhelming majority of individuals report a positive state of happiness. In fact, more than 80 per cent report they are either *fairly* or *very happy* with their life.

For the case of sport, nearly 30 per cent of the respondents are not physically active; where, including the 'several times a year or less often' frequency to those never practising sport, this statistic increases to 42 per cent. Of those participating more actively, the majority does so on a weekly basis, followed by a monthly basis and then by a daily basis.

Tables 11.2 and 11.3 report the regression results of interest. For succinctness, a baseline regression of happiness on all personal controls is

Table 11.1 Descriptive statistics

	% of sample
Happiness: very happy	26.5
Happiness: fairly happy	56.5
Happiness: not very happy	14.5
Happiness: not at all happy	2.5
Participate in sport	70.7
Sport Frequency: daily	14.9
Sport Frequency: several times a week	25.3
Sport Frequency: several times a month	18.3
Sport Frequency: several times a year or less often	12.1

Table 11.2 Happiness and sports participation

	With income	Without income
Participate in sport	0.191*** (0.02)	0.211*** (0.024)
Personal controls	Yes	Yes
Country effects	Yes	Yes
Observations	37188	46012
Log pseudolikelihood	−36,424.869	−44,978.302
Pseudo R^2	0.066	0.063

Notes:
Regressions are ordered probits of self-reported happiness.
Standard errors clustered at the country level are reported in parentheses.
***, ** and * denote significance at the 1 per cent, 5 per cent and 10 per cent level, respectively.

Table 11.3   Happiness and sports participation frequency

	With income	Without income
Daily	0.179*** (0.032)	0.203*** (0.028)
Several times a week	0.095*** (0.019)	0.113*** (0.019)
Several times a month	0.032* (0.017)	0.046*** (0.016)
Never	−0.115*** (0.022)	−0.119*** (0.024)
Personal controls	Yes	Yes
Country effects	Yes	Yes
Observations	37 188	46 012
Log pseudolikelihood	−36 387.457	−44 921.422
Pseudo R^2	0.066	0.064

Notes:
Regressions are ordered probits of self-reported happiness.
Standard errors clustered at the country level are reported in parentheses.
***, ** and * denote significance at the 1 per cent, 5 per cent and 10 per cent level,
respectively.

presented in the Appendix, where, as in the literature, a positive correlation is estimated between happiness and marriage, cohabitation, some
levels of education and income. Regarding the latter, note that the level of
happiness is increasing for each income quartile. Age and disability have
a negative impact on happiness, although the former exhibits a diminishing effect. Moreover, unemployed, separated and widowed individuals all
report lower levels of happiness, on average.

The results of the regression of happiness on participation (equation
11.1) are presented in Table 11.2. Notably, the number of observations
decreases substantially due to individuals' refusal to disclose family
income. The estimation is thus repeated by excluding income and the
results are presented in the adjacent column. In both cases the relationship
between sports participation and subjective happiness is positive and statistically significant, where not controlling for income leads to an upward
bias of the estimated coefficient by 2 percentage points.

Although the statistical significance of this finding is quite large, a question remains on its economic significance. Based on the estimated model,
participating in sport and belonging to the third income quartile have an
almost equivalent relation to well-being (0.191/0.211 = 0.905, where 0.211
is the estimated coefficient for the third income quartile, significant at the
1 per cent level).

Having established a significantly positive relation between sports participation and self-reported states of well-being, I now move on to examine
the partial correlations between happiness and measures of participation

frequency. This involves the estimation of equation (11.2). Results are reported in Table 11.3.

As in the results of Table 11.2, omitting income controls from the estimation appears to be inflating the estimated coefficients by about 2 percentage points, with the exception of the 'never participating' category. In any case, the results are very informative. All frequency variables are statistically significant, where in addition their size decrease along with the decrease in frequency. Never participating in physical activity is associated with a significantly negative estimate, which is in absolute terms greater than that corresponding to the weekly frequency and about four times as large as that corresponding to the monthly frequency.

Assuming for a moment that causality is indeed running from participation to happiness, as some medical studies seem to be suggesting, being entirely inactive in sport has an equivalent effect on well-being as moving from the fourth (highest) to the third income quartile $(0.115/(0.321 - 0.211) =$ 1.045, where 0.321 and 0.211 are the estimated coefficients for the fourth and third income quartile, respectively, both significant at the 1 per cent level).

5. CONCLUSION

Following an extensive and currently growing literature on the health and welfare implications of obesity, this study examines a slightly different hypothesis relating the sports participation and frequency decision with individual self-reported states of happiness. Using a wide cross-sectional data-set of 34 countries, a positive relationship between happiness and participation is found. In greater detail, not only do sporty types report higher levels of happiness on average, but this measure of well-being appears to be increasing with the frequency of participation as well. Notably, inactive individuals tend to report significantly lower levels of happiness.

Although there is sufficient evidence from the psychology and medical literatures suggesting that the direction of causality is running from participation to happiness, the econometric analysis performed here is inadequate to providing a concrete answer regarding causality. Future studies are likely to use longitudinal data-sets to further enlighten the picture.

NOTES

1. See Burkhauser and Cawley (2008) for limitations regarding the use of BMI as an appropriate indicator of obesity.
2. Note that 'can't choose' responses are excluded from the analysis.

REFERENCES

Barron, J., Ewing, B. and Waddell, G. (2000), 'The effects of high school athletic participation on education and labor market outcomes', *Review of Economics and Statistics*, **82** (3), 409–21.

BHF National Centre (2007), 'Obesity and physical activity: adults', The British Heart Foundation National Centre for Physical Activity and Health, School of Sport and Exercise Sciences, Loughborough University.

Biddle, S.J.H., Fox, K.R. and Boutcher, S.H. (2000a), *Physical Activity and Psychological Well-Being*, London: Routledge.

Biddle, S.J.H., Fox, K.R., Boutcher, S.H. and Faulkner, G.E. (2000b), 'The way forward for physical activity and the promotion of psychological well-being', in S.J.H. Biddle, K.R. Fox and S.H. Boutcher (eds), *Physical Activity and Psychological Well-Being*, London: Routledge, pp. 154–68.

Blanchflower, D.G., Oswald, A.J. and Van Landeghem, B. (2009), 'Imitative obesity and relative utility', *Journal of the European Economic Association*, **7** (2/3), 528–38.

Burkhauser, R.V. and Cawley, J. (2008), 'Beyond BMI: the value of more accurate measures of fatness and obesity in social science research', *Journal of Health Economics*, **27**, 519–29.

Chaouloff, F. (1997), 'The serotonin hypothesis', in W.P. Morgan (ed.), *Physical Activity and Mental Health*, Abingdon: Taylor and Francis, pp. 179–98.

Commission of the European Communities (2005), 'Promoting healthy diets and physical activity: a European dimension for the prevention of overweight, obesity and chronic diseases', European Commission Green Paper, December, Brussels.

Cornelissen, T. and Pfeifer, C. (2007), 'The impact of participation in sports on educational attainment: new evidence from Germany', IZA discussion paper, No. 3160.

Dolan, P., Peasgood, T. and White, M. (2008), 'Do we really know what makes us happy? A review of the economic literature on the factors associated with subjective well-being', *Journal of Economic Psychology*, **29**, 94–122.

Glenister, D. (1996), 'Exercise and mental health: a review', *Journal of the Royal Society of Health*, **116**, 7–13.

Hoffmann, P. (1997), 'The endorphin hypothesis', in W.P. Morgan (ed.), *Physical Activity and Mental Health*, Abingdon: Taylor and Francis, pp. 163–77.

Kavetsos, G. and Szymanski, S. (2010), 'National wellbeing and major sports events, *Journal of Economic Psychology*, **31** (2), 158–71.

Long, J. and Caudill, S. (1991), 'The impact of participation in intercollegiate athletics on income and graduation', *Review of Economics and Statistics*, **73** (3), 525–31.

Mazzocchi, M., Traill, W.B. and Shogren, J.F. (2009), *Fat Economics: Nutrition, Health, and Economic Policy*, Oxford: Oxford University Press, pp. 114–57.

Melin, R., Fugl-Meyer, K.S. and Fugl-Meyer, A.R. (2003), 'Life satisfaction in 18- to 64-year-old Swedes: in relation to education, employment situation, health and physical activity', *Journal of Rehabilitation Medicine*, **35**, 84–90.

Oswald, A.J. and Powdthavee, N. (2007), 'Obesity, unhappiness, and the challenge of affluence: theory and evidence', *Economic Journal*, **117**, 441–59.

Philipson, T. and Posner, R. (2008), 'Is the obesity epidemic a public health problem? A decade of research on the economics of obesity', NBER working paper No. 14010.

Pollock, K.M. (2001), 'Exercise in treating depression: broadening the psycho-therapist's role', *Journal of Clinical Psychology*, **57** (11), 1289–300.

Roberts, R.E., Kaplan, G.A., Shema, S.J. and Strawbridge, W.J. (2000), 'Are the obese at greater risk for depression?', *American Journal of Epidemiology*, **152** (2), 163–70.

Robst, J. and Keil, J. (2000), 'The relationship between athletic participation and academic performance: evidence from NCAA Division III', *Applied Economics*, **32** (5), 547–58.

Schroeter, C., Lusk, J. and Tyner, W. (2008), 'Determining the impact of food price and income changes on body weight', *Journal of Health Economics*, **27**, 45–68.

Stubbe, J.H., de Moor, M.H.M., Boomsma, D.I. and de Geus, E.J.C. (2007), 'The association between exercise participation and well-being: a co-twin study', *Preventive Medicine*, **44**, 148–52.

Stutzer, A. (2007), 'Limited self-control, obesity and the loss of happiness', IZA discussion paper No. 2925.

Yaniv, G., Rosin, O. and Tobol, Y. (2009), 'Junk-food, home cooking, physical activity and obesity: the effect of the fat tax and the thin subsidy', *Journal of Public Economics*, **93**, 823–30.

APPENDIX: BASELINE HAPPINESS REGRESSION

Table 11A.1   Happiness regression

Male	−0.012 (0.023)
Age	−0.036*** (0.005)
Age^2	0.0003*** (0.0001)
Married	0.305*** (0.032)
Cohabiting	0.156*** (0.018)
Divorced	0.005 (0.031)
Separated	−0.11*** (0.041)
Widowed	−0.112*** (0.034)
Lower education	−0.023 (0.048)
Secondary education	0.057 (0.045)
Higher education	0.094* (0.056)
Employed full-time	−0.066 (0.079)
Employed part-time	−0.094 (0.074)
Employed less than part-time	−0.126 (0.09)
Helping family member	−0.068 (0.105)
Unemployed	−0.261*** (0.086)
At School	0.007 (0.09)
Retired	−0.048 (0.088)
Taking care of home	−0.004 (0.085)
Permanently disabled	−0.441*** (0.093)
Income quartile (2)	0.125*** (0.025)
Income quartile (3)	0.223*** (0.033)
Income quartile (4)	0.343*** (0.05)
Urban resident	−0.01 (0.06)
Suburb resident	−0.074* (0.04)
Town/small city resident	−0.028 (0.037)
Country village resident	0.014 (0.053)
Country effects	Yes
Observations	37 480
Log pseudolikelihood	−36 823.408
Pseudo R^2	0.063

Notes:
Regressions are ordered probits of self-reported happiness.
Standard errors clustered at the country level are reported in parentheses.
***, ** and * denote significance at the 1 per cent, 5 per cent and 10 per cent level, respectively.

12. Sport opportunities and local well-being: is sport a local amenity?

Tim Pawlowski, Christoph Breuer and Jorge Leyva

1. INTRODUCTION

For centuries, happiness has been a central theme of famous philosophers like Aristotle or Kant. However, recent important contributions have been developed by psychologists (for example, Nettle, 2005), sociologists (for example, Veenhoven, 1999), political scientists (for example, Lane, 2000) and economists (for example, Oswald, 1997). In the context of economics, happiness can be seen as a subjective approach to utility, and therefore it offers a wide range of possibilities to understand human behaviour. It is considered to be the ultimate goal in life and consequently appears to be a far better measure of individual welfare than income (Frey, 2008).

A number of studies have explored the relationship between sport and self-reported, subjective well-being (SWB).[1] With few exceptions, most of the research focused on the direct health benefits associated with physical activity and leisure. Empirical proof was found that physical activity in general, increases SWB. Since previous research could detect that the frequency and intensity with which a sport is practised depends on the allocation of sport facilities (Pawlowski et al., 2009; Wicker et al., 2009), a certain allocation of sport facilities itself might contribute to SWB. In order to make strategic political decisions, it is of great importance to know if the allocation of public sport facilities (decentralized versus centralized allocation), that is, the time people need to reach a public sports facility, has a direct impact on SWB. Therefore, this chapter primarily analyses the relationship between SWB and the availability of public sport facilities, while controlling for other factors.

The chapter is organized as follows: section 2 discusses the state of research and the theoretical background of happiness research; section 3 discusses the used data and the applied methods; section 4 presents the results of our analysis of the relationship of individual well-being and the availability of public sports facilities; and section 5 discusses the implications of the results and possible policy responses.

2.   PREVIOUS RESEARCH AND THEORETICAL BACKGROUND

For many years, it was assumed that utility could not be measured directly. However, during the recent past, it became generally accepted that SWB is a suitable measure for utility. Therefore, similarly to theoretical models based on utility, that is, classical demand theory (for example, Hicks, 1939), socio-economic demand theory (for example, Lavoie, 2004), or household production theory (for example, Becker, 1965; Lancaster, 1966; Stigler and Becker, 1977), there might be various factors that influence SWB. In the following, we provide an overview on the factors influencing SWB. We start by summarizing some empirical findings on general correlates of SWB before discussing some findings on sport-specific correlates.

Looking at the general determinants that have an impact on SWB, income is the most often analysed variable with results leading to different conclusions. While some researchers found empirical proof that income and SWB are independent (for example, Easterlin, 1974; Moghaddam, 2008), others confirmed (at least a slight) positive relationship (for example, Di Tella et al., 1999). Veenhoven and Ouweneel (1995) as well as Diener and Diener (1995) could also detect that SWB in richer countries is higher than in poorer countries. Cummins (2000) showed that there is a significant and positive effect on well-being as long as a minimum subsistence threshold has not been reached. On the other hand, Diener et al. (1993), using aggregate data, showed that gross domestic product (GDP) growth is inversely correlated with happiness. Further research focused on how people perceive their income in relation to reference groups or an aspired consumption level. In this context, Stutzer (2004) detected that relative income appears to have a larger impact on SWB than absolute income. In addition, Pedersen and Schmidt (2009) showed that the self-assessed financial situation has a significant positive impact on SWB.

In recent years, the analysis of further (non-pecuniary) micro and macro factors influencing SWB has gained relevance. On the micro level, level of education, health status and age are among the most investigated variables. For example, it was shown in different countries that higher education has a significant positive impact on SWB (Gerdtham and Johannesson, 2001; Pedersen and Schmidt, 2009; Veenhoven, 1993). Health was operationalized in the studies of Gerdtham and Johannesson (2001) as a dummy variable. They could detect a significant positive effect on SWB for a body mass index lower than 30. Age was detected to have a U-shaped relationship with SWB, which means that younger and older people are happier compared with middle-aged individuals (for example, Angeles, 2009). Furthermore, Graham and Pettinato (2000) found that individuals living in Latin America have the lowest level of SWB at approximately 50 years of age. In addition, Frey and Stutzer (2000) found that people older than 60 years are happier than people aged 30 years and younger. Furthermore, living in a couple or being married shows a strong positive effect on SWB (Moghaddam, 2008; Pedersen and Schmidt, 2009). Regarding further social relationships, Flouri (2003) detected that the involvement of parents in early years of life has a significant positive effect on the SWB while Pedersen and Schmidt (2009) found empirical proof that persons who are members of a social, political or sporting club are happier than those who do not belong to any club.

On the macro level, Dorn et al. (2007) showed that people living in democratic countries are happier than those living in countries with non-democratic governments. In addition, militarism, investigated by Chang-Tsai (2009) as an index of military expenditures as a percentage of the GDP and the ratio of military personnel to the total labour force, shows a strong negative relation to SWB. A further branch of analysed macro factors on SWB regards the environment. For example, Brereton et al. (2007) showed that weather conditions, such as high temperatures are positive and significant, and precipitation slightly increases happiness, while Luechinger (2009) and Rehdanz and Maddison (2008) proved that higher air pollution and noise levels significantly reduce SWB. Especially during recent years, the analysis of effects caused by geographical and infrastructural amenities on SWB has increased in importance. For instance, Brereton et al. (2007) used the geographical information system from Ireland to show that proximity to coast has a significant positive impact on SWB, while other variables, such as the proximity to landfills, are negatively related to SWB. Furthermore, Brereton et al. (2007) could detect that living too close to, as well as living too far from, an international airport decreases SWB. The authors conclude that the first might be caused by the noise of the aircraft while the latter might be the result of the long commuting time that individuals have to spend to reach the airport. Therefore, the highest SWB is reported by those living between 30 and 60 km from an international airport. Other transportation amenities, such as major roads were found to have a linear relationship to SWB. While reported well-being is at the lowest level for those living close to a major road, it is considerably higher for those living farther away.

Finally, the number of studies linking sport to SWB has increased during recent years. So far, most of the research focuses on the direct health benefits associated with physical activity and leisure. For example, Blanchflower and Oswald (2008) showed that countries whose population has low blood pressure, readings are happier. Empirical proof was found that special sports programmes (Kara et al., 2005) and the frequency (Sila, 2003) or intensity (Lafont et al., 2007) of physical activity positively influences SWB. Similarly, different dimensions of athletic involvement positively affect mental well-being, as shown by Miller and Hoffman (2009). Rasciute and Downward (2010) showed that active travelling (utilitarian cycling or walking) also increases well-being.

Other dimensions of sport, such as hosting major sporting events have been studied by Kavetsos and Szymanski (2008), who analysed data from 12 European countries and detected that hosting the Olympic Games has a negative impact on SWB. By contrast, hosting a major football event like the European Cup or the FIFA World Cup has a temporary but significant positive effect on SWB. Interestingly, Wei-Ping (2007) detected that hosting the Olympic Games 2008 in Beijing had a significant positive impact on the Gross National Happiness index of China.

The first and, to our knowledge, only study that combines the effect of the general factor (infrastructure) with a sport-related aspect was developed by England et al. (1980). They investigated the effect of the presence of ski resorts on SWB and were able to detect that living close to a ski resort slightly increases SWB.

Summing up, there is a rich literature that has analysed general and sport-specific factors and their effects on SWB. However, the following study is the first to explore the relationship between the availability of public sports facilities and SWB.

3.   APPLIED METHODS

To detect the relationship between the availability of public sports facilities and SWB, data from the German Socio-Economic Panel (SOEP) are used. This panel is a representative repetitive survey that has been carried out for more than 25 years to observe the stability and change of living conditions in Germany over a long period of time. Every year, more than 21 000 people living in around 11 600 households answer 215 different questions on income, employment, housing, family, education, health, self-assessed well-being and personal attitude. A particularity of this study is the high representativeness of immigrants, East Germans, and higher-income households. For the SOEP, all members over 16 years of age living in the selected households are considered and all surveyed persons are requested to take part in the next survey, even if they move to a different household before the next survey takes place. The stability of this panel is 95 per cent (2007), which is high and means that 95 per cent of the sample surveyed that year took part in the survey the previous year. The survey itself consists of two questionnaires, one to be answered individually by each member of the household, and the other to be answered per household. To serve as variables in our model, socio-economic and SWB indicators can be identified from the first section of the survey, and from the latter section, several spatial indicators can be extracted. By matching the data of individuals and households of the year 2004, it is possible to implement several different characteristics in our model. Overall, n = 22 019 cases are available for analysis for this research.

Following Nettle (2005), the research of happiness is focused on the concept of 'life satisfaction' (happyli), which reflects the overall contentment with life. In addition, we have access to data of individuals' 'satisfaction with leisure' (happyle) as well as 'satisfaction with health' (happyhe). On an 11-point scale, participants answer the question, how satisfied are they currently with their life, leisure and health status? In econometric terms, we are faced with a limited dependent variable. This implies that a linear regression model with ordinary least squares (OLS) estimates is not appropriate. In the literature, at least two general branches of models are generally accepted for implementation in the case of a limited dependent variable: probit or logit models (for example, Pedersen and Schmidt, 2009) as well as ordered probit or ordered logit models (for example, Borooah, 2006; Brereton et al., 2007; Di Tella et al., 1999; Graham and Pettinato, 2000; Kavetsos and Szymanski, 2008). Following Rascuite and Downward (2010), we focus on a binary probit model for which dummy variables happyli, happyle and happyhe were created, where zero represented all self-assessed well-being, satisfaction with leisure or satisfaction with health notes between 0 and 5, and one was for notes ranging from 6 to 10. The estimation of a probit model is done by applying the maximum likelihood and the results indicate the increase or decrease in the probability of happiness with regard to the explanatory variables. The three probit models to be estimates are defined as (see Long and Freese, 2006)

$$\Pr(happyli_i \neq 0 | x_i) = \Phi(x_i b)$$
$$\Pr(happyle_i \neq 0 | x_i) = \Phi(x_i b) \qquad (12.1)$$
$$\Pr(happyh_i \neq 0 | x_i) = \Phi(x_i b)$$

where $x_i b$ is called the probit score, which is based on different explanatory variables and their corresponding estimates, and Φ is the standard cumulative normal probability distribution. Based on the estimates one can observe the marginal effects for continuous variables (meaning the change in the probability calculated at the mean) as:

$$MFX_{continous} \equiv \frac{\partial \Phi}{\partial x_1} = \phi(\bar{x}b)b_i \tag{12.2}$$

where ϕ is the normal density function. In contrast, the marginal effect associated with a dummy changing from zero to one is calculated as:

$$MFX_{discrete} \equiv \Phi(\bar{x}_1 b) - \Phi(\bar{x}_0 b) \tag{12.3}$$

The purpose of this chapter is to observe the effect of the distance to sports and leisure facilities on happyli, happyle and happyhe. This indicator is computed with three variables: dsport10 for those living in a distance less than 10 walking minutes away, dsport1020 for those living between 10 and 20 minutes, and dsport20 for those living more than 20 minutes away from a public sports facility. The reference category, which is, for reasons of multicollinearity, excluded from our estimation, relates to the category of people that are not able to reach public sports facilities by walking.

To control for other covariates, we also implemented further spatial factors. Following the above-mentioned definition, closeness to daily consumption shops was operationalized with dshops10, dshops1020 and dshops20. In the same way, distances to restaurants and bars (dbar10, dbar1020 and dbar20), banks (dbank10, dbank1020 and dbank20), family doctor (ddoc10, ddoc1020 and ddoc20), kindergarten (dkinder10, dkinder1020 and dkinder20), primary school (dschool10, dschool1020 and dschool20), high school (dhighs10, dhighs1020 and dhighs20), facility or meeting place for young people (dyouth10, dyouth1020 and dyouth20), facility or meeting place for seniors (dseniors10, dseniors1020 and dseniors20), public park (dpark10, dpark1020 and dpark20), and public transportation stop (dpubtr10, dpubtr1020 and dpubtr20) were also observed in the model. In order to measure the degree of urbanization of the household's area, further variables were created: city for households located in the downtown of a large city, city10 was created for households situated less than 10 km away, city1025 was created for those living between 10 and 25 km away, city2540 for those living between 25 and 40 km, and city4060 for those living between 40 and 60 km away.

In line with previous studies, different socio-demographic indicators are implemented as well. Age of respondents is given by the variable with the same name. To cover possible curve, non-linear effects of age on happyli, happyle, and happyhe, age squared (age2) is implemented as an additional variable in our model. The variable male was created for gender, and married and single for marital status. Income is observed in the model as a metric variable. Regarding occupational indicators, the following variables were created: public official, blue collar worker, white collar worker, self employed, trainee, and unemployed. The effect of the commuting distance to work on SWB is also analysed in our model (metrical scaled variable). Furthermore, health was represented with the dummy variable goodhealth and the responses were 'good', 'very good' and zero for 'satisfactory', 'not quite good' and 'bad'. The amount of leisure time per day is also included in the model as a metrical scaled variable.

The effect of physical inactivity on SWB is covered in our model with the variable nosport, which takes the value zero, for those stating they do sport regularly or occasionally and one, for those reporting they never do sport. Summing up, most of the variables included in the model emerge regularly in other well-being studies. Table 12.1 provides a summary and overview of the different variable labels.

4. RESULTS

The average monthly net income of households is around €2662 per month. The data show that 10.3 km is the mean commuting distance to work. Furthermore, on average, Germans dedicate 2.38 hours for leisure and hobbies daily (see Table 12.2).

Table 12.3 shows the frequency distribution of the dependent variables. Females represent 52 per cent and males 48 per cent of the sample; 60 per cent of the respondents are married and 24.8 per cent are single. In the three cases, the percentages of participants who are happy with their life, leisure and health are very similar, ranging between 69 per cent and 76 per cent. Around 36 per cent of the respondents affirmed that they were never engaged in physical activities. On the occupational variables, white collar workers represent the largest type of employment at 27.5 per cent, followed by blue collar workers (15 per cent), self employed (6 per cent), public officials (4.3 per cent), and unemployed (3.1 percent).

When we look at the spatial variables, it can be seen that most of the participants live in suburban areas; 24.7 per cent of the respondents live within 10 km of the city centre and an almost equal portion of respondents (27.7 per cent) live within 10 and 25 km of the city centre. With n = 8641, around 40 per cent of the surveyed individuals have access to public sports facilities within 10 minutes' walking distance from their homes, 35 per cent need to commute between 10 and 20 minutes, and slightly more than 10 per cent state that a public sports facility is not within walking distance. Furthermore, 54.6 per cent of the respondents live within 10 minutes' or

The economics of sport, health and happiness

Table 12.1   Description of variables

	Variable	Description	Variable	Description	Variable	Description
Socio-demographic	Age	Metric (years)	age2	Metric (years*years)	Men	1 for 'men'; 0 otherwise
	income	Metric (net income per month in €)	married	1 for 'married'; 0 otherwise	Single	1 for 'single'; 0 otherwise
	good health	1 for 'good', 'very good': 0 for 'satisfactory'	nosport	1 for 'never do sport': 0 for 'regularly', 'occasionally'	Ltime	Metric (hours per day)
	public official	1 for 'public official'; 0 otherwise	blue collar worker	1 for 'blue collar worker'; 0 otherwise	white collar worker	1 for 'white collar worker'; 0 otherwise
	self employed	1 for 'self employed'; 0 otherwise	trainee	1 for 'trainee'; 0 otherwise	unem-ployed	1 for 'unem-ployed'; 0 otherwise
	dwork	Metric (km)				
Spatial	city	1 for 'living in a downtown of a large city'; 0 otherwise	city10	1 for 'living within 10 km from the downtown of a large city'; 0 otherwise	city 1025	1 for 'living between 10 and 25 km from the downtown of a large city'; 0 otherwise
	city 2540	1 for 'living between 25 and 40 km from the downtown of a large city'; 0 otherwise	city4060	1 for 'living between 40 and 60 km from the downtown of a large city'; 0 otherwise	dshops 20	1 for 'living more than 20 walking minutes away from shops'; 0 otherwise
	dshops 10	1 for 'living within 10 walking minutes from shops'; 0 otherwise	dshops 1020	1 for 'living between 10 and 20 walking minutes from shops'; 0 otherwise	dbar20	1 for 'living more than 20 walking minutes away from bars and restaurants'; 0 otherwise

Table 12.1   (continued)

	Variable	Description	Variable	Description	Variable	Description
Spatial	dbar10	1 for 'living within 10 walking minutes from bars and restaurants'; 0 otherwise	dba1020	1 for 'living between 10 and 20 walking minutes from bars and restaurants'; 0 otherwise	dbank 20	1 for 'living more than 20 walking minutes away from bank'; 0 otherwise
	dbank 10	1 for 'living within 10 walking minutes from bank'; 0 otherwise	dbank 1020	1 for 'living between 10 and 20 walking minutes from bank'; 0 otherwise	ddoc20	1 for 'living more than 20 walking minutes away from family doctor'; 0 otherwise
	ddoc10	1 for 'living within 10 walking minutes from family doctor'; 0 otherwise	ddoc 1020	1 for 'living between 10 and 20 walking minutes from family doctor'; 0 otherwise	dkinder 20	1 for 'living more than 20 walking minutes away from kinder-garten'; 0 otherwise
	dkinder 10	1 for 'living within 10 walking minutes from kindergarten'; 0 otherwise	dkinder 1020	1 for 'living between 10 and 20 walking minutes from kindergarten'; 0 otherwise	dschool 20	1 for 'living more than 20 walking minutes away from primary school'; 0 otherwise
	dschool 10	1 for 'living within 10 walking minutes from primary school'; 0 otherwise	dschool 1020	1 for 'living between 10 and 20 walking minutes from primary school'; 0 otherwise	dhighs 20	1 for 'living more than 20 walking minutes away from high school'; 0 otherwise

The economics of sport, health and happiness

Table 12.1   (continued)

<table>
<tr><th></th><th>Variable</th><th>Description</th><th>Variable</th><th>Description</th><th>Variable</th><th>Description</th></tr>
<tr><td rowspan="5">Spatial</td><td>dhighs 10</td><td>1 for 'living within 10 walking minutes from high school'; 0 otherwise</td><td>dhighs 1020</td><td>1 for 'living between 10 and 20 walking minutes from high school'; 0 otherwise</td><td>dyouth 20</td><td>1 for 'living more than 20 walking minutes away from youth centre'; 0 otherwise</td></tr>
<tr><td>dyouth 10</td><td>1 for 'living within 10 walking minutes from youth centre'; 0 otherwise</td><td>dyouth 1020</td><td>1 for 'living between 10 and 20 walking minutes from youth centre'; 0 otherwise</td><td>dseniors 20</td><td>1 for 'living more than 20 walking minutes away from senior centre'; 0 otherwise</td></tr>
<tr><td>dseniors 10</td><td>1 for 'living within 10 walking minutes from senior centre'; 0 otherwise</td><td>dseniors 1020</td><td>1 for 'living between 10 and 20 walking minutes from senior centre'; 0 otherwise</td><td>dpark 20</td><td>1 for 'living more than 20 walking minutes away from park or green area'; 0 otherwise</td></tr>
<tr><td>dpark 10</td><td>1 for 'living within 10 walking minutes from park or green area'; 0 otherwise</td><td>dpark 1020</td><td>1 for 'living between 10 and 20 walking minutes from park or green area'; 0 otherwise</td><td>dsport 20</td><td>1 for 'living more than 20 walking minutes away from sport facility'; 0 otherwise</td></tr>
<tr><td>dsport 10</td><td>1 for 'living within 10 walking minutes from sport facility'; 0 otherwise</td><td>dsport 1020</td><td>1 for 'living between 10 and 20 walking minutes from sport facility'; 0 otherwise</td><td>dpubtr 20</td><td>1 for 'living more than 20 walking minutes away from p. transportation stop'; 0 otherwise</td></tr>
</table>

Table 12.1   (continued)

	Variable	Description	Variable	Description	Variable	Description
Spatial	dpubtr 10	1 for 'living within 10 walking minutes from public transportation stop'; 0 otherwise	dpubtr 1020	1 for 'living between 10 and 20 walking minutes from public transportation stop'; 0 otherwise		

Table 12.2   *Descriptive statistics of metrical scaled variables*

Variable	Observations	Mean	Standard deviation	Min	Max
Age	22 019	47.20	17.46	17	99
ltime[1]	22 019	2.38	2.01	0	24
dwork[2]	22 019	10.29	36.88	0	960
income[3]	22 012	2 662.21	2 260.45	0	99 999

Notes:
[1] In hours per day,
[2] In km.
[3] Net euros per month.

less walking distance of shops selling daily consumption goods. It is also interesting that a high percentage of the respondents (61 per cent) live within 10 minutes' walking distance from bars and restaurants. Nearly all respondents (84 per cent) have a public transportation stop nearby. Banks and doctors can be reached within 10 minutes by 47 per cent and 36 per cent of the participants, respectively. While we can observe similar portions for nursery schools (kindergartens) (46 per cent) and primary schools (40 per cent), only 21 per cent of respondents can reach a high school in a 10-minute walk from their homes. This seems plausible since there are fewer high schools per district than primary schools (see Table 12.3).

Table 12.4 shows the estimation results of the three probit models. Our findings confirm the often observed U-shaped relationship between age and SWB (while age has a significant negative impact on SWB, age2

Table 12.3   Frequencies

Variable	Frequency	Percentage
happyli	16838	76.66
happyle	16519	75.02
happyh	15294	69.46
men	10567	47.99
goodhealth	11353	51.56
married	13278	60.30
single	5461	24.80
nosport	7956	36.13
public official	953	4.33
blue collar worker	3328	15.11
white collar worker	6060	27.52
self employed	1327	6.03
trainee	674	3.06
unemployed	686	3.12
city	2196	9.97
city10	5434	24.68
city1025	6097	27.69
city2540	3330	15.12
city4060	2353	10.69
dshops10	12025	54.61
dshops1020	6248	28.38
dshops20	1452	6.59
dbar10	13417	60.93
dbar1020	6166	28.00
dbar20	1185	5.38
dbank10	10500	47.69
dbank1020	6931	31.48
dbank20	1962	8.91
ddoc10	7948	36.10
ddoc1020	6802	30.89
ddoc20	3239	14.71
dkinder10	10186	46.26
dkinder1020	6219	28.24
dkinder20	1802	8.18
dschool10	8676	39.40
dschool1020	6740	30.61
dschool20	2223	10.10
dhighs10	2995	13.60
dhighs1020	4747	21.56
dhighs20	4299	19.52
dyouth10	5480	24.89
dyouth1020	6314	28.68

Table 12.3   (continued)

Variable	Frequency	Percentage
dyouth20	3 174	14.41
dseniors10	4 928	22.38
dseniors1020	5 589	25.38
dseniors20	3 423	15.55
dpark10	12 503	56.78
dpark1020	4 950	22.48
dpark20	1 562	7.09
dsport10	8 641	39.24
dsport1020	7 774	35.31
dsport20	3 078	13.98
dpubtr10	18 524	84.13
dpubtr1020	2 878	13.07
dpubtr20	291	1.32

Note: Total observations are 22 019 except for the variable happy1 for which 21 964 responses were considered.

has a significant positive effect on SWB). Males tend to be more satisfied with their health and leisure while we could not observe a gender effect on the probability of being happy with life. Single people and married people (which is in accordance with Pedersen and Schmidt, 2009) have a higher probability of being happy compared with others (for example, divorced individuals). This holds true for all measures (except for the combination single and happyh). Not engaging in sport, fitness or gymnastics is negatively related to our three constructs of well-being. For example, not practising sport decreases the probability of people being satisfied with their leisure status by about 8 per cent. In contrast, reporting good health has a very strong positive impact on all three dependent variables of SWB. As might be expected, good health increases the probability of being satisfied with one's health status by around 50 per cent. However, the probability of being satisfied with ones life and leisure is also considerably increased (23 per cent and 12 per cent, respectively). This ratifies the evidence found by Gerdtham and Johannesson (2001) and Moghaddam (2008) acknowledging the high influence of good health on SWB.

As could be expected, the amount of daily leisure time shows a considerable impact on satisfaction with leisure, significant to the .01 level. In contrast, the impact of leisure time on the other dependent variables is positive but quite low. A possible reason for this can be found in the decreasing

Table 12.4 *Probit estimates and marginal coefficients for happyli, happyle and happyh (statistical test in parentheses)*

Variable	happyli coefficient	dF/dx	happyle coefficient	dF/dx	happyh coefficient	dF/dx
age	−.0351***	−.0099	.0052	.0015	−.0227***	−.0068
	(-8.74)		(1.26)		(-5.24)	
age2	.0004***	.0001	.0001**	.0000	.0002***	.0000
	(10.88)		(2.34)		(3.88)	
men	.0240	.0068	.0699***	.0209	.0497**	.0148
	(1.15)		(3.45)		(2.26)	
goodhealth	.8221***	.2315	.3956***	.1189	1.6915***	.4861
	(36.55)		(18.55)		(68.37)	
married	.3236***	.0934	.0639 **	.0193	.0956***	.0287
	(11.33)		(2.17)		(3.17)	
single	.1155***	.0317	.1677***	.0486	−.0211	−.0063
	(2.85)		(4.17)		(−.47)	
nosport	−.1951***	−.0561	−.2555***	−.0785	−.2000***	−.0607
	(-9.18)		(-12.23)		(-8.98)	
ltime	.0130**	.0037	.1398***	.0419	.0161***	.0048
	(2.50)		(22.74)		(2.93)	
dwork	−.0003	−.0001	−.0014***	−.0004	.0000	.0000
	(−1.10)		(−5.29)		(.10)	
public official	.4502***	.1044	−.1016*	−.0315	.2323***	.0634
	(7.24)		(−1.96)		(3.80)	
blue collar worker	.1452***	.0391	−.2466***	−.0785	.0395	.0116
	(4.39)		(−7.68)		(1.11)	
white collar worker	.3010***	.0797	−.2228***	−.0692	.1432***	.0415
	(10.16)		(−7.91)		(4.52)	
self employed	.1859***	.0487	−.6339***	−.2229	.1749***	.0489
	(3.85)		(−14.88)		(3.38)	
trainee	.1714**	.0449	−.0172	−.0052	−.0502	−.0152
	(2.57)		(−.28)		(−.65)	
unemployed	−.7400***	−.2574	−.2501***	−.0812	−.4499***	−.1530
	(−14.25)		(−4.70)		(−7.72)	
income	.0000***	.0000	.0001	.0000	.0000***	.0000
	(13.07)		(.64)		(3.49)	
city	.0347	.0097	−.0559	−.0171	−.1467***	−.0456
	(.79)		(−1.30)		(−3.11)	
city10	.0616*	.0171	−.0488	−.0148	−.0835**	−.0253
	(1.74)		(−1.40)		(−2.21)	
city1025	.1200***	.0330	.0228	.0068	−.0042	−.0012
	(3.50)		(.67)		(−.11)	
city2540	.1175***	.0319	.0448	.0133	.0371	.0109
	(3.08)		(1.19)		(.91)	
city4060	.1301***	.0350	.0628	.0185	−.0347	−.0104
	(3.11)		(1.53)		(−.78)	

Table 12.4 (continued)

Variable	happyli coefficient	dF/dx	happyle coefficient	dF/dx	happyh coefficient	dF/dx
dshops10	−.0884*	−.0248	−.0886*	−.0265	−.0162	−.0048
	(−1.79)		(−1.85)		(−.31)	
dshops1020	−.0498	−.0141	−.0678	−.0205	−.0760	−.0229
	(−.97)		(−1.36)		(−1.39)	
dshops20	.0350	.0097	.0717	.0210	.0272	.0080
	(.54)		(1.14)		(.40)	
dbar10	.0520	.0147	−.0082	−.0024	.0686	.0205
	(.98)		(−.15)		(1.21)	
dbar1020	.0646	.0179	−.0332	−.0100	.0611	.0180
	(1.16)		(−.60)		(1.03)	
dbar20	.0421	.0117	.0059	.0018	.1249*	.0356
	(.61)		(.09)		(1.72)	
dbank10	.0936*	.0263	.0039	.0012	.0556	.0165
	(1.92)		(.08)		(1.07)	
dbank1020	.0349	.0098	.0357	.0106	−.0357	−.0107
	(.70)		(.73)		(−.68)	
dbank20	.0149	.0042	.1098*	.0318	−.0731	−.0223
	(.25)		(1.89)		(−1.17)	
ddoc10	−.0743*	−.0211	.0483	.0144	−.0457	−.0137
	(−1.90)		(1.28)		(−1.11)	
ddoc1020	−.0684*	−.0195	.0133	.0040	−.0394	−.0118
	(−1.75)		(.35)		(−.96)	
ddoc20	−.0982**	−.0284	.0043	.0013	−.0425	−.0128
	(−2.26)		(.10)		(−.93)	
dkinder10	−.0269	−.0076	−.0414	−.0124	−.0261	−.0078
	(−.64)		(−1.02)		(−.58)	
dkinder1020	.0184	.0052	−.0497	−.0150	.0179	.0053
	(.42)		(−1.17)		(.39)	
dkinder20	−.0399	−.0114	−.1086**	−.0336	.0177	.0052
	(−.72)		(−2.03)		(.30)	
dschool10	.0470	.0132	.1189***	.0353	−.0026	−.0008
	(1.06)		(2.76)		(−.06)	
dschool1020	.0454	.0127	.1106**	.0326	.0400	.0118
	(1.02)		(2.56)		(.85)	
dschool20	.0997*	.0271	−.0285	−.0086	.0163	.0048
	(1.85)		(−.55)		(.29)	
dhighs10	.0463	.0128	−.0603	−.0184	−.0168	−.0050
	(1.20)		(−1.62)		(−.41)	
dhighs1020	.0011	.0003	−.0483	−.0146	.0091	.0027
	(.04)		(−1.53)		(.26)	
dhighs20	.0004	.0001	−.0823***	−.0251	−.0436	−.0131
	(.01)		(−2.65)		(−1.28)	

Table 12.4   (continued)

Variable	happyli coefficient	dF/dx	happyle coefficient	dF/dx	happyh coefficient	dF/dx
dyouth10	−.0056	−.0016	.0224	.0067	.0124	.0037
	(−.17)		(.68)		(.34)	
dyouth1020	.0340	.0095	.0631**	.0187	.0164	.0049
	(1.06)		(2.01)		(.48)	
dyouth20	.0909**	.0249	.0731*	.0215	.0416	.0122
	(2.32)		(1.93)		(1.01)	
dseniors10	−.0197	−.0056	.0233	.0069	−.0172	−.0051
	(−.57)		(.69)		(−.47)	
dseniors1020	.0187	.0052	−.0152	−.0046	.0559	.0165
	(.58)		(−.48)		(1.63)	
dseniors20	−.0401	−.0114	−.0374	−.0113	.0349	.0103
	(−1.09)		(−1.04)		(.89)	
dpark10	.0527	.0149	.0281	.0084	.0670 *	.0200
	(1.53)		(.84)		(1.84)	
dpark1020	−.0405	−.0115	−.0027	−.0008	−.0091	−.0027
	(−1.06)		(−.07)		(−.23)	
dpark20	−.0429	−.0123	−.1169**	−.0364	−.0137	−.0041
	(−.87)		(−2.43)		(−.26)	
dsport10	.1605***	.0445	.1054***	.0313	.1277***	.0376
	(4.02)		(2.68)		(3.02)	
dsport1020	.1153***	.0320	.0925**	.0274	.0460	.0136
	(2.93)		(2.38)		(1.10)	
dsport20	.0872*	.0239	.0099	.0030	.0149	.0044
	(1.96)		(.23)		(.32)	
dpubtr10	−.0806	−.0222	−.0435	−.0129	−.0093	−.0028
	(−.93)		(−.51)		(−.10)	
dpubtr1020	−.1137	−.0331	−.0518	−.0157	.0045	.0013
	(−1.26)		(−.58)		(.05)	
dpubtr20	0.1471	−.0438	−.1019	−.0317	−.0033	−.0010
	(−1.23)		(−.87)		(−.03)	
_cons	.3133**		−.1668		.3145**	
	(2.33)		(−1.26)		(2.18)	
Number of observations	21 957		22 012		22 012	
Log likelihood ratio	−10 370.15		−11 204 363		−93 055 186	
LR chi2(57)	3121.01		2336.52		8479.27	
Pseudo R^2	13.08		9.44		31.30	

Note: *p < .1; ** p < .05; *** p < .01.

marginal rates of leisure time consumed. Among the Organisation for Economic Co-operation and Development (OECD) countries, Germany enjoys one of the largest percentages of leisure time per day (OECD, 2009). Therefore, the average leisure time among Germans is already at a level that produces only small positive effects on SWB with increasing consumption. The commuting distance to work shows slight negative impacts but is only significant in relation to satisfaction with leisure. In addition, we can observe that the occupational indicators (reference category: family members involved in domestic work) have a significant impact on SWB. Public officials, white- or blue-collar workers, as well as self-employed individuals, have a significant higher probability to be satisfied with their life and health compared with family members involved in domestic work. Interestingly, all employed individuals have a significant lower probability to be satisfied with their leisure compared with the latter mentioned individuals. In addition, this study confirms the findings of Di Tella et al. (1999) and Graham and Pettinato (2000), showing a strong negative correlation for unemployment in relation to the three constructs of SWB. Income appears to have a negligible effect on SWB.

In general, the spatial factors that have been analysed in our study appear to be less relevant for SWB. For all distances, closeness to a city centre is positively related to satisfaction with life, while there is little evidence of an impact on satisfaction in relation to leisure or health. The estimates show also that living too close to shops selling daily consumption goods is negatively related to happyli and happyle. The inconvenience caused by traffic, noise and visual pollution around commercial areas could be a reason for this. Additionally, it was estimated that living close to parks (10 minutes or less) increases satisfaction with health and leisure and, in line with this, living more than 20 walking minutes away from them reduces satisfaction with leisure. This confirms the important role of parks and green areas for recreational purposes. Of interest to our study is the strong positive relationship detected between closeness to a public sports facility and respondents' self-reported satisfaction with life, health and leisure. It can be seen that the regression coefficients decrease as distances from a sports facility increase. All estimated regression models show this significant negative impact between the time needed to reach a sports facility and SWB. This implies that people are less likely to be satisfied with their life, health and leisure the longer they have to walk to a public sport facility. On average, individuals living less than 10 or 10–20 minutes' walking distance to public sports facilities are around 3–4 per cent more likely to be satisfied with their life, health, and leisure based on the estimation results (see Table 12.4).[2]

5.   DISCUSSION

Physical activity (in sports clubs) satisfies personal needs (internal effects) and provides notable external effects through, for example, social integration or public health. This implies that social benefits might exceed private benefits, suggesting an under-provision of sports participation without market regulation. Therefore, physical activity is seen as merit good (Sandy et al., 2004) and receives considerable public funds in Europe (Downward et al., 2009). Since sports facilities provide the basis for physical activity, a large portion of public funds is allocated to the construction, renovation, and operation of sports facilities (Breuer, 2009).

Given the increasing scarcity of public funds, measures to allocate public funds efficiently become increasingly important. In general, the allocation of public funds becomes more efficient as more social welfare is generated. Furthermore, welfare is defined as aggregated individual utility. Since SWB appears to be a suitable measure for utility, policy decisions should increasingly target well-being/happiness (Clarke and Islam, 2004). Therefore, it is of great importance to know if a certain allocation of sports facilities has a direct impact on SWB. While some studies have already focused on the economic impact of (professional) sports facilities on the welfare of inhabitants of urban areas (for example, Coates and Humphreys, 2003; Crompton, 1995; Johnson et al., 2001; Noll and Zimbalist, 1997a, 1997b; Rosentraub, 1997; Siegfried and Zimbalist, 2000), this study is the first to focus on the relationship between SWB and the availability of public sport facilities, that is, the time people need to reach a public sports facility.

Our estimation results indicate that the availability of public sports facilities positively influences SWB. In detail: empirical proof was found that (beside other important factors) people are more likely to be satisfied with their life, health and leisure status, the closer they live to a public sports facility. Since governments are not only composed of benevolent politicians (Frey, 2008), in reality, the maximization of a national happiness indicator is not the obvious ultimate goal of the public. However, these insights might serve as inputs into the political process when deciding on the allocation of sports facilities.

NOTES

1. While few studies distinguish between 'subjective well-being' and 'happiness' (for example, Ouweneel, 2002), most studies use these terms interchangeably, as we have done in our study.

2. We tested the robustness of our results based on different dependent variable classifications. Beside the main models, where the dummy variables happyli, happyle, and happyhe were zero, representing all self assessed well-being, satisfaction with leisure or satisfaction with health notes between 0 and 5 and one for notes ranging from 6 to 10. We also tested models based on the two further classification clusters: (a) zero representing all self assessed well-being, satisfaction with leisure, or satisfaction with health notes between 0 and 4 and one for notes ranging from 5 to 10, and (b) zero representing all self assessed well-being, satisfaction with leisure, or satisfaction with health notes between 0 and 6 and one for notes ranging from 7 to 10. The estimates for dsport10 remain significant and positive for all models and all applied classification clusters.

REFERENCES

Angeles, L. (2009), 'Children and life satisfaction', *Journal of Happiness Studies*, **11** (4), 523–38, DOI: 10.1007/s10902-009-9168-z.

Becker, G.S. (1965), 'A theory of the allocation of time', *Economic Journal*, **75** (299), 493–517.

Blanchflower, D.G. and Oswald, A.J. (2008), 'Hypertension and happiness across nations', *Journal of Health Economics*, **27** (2), 218–33.

Borooah, V.K. (2006), 'What makes people happy? Some evidence from Northern Ireland', *Journal of Happiness Studies*, **7** (4), 427–65.

Brereton, F., Clinch, J.P. and Ferreira, S. (2007), 'Happiness, geography and the environment', *Ecological Economics*, **65** (2), 386–96.

Breuer, C. (ed.) (2009), Sportentwicklungsbericht für Deutschland 2007/2008 (*Sports development report for Germany 2007/2008*). Wissenschaftliche Berichte und Materialien des Bundesinstituts für Sportwissenschaft. Köln: Sportverlag Strauß.

Chang-Tsai, M. (2009), 'Market openness, transition economies and subjective wellbeing', *Journal of Happiness Studies*, **10** (5), 523–39.

Clarke, M. and Islam, S.M.N. (2004), *Economic Growth and Social Welfare. Operationalising Normative Social Choice Theory*, Amsterdam: Elsevier.

Coates, D. and Humphreys, B.R. (2003), 'Professional sports facilities, franchises and urban economic development', *Public Finance and Management*, **3** (3), 335–57.

Crompton, J.L. (1995), 'Economic impact analysis of sports facilities and events: eleven sources of misapplication', *Journal of Sport Management*, **9** (1), 14–35.

Cummins, R.A. (2000), 'Personal income and subjective well-being: a review', *Journal of Happiness Studies*, **1** (2), 133–58.

Di Tella, R., MacCulloch, R. and Oswald, A. (1999), *The Macroeconomics of Happiness*, Bonn: ZEI.

Diener, C. and Diener, E. (1995), 'The wealth of nations revisited: income and quality of life', *Social Indicators Research*, **36** (3), 275–86.

Diener, E., Sandvik, E., Seidlitz, L. and Diener, M. (1993), 'The relationship between income and subjective well-being: relative or absolute', *Social Indicators Research*, **28**, 195–223.

Dorn, D., Souza-Poza, A., Fischer, J. and Kirchgassner, G. (2007), 'Is it culture or democracy? The impact of democracy and culture on happiness', *Social Indicators Research*, **82** (3), 505–26.

Downward, P., Dawson, A. and Dejonghe, T. (2009), *Sports Economics – Theory, Evidence and Practice*, Oxford: Elsevier.

Easterlin, R. (1974), 'Does economic growth improve the human lot?', in P.A. David and M.W. Reder (eds), *Nations and Households in Economic Growth Essays in Honor of Moses Abramovitz*, New York: Academic Press, 89–125.

England, J.L., Gibbons, W.E. and Johnson, B.L. (1980), 'The impact of ski resorts on subjective well-being', *Leisure Sciences*, **3** (4), 311–49.

Flouri, E. (2003), 'Subjective well-being in midlife: the role of involvement of and closeness to parents in childhood', *Journal of Happiness Studies*, **5** (4), 335–58.

Frey, B.S. (2008), *Happiness: A Revolution in Economics*, Munich Lectures in Economics, Cambridge, MA: MIT Press.

Frey, B.S. and Stutzer, A, (2000), 'Happiness, economy and institutions', *The Economic Journal*, **110** (466), 918–38.

Gerdtham, U.G. and Johannesson, M. (2001), 'The relationship between happiness, health and socioeconomic factors: results based on Swedish microdata', *The Journal of Socio-Economics*, **30** (6), 553–7.

Graham, C. and Pettinato, S. (2000), 'Happiness, markets and democracy: Latin America in comparative perspective', *Journal of Happiness Studies*, **2** (3), 237–68.

Hicks, J.R. (1939), *Value and Capital. An Inquiry into Some Fundamental Principles of Economic Theory*, Oxford: Clarendon Press.

Johnson, B.K., Groothuis, P.A. and Whitehead, J.C. (2001), 'The value of public goods generated by a major league sports team: the CVM approach', *Journal of Sport Economics*, **2** (1), 6–21.

Kara, B., Pinar, L., Ugur, F. and Oguz, M. (2005), 'Correlations between aerobic capacity, pulmonary and cognitive functioning in the older women', *International Journal of Sports Medicine*, **26** (3), 220–24.

Kavetsos, G. and Szymanski, S. (2008), 'National well-being and international sport events', International Association of Sports Economists, working paper series, paper 08-04.

Lafont, L., Dechamps, A. and Boudel-Marchasson, I. (2007), 'Effects of tai chi exercises on self-efficacy and psychological health', *European Review of Aging and Physical Activity*, **4** (1), 25–32.

Lancaster, C. (1966), 'A new approach to consumer theory', *Journal of Political Economy*, **74** (2), 132–57.

Lane, R. (2000), *The Loss of Happiness in Market Democracies*, New Haven, CT: Yale University Press.

Lavoie, M. (2004), 'Post Keynesian consumer theory: potential synergies with consumer research and economic psychology', *Journal of Economic Psychology*, **25**, 639–49.

Long, J.S. and Freese, J. (2006), *Regression Models for Categorical Dependent Variables Using Stata*. College Station, TX: Stata Press.

Luechinger, S. (2009), 'Valuing air quality using the life satisfaction approach', *The Economic Journal*, **119** (536), 482–515.

Miller, K. and Hoffman, J. (2009), 'Mental well-being and sport-related identities in college students', *Sociology of Sport Journal*, **26** (2), 335–56.

Moghaddam, M. (2008), 'Happiness, faith, friends and fortune-empirical evidence from the 1998 US survey data', *Journal of Happiness Studies*, **9** (4), 577–87.

Nettle, D. (2005), *Happiness: The Science Behind Your Smile*, New York: Oxford University Press.

Noll, R.G. and Zimbalist, A. (1997a), 'Build the stadium – create the jobs', in R.G. Noll and A. Zimbalist (eds), *Sports, Jobs and Taxes: The Economic Impact of Sports Teams and Stadiums*, Washington, DC: Brookings Institution, pp. 1–54.

Noll, R.G. and Zimbalist, A. (1997b), *Sports, Jobs and Taxes: The Economic Impact of Sports Teams and Stadiums*, Washington, DC: Brookings Institution.

OECD (2009), *Society at a Glance: OECD Social Indicators*, Paris: Organisation for Economic Co-operation and Development.

Oswald, A. (1997), 'Happiness and economic performance', *Economic Journal*, **107** (445), 1815–31.

Ouweneel, P. (2002), 'Social security and well-being of the unemployed in 42 nations', *Journal of Happiness Studies*, **3** (2), 167–92.

Pawlowski, T., Breuer, C., Wicker, P. and Poupaux, S. (2009), 'Travel time spending behavior in recreational sports: an econometric approach with management implications', *European Sport Management Quarterly*, **9** (3), 215–42.

Pedersen, P.J. and Schmidt, T.D. (2009), 'Happiness in Europe: cross country differences in determinants of subjective well-being', The Institute for the Study of Labor, discussion paper No. 4538.

Rasciute, S. and Downward, P. (2010), 'Health or happiness? What is the impact of physical activity on the individual?', *Kyklos*, **63** (2), 256–70.

Rehdanz, K. and Maddison, D. (2008), 'Local environmental quality and life satisfaction in Germany', *Ecological Economics*, **64** (4), 787–97.

Rosentraub, M.S. (1997), 'Stadiums and urban space', in R.G. Noll and A. Zimbalist (eds), *Sports, Jobs and Taxes: The Economic Impact of Sports Teams and Stadiums*, Washington, DC: Brookings Institution, pp. 178–207.

Sandy, R., Sloane, P.J. and Rosenstraub, M.S. (2004), *The Economics of Sport. An International Perspective*, New York: Palgrave Macmillan.

Siegfried, J. and Zimbalist, A. (2000), 'The economics of sport facilities and their communities', *Journal of Economic Perspectives*, **14** (3), 95–114.

Sila, B. (2003), 'People's estimation of their state of health in relation to frequency of their sports activity', *Kinanthropologica*, **39** (1), 99–108.

Stigler, G.J. and Becker, G.S. (1977), 'De Gustibus Non Est Disputandum', *The American Economic Review*, **67** (2), 76–90.

Stutzer, A. (2004), 'The role of income aspirations in individual happiness', *Journal of Economic Behaviour and Organization*, **54** (1), 89–109.

Veenhoven, R. (1993), *Happiness in Nations. Subjective Appreciation of Life in 56 Nations 1946–1992*, Rotterdam: RISBO.

Veenhoven, R. (1999), 'Quality-of-life in individualistic society: a comparison in 43 nations in the early 1990s', *Social Indicators Research*, **48** (2), 159–88.

Veenhoven, R. and Ouweneel, P. (1995), 'Livability of the welfare state: appreciation of life and length of life in nations varying in state welfare effort', *Social Indicators Research*, **36** (1), 1–48.

Wei-Ping, L. (2007), 'Research on the relations between the 2008 Olympic Games and the Gross National Happiness', *Journal of Beijing Sport University*, **30** (3), 161–4.

Wicker, P., Breuer, C. and Pawlowski, T. (2009), 'Promoting sport for all to age-specific target groups – the impact of sport infrastructure', *European Sport Management Quarterly*, **9** (2), 103–18.

Index